DEVCALE

TRAVEL

Westra Øy

Papa

Holm of Pap

Fara

Calf of Sixth Øy

Calf Sound

Heth Øy, or Eda

Green Teiles

The Rowlings

Simon holms

Linga

Fringe

Redenghead

SAND ØY

Streams Øy
Vulganle
Stronfa

Oulkerrie

Eglis Øy

The Beadlings

Siapins Øy

Dert Sound

GERMANI

MARE

ORCADES

PARISH LIFE ON THE PENTLAND FIRTH

Morris Pottinger

PARISH LIFE
ON THE
PENTLAND FIRTH

Morris Pottinger

1997

Published by
Whitemaa Books, Isauld House, Reay, Thurso, Caithness, KW14 7RW

Text, © Morris Pottinger

Illustrations (except pages XV and 182), © Isobel Gardner

Illustration page 182, © Alice Calder

Endpapers from Maps, circa 1600
by Timotheo Pont, Minister of Dunnet

ISBN 0 9530709 0 5

First Edition – 1997

Printed by The Orcadian Limited (Kirkwall Press), Hatston,
Kirkwall, Orkney

— Contents —

DEDICATED TO

NETTIE

— Foreword —

⟫◆⟪

Ore than three years have passed since Morris Pottinger
began contributing his articles about "Parish Life on
the Pentland Firth" to the *John O'Groat Journal*. Having
focused initially on the Session Records of Canisbay from the
middle of the 17th century, the series meandered down the east
coast of Caithness to encompass the civic affairs of the Royal
Burgh of Wick from 1660 to the 1700s. Those studies have now
evolved into this invaluable book which offers a history lesson
to us all, delivered in Morris's own inimitable style.

The language of the period is faithfully reproduced, inviting
us to travel back in time to a period far beyond living memory.
Throughout it all, Morris's warm, conversational style,
peppered with the occasional wry aside, guides the reader
through the stuffy terminology of officialdom in the 1600s.

These aren't wistful, sentimental reflections on the good old
days; Morris gives us the nitty-gritty of day-to-day life – from
Counsell deliberations over weights and measures, taxes,
customs and building works, to goings-on of a rather more racy
nature – marital strife, shadowy liaisons, petty theft, fisticuffs
among fishermen and other misdemeanours that were frowned
upon by respectable, God-fearing citizens more than three
centuries ago.

Despite the passage of time, many of the locations featured
here will be familiar to the contemporary reader – and therein
lies a large part of the book's appeal. For instance, anyone with

any knowledge of the old town of "Weik" will, with a little imagination, be able to visualise the "Camps" or the "Shoar" as described in Morris's vivid text. The *dramatis personae* have moved on, but the backdrop is still more or less there.

After one of the articles had appeared in the *Groat*, I told Morris in conversation that his intriguing yarns had encouraged me to gaze "with new eyes" upon many of the Royal Burgh's familiar old landmarks. I think he was quite pleased with that modest endorsement.

The painstaking and time-consuming nature of the work involved in transcribing, interpreting and writing the material for this book must not be overlooked. It is the work of a man who is truly dedicated to the cause of local history. In researching and deciphering the old records, and presenting us with an insight into that distant era in his own illuminating and entertaining way, Morris Pottinger has done a great service to Caithness as a whole and to Weik in particular.

Alan Hendry,
Editor,
John O'Groat Journal
and Caithness Courier,
February, 1997.

In the Beginning

———✦———

History to the school memory of most of us was of being drilled to remember the names of Kings and Queens, of battles won, of battles lost, of lists of dates to be memorised. Of the common man, or woman, little was taught, less was remembered. The Nobles and the Lairds had their family records, their estates, their genealogies. Their workers rarely had even a tombstone, remembered if at all only by some heroic deed on a long gone battlefield.

Yet old records of many aspects of life long ago still exist, lying moldering in many an attic, in Archives and Museums dotted around the country, patiently waiting to be dusted off and read. Modern technology has given us the computer, desktop publishing, ultra violet light which will bring up and make legible faint and faded and unreadable writing. All that is needed is time, and lots of it. And an interest in finding out more about our fore-bears.

My own early years were on the Island of Stronsay in the far North Isles of the Orkneys, born on the farm of Whitehall, watching as a young boy the dying days prewar of the herring fishing. The herring drifter Rose Three, from Buckie, died on the rocks below Odness, running onshore in thick fog. No loss of life. Our father took us to view the wreck. Dutch boats came in to buy and cure the mackerel unwanted by the herring curers, their crews wearing the wooden clogs and baggy trousers of legend. German and Russian ships came to load cured herring for Hamburg, Stettin, Danzig, St Petersburg. The gutter girls came in their hundreds early July and departed again mid August as swiftly as they came, usually on a drifter going South to Wick and following the fish. James More and James

Donaldson, two of the fish curers I remember, had their curing yards in Stronsay, and came from Wick.

On a clear summer morning our first look from the bedroom window, or more correctly the boxroom that did service as a bedroom for my brother David and I, was to the Eastern horizon to catch the first black stain of smoke from a returning drifter, sharp against the quickening sky, then a second, then a hundred, all hurrying to get in to market. Among them were the very last of the old sailing drifters and I believe they came from Burray, brown sails tall against the rising sun, frequently coming into Whitehall Harbour by the quicker, shorter and shallower Eastern channel only taken by the drifters on the top of the tide, the more usual route skirting the North side of Papa Stronsay and in by the Western Channel. Coal hulks lay in the Bay of Franks below Whitehall Farm to fill and refill the drifters all summer, themselves being in turn filled by colliers earlier in the year. Most were broken up for scrap iron during the war but a concrete hulled vessel still lies there. She was a three masted sailing ship in her prime, and can rest in Stronsay for ever.

Drifters careened themselves on a shingle bank on Papa Stronsay near the top of tide, allowing the hull to be cleaned when the tide went out, and refloated when it returned. We crossed on a bridge of boats from the New pier to the Old, a Sunday afternoon frolic. Most of the year our father farmed the farm, in the herring season he farmed the sea, providing carts and low loading four wheel horse lorries and horses and men to service the herring industry. Busy times, and good company for an "after-day-set".

It was a great honour a few years back to meet by chance a Wicker watching a Rugby game on the Harmsworth Park in Wick, and to find he had, in his youth, carted herring and guts and barrels and salt for my father in Stronsay. And on a stormy day when the boats did not get to sea, sent along the beach to cart rotting and putrid seaweed onto the farm. Organic. No work, no pay. We forgot the match!

On occasion our father went out with the Christmas Morn, a Banff drifter, for a night's entertainment, coming home in the early morning with a fry of fresh herring to have later for dinner with Duke of York new tatties and melted butter. A feast fit for a king.

All now gone into the discard of History.

X

Small boys had much to do around a farm, feeding hens, gathering eggs, taking a sheep off its back, carrying lambs, dodging higher authority. We took teeick eggs (green plover) in season, trained to always leave one so the bird would not desert the nest, never to take out of a nest of four which was her clutch and on which she could be sitting. We went to Midgarth Holm with our father to gather maa's eggs, dodging the ferocity of the tern's defensive swoop. We went to Rousam Head for our father to disappear below the cliff, banned to us, and reappear with a hat full of eggs. Or to gather heather berries for the best jam there ever was.

We set off to sea below Yernesetter with Jacky and Hecky to row an old tub to Kirkwall but came home wiser and wetter. We took our father's 14 foot dinghy down the beach and set off for the concrete barge. The rowlocks had been taken home by our father for safety but we put driftwood sticks in the holes and set off. Got to the barge which we examined in detail, noted a boat speeding towards us, little thinking we were the target. Towed back to the village in ignomy and disgrace and never got a hammering. I think our parents were too relieved at our safety. We were absolutely non swimmers.

On the farm we killed mice out of the cornstack on threshing days, sometimes rats. Had rat hunts down at the quarry where the henhouses were, watching Willy Peace put his hand down a rathole and extract his victim in bare fist. One less. Sent to chase corncrakes out of the last bout of hay before it fell to the reaper, conservation.

Played in the stooks at harvest time, in the straw barn in winter.

On the farm we got an education in biology denied to our city cousins, though sent indoors when the stallion visited. Strictly adult viewing. Out through the front door, peedie legs doon the dyke and around the back of the steading and up the loft stairs to a small window. Spotted, and got a hammering later. No complaints. Worth it!

My early education was the first years of primary in the North School, with Miss Sutherland my very first teacher. Then at the age of nine on to the Central School, a two mile daily walk each way, no school transport in those days, finishing there at the age of eleven after the first year of Secondary with John Drever, Headmaster.

A furious man who drove learning into us willy nilly.

XI

And it was he who taught us quite a bit of local history from his fund of local knowledge, aided somewhat by the Orkneyinga Saga, an ancient sheepskin manuscript surviving in Iceland and taken to Denmark where it was deciphered. As it contained portions of Orkney and of Caithness History it was the more interesting to us at school. We even had to do an essay on it for the Orkney and Shetland Competition. Still got a copy of the prize list from the back files of the Orcadian, sent to me recently by an Orkneyman whom I will not name - dare I say it, he was lower down the list!!

John Drever also had the knack of pointing out to us on the ground the small part Stronsay played in the affairs of Orkney, the killing of Earl Rognvald in the ebb on Papa Stronsay, given away to his foes by the bark of his pet dog, the Dane's Pier near Housebay, the Pict's Houses at Lamb Head, the Jacobite Cave at Brough Head. The lands of Clestrain, owned by James Fea, disponed to him in 1720 by his father, and best remembered for his capture, in February 1725, at the House of Carrick in Eday where he was then living, of John Gow the Stromness pirate born in Wick. Gow's father William had come from Wick in Caithness to Stromness in Orkney in April, 1710, setting up there as a merchant. The "Revenge", Gow's pirate ship, was refloated off the Calf of Eday and the prize was moored by Fea for a while below Clestrain in Linga Sound.

It did, and I have no doubt still does, bring History home to scholars if local interest can be added, and I think this is a subject receiving more attention than once it did, deservedly so. And of course the Orcadian has always had a certain conceit of his History.

The 1939-45 war was on, for further secondary education we North Islanders had to go into the Grammar School in Kirkwall, the Germans were having a go at Scapa Flow from time to time, the Royal Oak was sunk. There was no hostel accommodation, lodging was usually with some friends in the "Toon", the place was seething with service men and women, the blackout was solid.

We in Stronsay lived through our own little patch of History without realising it at the time. The Island was a quiet back-water, living it's own life, interfering with no one. No guns or service men stationed there, only a small wireless station on the top of the Island and an Observer Post on Brough Head. Dad's army, and my dad was the sergeant.

XII

Rationing was a laugh in a farming environment. Turnip shaws were cut, bagged up and sold to the Royal Navy in Scapa Flow as cabbages. Prevented scurvy, I am reliably told. Half and half cabbage and swede shaws were quite tasty, no doubt! No more herring fishing, dying away a few years previously, but trawlers took their place, having to come in to harbour every night for safety. Some hard drinking men aboard, bloody heroes everyone. Some did not make it.

The Norway boats came in, some leaking, some just afloat and no more, overloaded with escapees from the Germans. Every now and then a dull boom of thunder told us another drifting mine had exploded on the beach or under the cliffs of Brough Head. We were forbidden to touch even a tin of "Cremola Foam" found on the shore in case the clever Germans had booby trapped it. We found a paravane in Mill Bay lost off some trawler sunk doing minesweeping duty and thought it was a torpedo. Reported it to the bobby. The Navy mine disposal boys enjoyed their trip to Stronsay.

Over the Mainland from time to time we watched the black bursts of anti-aircraft fire as some raid or other went on, the quiet thunder only just reaching us across some twenty miles of sea if the day was mild and the wind was Southerly. At night the searchlights swept the heavens to the South , a mirror image of the Merry Dancers in the heavens to the North. The "Village" lay to the lee of the Island from Kirkwall but by some intuition when a raid was on the villagers already had ringside seats at the top of the Island. A German plane was brought down, a plume of black smoke indicating its demise, near Wideford Hill I think, and the "villagers" knew about it before it happened!

On Stronsay a Spitfire, its engine damaged in shooting down a long range Me109 some 20 miles East of Stronsay, force landed at the "Hill." Taken apart by a recovery crew and shipped into Kirkwall. An American plane, a Corsair, short of fuel, landed somewhere in the South end, on Holland Farm I believe, and took off again, after Stronsay hospitality for the crew and some petrol for the plane. Returned to "bomb" their generous hosts with acceptable largesse. A British plane, I think a Skua and out of control, crash landed on Tor Ness. Both crew men died, one on the way to Kirkwall. We went to see the wreckage.

XIII

Unpleasant. An Oxford bomber crash landed on uninhabited lighthouse Auskerry, what was left after salvage and the Stronsay natives is still there.

On some quiet days we would hear the recognisable undulating throbbing beat of German engines as a plane skirted Westwards to the North of Sanday, lying to the North of us. Up to the top of the Island and half an hour later the guns would open up as the German reconnaissance plane belted Eastwards over Scapa Flow after his roundabout approach from the Atlantic west of Hoy, heading home with his photographs. Not every time.

Once, and once only, did we see one. We were playing in the stackyard at Whitehall when we heard the engine noise of a low flying plane coming straight towards us in a hurry. Eyes aloft, and this funny plane crossed right above us just missing the buildings. Twin booms and rudders. Black crosses on the wings. Down over the low lying Ness and on Eastwards. A minute later two Spitfires, we all knew *their* shape, following in tearing pursuit and also heading out to sea. Only later did we learn that the first plane was a German Dornier and, stripped down for reconnaissance, a match in speed for any Spitfire. No hope of catching up.

Convoys passed, wreckage came ashore, dead seamen also which perhaps coloured my mind in favour of home produced food. Young men went off to War, most came back. One of my school acquaintances, older, went off to be a Bevin Boy down the coal mines. He did not come back. One went to Sanday to erect masts, for Radar I suppose. Fell, and did not come back. Somebody took appendicitis and was taken into Kirkwall, and did not come back. Davie Shearer was on the pier waiting for the steamer to take him into hospital in Kirkwall. Died on the pier.

Steven Colman, from the village, took apendicitis. He did not get to Kirkwall. He died, October 1939. He was eleven. From the school all the older boys joined the horse drawn cortege as it passed from the village to follow the two mile walk to the Bay Cemetery. It was my first funeral. I was ten.

Our sister Anne took appendicitis.

Captain Clements, who had been Harbour Master in Stronsay prewar but called back to Service as King's Harbourmaster in charge in Kirkwall, and also I think involved with Contraband Control, and a friend of our father, had a drifter standing by with steam up ready to go out to check potential Swedish blockade runners. Our father phoned in his despair and Clements immediately cut red tape and sent the drifter out to Stronsay to take Anne into Kirkwall and the surgeon. She was five. Peritonitis. Measles at the same time. She came back. Some debts can never be repaid.

Higher authority in the Education Dept. decided that the Secondary scholars from the Islands should be offered Correspondence Courses at home towards their Highers and eventual University if for no other reason than the risk in Kirkwall of bombing by the Germans, a very real risk at that time. Indeed the very first civilian casualty from German bombing in World War II was James Isbister at the Brig of Waithe, when on the 16th March, 1940, raiders bombed that innocuous huddle of houses near Stromness. Many took up that offer, including our youngest two Pottinger cousins from Cleat in Westray. One of my former teachers, John D. Mackay, a Westrayman, went into Kirkwall to organise these courses. Many a scholar graduated from University in those years in spite of the problems of wartime education.

I did not go to Kirkwall nor took Correspondence Courses. David Macrae, whose father had owned the Stronsay Hotel, spectacularly burnt out one day, had gone to school in Inverness to the Royal Academy there. My mother contacted the school and there I went the next year, with my brother David in due course the year after. Wartime travel. Passes everywhere. Identity cards. Ration books.

Stronsay to Kirkwall by the Thorfinn, sometimes the Sigurd. Forget about the title "Earl", we never used it. Guns mounted on the stern, Oerlikons I think, two Navy men in attendance. Bored. Fired the guns one day to entertain us boys. Never batted an eye when they told the Captain "Thought it was a bloody periscope, Sah." The seal maintained its gentle course for the Green Holms.

Pass control at Kirkwall and Stromness and Scrabster. Crossed over the Pentland Firth many times in those years 1941 to 1944, both on and above the water. On the sea with the old and first St Ola and Captain Swanson, watching with interest the sea sick sailors from the Navy. Above that same sea with Capt Fresson and his Dragon Rapides, a photograph of which is in front of me as I sit at my desk, G-AIYK, not one of Fresson's but built in 1944 and still going strong, preserved at Duxford and maintained in flying condition. Flew in it from Dalcross on the 29th May 1994 to commemorate the 60th Anniversary of the Royal Mail Pennant being presented to Capt. Fresson for the new Air Mail Service to Orkney. Brought back many memories.

Flew with Fresson from Skaebrae in the West Mainland to Inverness to land on the Longman Airfield, long since disused in favour of Dalcross and built entirely over. Routed West round Hoy, no flying over Scapa Flow in case of accidents. Sometimes as far West as Strath-halladale in Sutherlandshire and South by Forsinard and Helmsdale, a circuitous route but considered safer from German aircraft. Safer from the Germans maybe, but Fresson was fired on once by an Australian battle cruiser shortly after leaving the safety of the Caithness shore to cross the Pentland Firth to the West of Hoy. Shell bursts around him and an important passenger on board in Clement Attlee, the Labour leader. The Aussie ship must have had a Tory Captain, but they missed anyway the opportunity to change the political future of Britain. On another occasion he came out of cloud to find himself flying *under* shells being fired by the Navy on one side of him at a target on the other, a practice shoot. Escaped that situation by skimming the waves. Plane windows were whitewashed to stop us from spying, but what there was to see I have no idea. Any man with a beard and in civilian clothes was looked at very carefully. Might be a spy. Navy beards were O.K.

We boys were privileged in being allowed to sit one at a time on the doorstep into Fresson's cockpit and get a full view. "Like to fly it?" Hands gingerly on the controls, a little this way, a little back. No bother, flying is easy!!

It was Fresson himself who landed early one summer morning in 1935 on Grice Ness, the field of Whitehall Farm used as the Stronsay airfield prewar, took my uncle John the surgeon from New Zealand, and his wife, my uncle Steven the doctor from Willenhall, Staffordshire, and his wife, my father, and his wife, and conveyed the three brothers and their spouses to land on Cleat in Westray to visit yet another brother, William, – a poor farmer! – and his wife. Fresson returned to Cleat in the evening to take them back to Stronsay, suitably wined and dined.

It was Fresson himself who, during the War when Grice Ness Airfield was unusable and peppered with stone pillars to stop the German intended invasion, for the building of which pillars our father got the contract , came with his Dragon Rapide to Whitehall Farm to ambulance Peter Irvine into Kirkwall. Peter, a year younger than myself, had a leg taken off tween ankle and knee at Midgarth by a mower, or as the Stronsay men called it, a "raper". Midgarth belonged to George (Dod) and Alec Tait, brothers of my father's mother and brothers of James of J. and W. Tait. The W. was their first cousin William who eventually retired to Midgarth and ended his days there. We remembered his long white beard and his habit of carrying on highly intelligent conversations with himself. A very clever man, and born in Caithness!

We were there, and watched Fresson come in low over the Bay of Franks, lift over the shore dyke of the Garth, a field of 12 acres and only 120 metres [133 yards] top to bottom, skim the grass and lift over the dyke into Peedie Cattaquoy, 5 acres and but 200 yards long, a field just below the farm steading.

I know that Islander aeroplanes nowadays have impressively short landings but it was some flying, even if Fresson had been a barnstormer in his early days. Landing was at least up the slope, turn at the top, stopped the door side engine, got Peter and the District Nurse in, and off down the field to skim the dyke and climb the sky.

And it was Fresson himself who landed on a field at Whitehall Farm in May 1944 to take my father, my mother, and the five younger members of the family on their flitting from Whitehall to Greenland Mains in Caithness. It would be a nice story to say he landed on a field at Greenland, door to door so to speak, but they actually landed at Thurdistoft Airfield next door. Near enough. Routed West over the North Isles, then South skirting Hoy to cross the Pentland Firth, past Dunnet Head and in over Dunnet Bay. A fast flitting, not permitted now I would think. We call it progress!!

Time moved on as it inexorably does. I went to Edinburgh to study medicine, a family failing!, left it to work a year or two at home, met Nettie Dunnet from Keiss just North of Wick, bought Lower Dounreay from Pat Oag in November 1953. I was 24 and I knew it all!!. We got married on the 23rd November, 1953, moved in, sold out to the U.K.A.E.A. in 1955 in which matter we had no choice, took over adjoining Isauld Farm in November 1955 and moved into Isauld House in May 1956 as the Authorities tenants of the combined farms.

Skip the intervening years, this is not yet my autobiography nor hopefully my epitaph, not yet anyway, though in a way it is Nettie's. With an infinity of patience and goodwill she put up with me for 41 years. She is no longer here, and I miss her.

Time has moved on a long way for me from school in Stronsay to the present, still farming at Isauld next door to the UKAEA at Lower Dounreay, our very first farm, and with most of the land of that farm still in hand.

Perhaps a latent interest or memory of John Drever directed me recently to taking a look at local History. Perhaps Hossack's book "Kirkwall in the Orkneys" set me off, after all he was a Stronsay man born at Hunton, the next door farm to Whitehall. Perhaps St Magnus Cathedral with its extraordinary history caught me. Perhaps I was just curious.

Anyway I looked at various material in the Kirkwall Archives and in the Archives in Inverness to where the Caithness Records had been removed and dungeoned after the Highland

Regional Council came into being. Some in Edinburgh. There I found the Caithness Valuations of 1666, 1667, 1683, 1701, 1702, 1751, 1760, 1798. The old writing took a bit of getting used to but eventually I managed a first transcription of these faded old Records, and printed copies are now available.

Locally I found some material still not removed to Inverness, or even Edinburgh, and on that I have done this present book, mostly on Parish Life on the Pentland Firth in the 1600s in the Parishes of Canisbay and Wick in Caithness, but touching here and there on Orkney, however briefly. These old records were firstly "The Canisbay Session Records of 1652 to 1666", compiled during the Ministry of William Davidson who was translated to Birsay in Orkney in 1666, dying there on 6th Sept. 1690 after becoming blind in 1673. These Session Records I transcribed from a manuscript copy done circa 1910 by Donald Beaton, Free Presbyterian Minister in Wick.

Then an original manuscript copy held in Wick of "A Short Geographical Survey of Caithness, 1735." by Aeneas Bayne, A.M.. Finally I managed a transcription from the original Toun Counsell Books of Wick for the years 1660 to 1711 and 1739 to 1772. The book for the intervening years is presently missing. There is much more material available, Kirkwall has Counsell records from 1669, exceedingly small but legible writing done by Andrew Corner, Toun Clerk, detailed and much more easily read than the Wick Counsell Books which are almost nightmarish at times. Transcribing all that is available will take a very long time indeed and is work for very many people.

What I have tried to do is to take glimpses of life as it was lived and recorded at the time, 1660 and all that, stories of very ordinary folk, of their alleged misdeeds which loomed large at the time in officialdom's eyes but now seem of very small account indeed, of local affairs such as superstitions and spells, school building, harbours, taxes, fights and fornication, toun accounts. My spellings will vary, as did the spellings in the originals. I make no apology. Sometimes I find myself using an old spelling in everyday writing. It is of no importance. Indeed I at times find the old spelling to be the better! Read on.

— Chapter 1 —

Superstitions and Spells of 1660

The Parish of Canisbay on the Pentland Firth, among it's many claims to fame and it's own little island of Stroma, has one claim to fame in the surviving records of 14 years of its Parish Life contained in the Church Session records of Cannesbey, 1652 to 1666. To my best knowledge they have never been printed or made easily available, even though various writers have delved into a manuscript held by North Highland Archives in Wick Library, or into the original copy held by the Scottish Record Office in Edinburgh, and have quoted, sometimes wrongly, what suited them out of that document.

This old manuscript was hand copied by the Rev. Donald Beaton during his tenure of the Free Presbyterian Ministry of Wick from 1901 to 1930, when he removed to another charge in Oban, later to Dornoch where he ended his days in 1953 in Evilix Manse, home of his son-in-law the Rev. Finlay MacLeod.

Donald Beaton's interest in Caithness History was intense, though he came from the South, and among many works he laid his hand to was the Record of the Births and Marriages of Canisbay, 1652 - 1666, printed by The Scottish Records Society in 1914 and still going the rounds among those interested in Caithness Family History. He also wrote "The Ecclesiastical History of Caithness", printed in 1909 by Wm Rae of Wick.

He took the time and the effort to copy the entire Session Records of Canisbay from 1652 to 1666, and his unsigned 220 page red ink manuscript, written about 1910, is the source of some of the material which we are going to use to give us a glimpse into "Parish Life on the Pentland Firth" some 340 years ago, even if as seen through the eyes of the Church. The original Session Record is now "dungeoned" in Edinburgh but is quite readable and in good shape. A copy of a small part of it is in the first pages of a Microfilm of the Old Parish Records of Canisbay Parish, available in most local Libraries, and a look

at these few pages will give an accurate indication of the task
Donald Beaton undertook in copying the original material into
his manuscript. His authorship I was able to prove by
comparing the handwriting with his signature in the
Registration by him of the birth of a child in Wick about 1905.
I have had the privilege of copying Donald Beaton's work and
copies are available in the Libraries of Wick, Thurso and
Kirkwall, though only in the Reference Sections at this time.
Enough of an introduction, though one could write on.

The period of Canisbay History we are dealing with was
during the Ministry of the Rev. William Davidson who came
to Canisbay in 1652 after the troubles in Ireland in 1643, where
he was a preacher, and he eventually crossed the Pentland Firth
to Birsay in Orkney in 1666, there ending his days in 1690 after
going blind in 1673. I suspect the very existence of these Session
Records was due to Davidson as I know not of any records
before or after for some considerable time. Perhaps the marriage of his daughter Mary to Robert Drummond, Sheriff and
Commissary Clerk in Orkney, had something to do with his
translation to Birsay.

The Session Records were very detailed, particularly during
the first years of Davidson's Ministry, becoming less full later
as perhaps his early zeal wore thin in the Northern air. They
were written by a succession of Session Clerks, and handwriting and spelling therefore varied, becoming less easy to read
at the later period of the Records.

From these Session Records I compiled an Index of names
and was staggered when, on completion, I counted them and
found that the Index contained 1,200 different names from 1652
to 1666 in the Parish of CANNESBEY, as it was then called,
extending from East Mey along the Pentland Firth to
"Dungasby" and on down the East Coast to "Ockingill". In
1735 Aneas Bayne recorded 1,200 "examinable persons" in
Canisbay Parish, i.e. persons over 8 years old, so my list must
contain practically all the family names in Canisbay in
1652-66, and indeed probably most of the individuals. By 1841
in the Census of that year there were 2,249 in the Parish in all,
of whom 186 lived on Stroma.

Of the Session Records themselves there are many differing
aspects we can look at, and I must make choice as to where to

begin. Perhaps Witchcraft or Superstition is as good as any, though the Church held there was no such thing. Nonetheless it pursued those who gave any hint of believing in it, arraigning them before the Session to enact what penalty seemed most fit. Stroma seemed to have it's fair share, or more, of superstition, and visits were made from the Island to various "Chappels" on the Mainland. A prime culprit was Donald Liell who in March of 1654 came out of Stroma on a stormie day in the company of Issobel Ham to go superstitiously to St Moddan's Chappell in Freswick. There must have been a very pressing reason to cross that stretch of turbulent sea on a "stormie" day, and both were ordained to make their public confession and promise not to do the like again, under pain of more severe censure. We shall hear of Donald Liell again.

Issobel Ham we can deal with and perhaps there was an association of connected events regarding her visit to the Chappel. In December 1653 she was charged as *"being with chyld"*, in February of 1654 she confessed her fornication with an Englishman, probably the father of her child and one of Cromwell's soldiers stationed in Canisbay. In March she was before the Session for going to St Moddans Chapel in Freswick, though this date was her appearance before the Session and not the day she went to St Moddans. In April she was referred to the Presbytery in Thurso for the serious nature of her "crime" but not till March of 1655 was she finally dealt with, being scourged for not naming the father of her child, whether the "Inglishman" or some other we do not know.

St Moddans had other visitors. In July 1652 Agnes Swanny, Issobel Watsone, Janet Warrs and Helene Mendtheplay were charged with "goeing, or kneeling", about the Chappell, all Freswick people, and promised before the Session not to repeat their fault. In August 1654 Elizabeth Mowat was similarly dealt with, having previously been charged in January 1653 with going superstitiously around St John's Heid, another Chapel site, in company with Elspet Cordiner, Margt Wright, Christane Harrow, Margt Miller, Janet Budge and Christane Plowman. In all the Session Records it was indeed odd that only women were charged with superstitious Chapel going, so it appears to have been a feminine characteristic, and what they were praying for I leave to the gentle reader's imagination.

No doubt love in some complicated form or other!

St Moddan must have had a powerful influence because, even after all the Church's efforts to stamp out this practice, we find Aneas Bayne, A.M., writing in his "Short Geographical Survey of the County of Caithness, 1735" :-

"There is a noted Chappell at Freswick in the Parish of Canesbay where some people, not long since, used to make superstitious journeys and Ceremonies such as eating in the Chappell and going thrice round it on their bended knees if any ways indisposed."

So the "Chappell" was still standing in 1735.

There was a case in Stroma in July, 1659, of Margaret Watson being before the Session charged with stooping thrice to the ground and taking three handfuls of grass from Margt Liell's cow's mouth with her left hand, putting it into her right hand, and with her right hand putting it under her belt, after which Margt Liell's cow was chased away. Another witness said she put the grass under her belt with her left hand. The evidence was further confused by other witnesses and nobody seemed to have the slightest idea what it was all about, so the Session moved on to other more exciting business.

This looked like a very local washing in Stroma of very dirty linen which was dealt with at the next Session meeting by stating that, for lack of evidence and corroboration, they could find no guilt, but not to do it again!

Spells were still being used, or "*libbes*" as they were termed. Janet Groat was an exponent of this art and, in May of 1655, was delated as being a charmer who "*libbed*" Andro Stevin in Okingill and Capt. Wood's child in Freswick. Capt. Wood was almost certainly one of Cromwell's men. She used small salt for this "*libbeing*" and it does not say what was wrong with either case. Small salt must have been fine ground table salt, not rough salt for fishcuring or meat pickling. Janet Liell in Huna was with Jannet Couper when she was "travelling" [travail:- pangs of childbirth] and, seeing she was in great danger, desired her to promise never to spin on a Saturday, and she would be relieved of her pain. This, favouring of sorcerie or superstition, Janet Liell was enacted never to put the lyke bond on any again under paine of the censure of the Kirk.

Effie Rosie, flitting from Stroma to Orkney, was alleged by

her father-in-law to be so well learned that she could make her stoup [small wooden pail with one handle] go and milk the cow by itself, while his second daughter-in-law foretold the death by the sea of her father. The same daughter-in-law, with Alex Simsone, going to lead her teynd [tax of one tenth of the crop] with his horse, she said he would never plow again with that horse, which accordingly lost the strength of his side and died, or as it was put, "came ower ye craige." [cliff]

Not a too unusual form of disposal of fallen farm animals even into modern times, though trouble could ensue when the tide turned!

Issobell Mowat, "alledged" to be the cause of an unnamed woman's husband's sickness, lifted up the bedclothes to have a look at him and said he would not die of that sickness, and after 8 dayes he recovered. Issobel was also charged by Findlay Groat that he fell out with her, and his tongue did swell for six weeks, which no doubt kept him quiet!

Spells on cattle, the mainstay of their economy, were common, even if the cows were of the smallest size and none the best of their kind [Aneas Bayne, 1735]. In March of 1655 Donald Miller complained to the Session that a stirk's head had been put in the way of his cattle going to the hill grazing, and his cattle immediately died. Margaret Wright said the stirk's head belonged to Alex Rosie. Walter Mendtheplay and Jon Rosie suspected it to be the cause of six of their cattle also dying. This was so serious it was referred to the Presbyterie. Incidentally, the tombstone of Walter Mendtheplay and his wife Issobel Paterson is still to be seen in good condition in Canisbay Kirkyard.

In September 1663 Issobel Sinclair complained that Anna Swanny in the Burneside of Freswick said she was a fool to bring her master's cattle there and they were always dying, and her master had not prospered since. Anna Swanny denied she said any such thing to Issobel Sinclair, but so vile was her language that she was referred to the civil judge to be punished.

In June 1657 Donald Liell, his wife, and Margt Water who was with them, came under charge by Andro Water that they said on his coming to live beside them that he would never milk his own cow, that his hen eggs went bad, that his goose died. Issobel McBeath said she wanted [missed] her cow's milk and suspected Margaret Water and Donald Liell and his wife for the loss.

Thomas Robsone said that Margt Water said, when he came to live beside her, "Is he comeing to our side of the toun with three ky?", wherupon one of them died, and another was in great danger, so he went and reproved Donald Liell etc., and his cow became better. It was referred to further tryall but a blank in the Records may explain why no further reference. Incidentally, this Donald Liell was on the Mainland and was not the Donald Liell who crossed from Stroma on a stormie day.

Perhaps a rather sweet one to end with. Issobell Skeall in Dungasbey was charged in June 26, 1659, that "*ye first day yt ye plough streiked [stroked,] sche did put ane blew threid about ane oxes foot wt several knots upon it, and yt sche removed [it] ye first day of sowing barland [bere or barley now] and put on a threid of another color.*" On 3rd July she appeared again and confessed that she had from Donald Gilbertsone a wustband [wristband? worsit? worsted? – take your choice] of "*reid threid which she put about hir oxes foot, being sore, and that the said Donald Gilbertsone did put it on, speiking some words by way of charme*". She was ordained to enter her obedience and to stand in sackcloth. As a farmer I was curious as to whether this would be a good cure for a sore foot on a cattle beast so consulted a local vet, who must remain nameless for professional reasons! if he or she would so prescribe and would it work. I was told that, while it would not be a normal prescription, there might be an occasion when it would work as well as anything else!

— Chapter 2 —

Demon Drink

It is well known that the Parish of Canisbay is one of the most abstemious to be found in the United Kingdom at the present time, though it was not always so. In the Session Records of Cannesbey circa 1660 there are references to which we may refer to illustrate the remarkable change that has come, since that time, over the drinking customs of the inhabitants of the "Parish on the Pentland Firth."

Probably the most outrageous, as seen through the eyes of the Church, was "Drinking in tyme of Sermon", which could also be taken with the dreadful crime of not attending Church. On 27th September 1652 the Session *"regrated"* that many ignorant people were going out into the Kirkyard in *"tyme of sermone"*, no names being mentioned, and to prevent this sin in future one of the Elders was appointed to go out of the Kirk and take note of those staying without so that they could be referred to the Session for censure. This obviously had effect because the very next Sabbath we find Hendrie Liell and Donald Liell delate for drinking and tulzeing [violent quarrelling] on the Lord's Day, as also was Issobell Mill. Additionally Helene Ham and Issobel Southerland were charged with selling drink on the Lord's day so it would appear that they were all apprehended together. Matters went from bad to worse because the very next Sabbath the names of Jon Mathesone and Rorie Mansone were added to the list. They must have been quite a friendly bunch because Rorie Mansone married Issobel

Southerland in August of the next year and Jon Mathesone, in December of 1652, was accused of being a bad boy with Issobel Mill!

In October they were all convicted, it looks like *"in absentia"*, and made their repentance later that month, being then absolved from Kirk Censure, almost a Catholic forgiveness of sin.

The same month of 1652 we find Alex Rosie and his wife accused of selling drink on the Sabbath. I think he came from about Hollandmey in the West of the Parish. In November Jon Liell appears along with Alex Rosie for selling drink, and Hendrie Miller's wife was also accused, on the 15th November, 1652, of selling drink and *"causing bear to be burne on the Lord's day"*. Sounds like toasting malt on a Sunday in readiness for brewing on Monday, which same offence Hendrie Miller denied. As Hendrie Miller had been appointed an Elder on the 11th October, 1652, one could say, "He would say that, wouldn't he?" The matter was referred to further trial, and in March of 1654 he was convicted of selling drink in his house, and in the same month he was discharged from sitting as an Elder, partly for being convicted of selling drink, partly as venting some evil speeches against Wm Mowat, merchant in Thurso, unbecoming for an Elder.

Alexr Rosie in January, 1653, was charged by the officers, Alex McBeath and Bernard Barnatsone [Barnie], to compeir to undergo censure for his profaning the Sabbath, and answered *"Is the Minister beginning to crow. I will mak 8/- & two tyme do his turne."* He was ordained to be charged again, with certification, and *"if he compeir not, a strict course sall be taken for correcting him in ane exemplary manner for ye terrification of others from the lyke impious boldness."*

Although it took Hendrie Miller until 1654 to lose his Eldership the seriousness of Elders setting an example was illustrated by an enactment of 27th December, 1652, that *"if any Elder, or other parochiner, be found drinking on the Sabbath, or extraordinarily upon a weekday, he should pay 40 shillings and make confession before the congregation, and if repeated, then to higher censure, **especially an Elder.**"*

There was an elder, John Manson, appointed for Stroma in October 1652, and it may have been he, in January 1653, taking his duties seriously, who reported David Angus and Issobel

Beg for drinking and tulzeing on the Sabbath, as well as Wm. Liell, elder and younger, and Donald Liell of St Moddan's Chapel fame, all Stroma people. The five people reported above made their public confession on 15th February, 1653, and were absolved from further censure.

It was not long, however, before Stroma again featured in the drinking on Sabbath lists with some other persons starring. Hendrie Liell's house in Stroma was the venue for this drinking in time of sermone by Alex Beg and his wyfe, Wm. Liell, elder, [again?], Wm Tennant and his wyfe, Mathew Water and his wyfe, and Gilbert Ham and his wyfe. They were each fined 6/8d, had to make public confession and, if found again in the like fault, to pay 40s. each. The 6/8d.was paid and receipted, the amount being half a merk Scots money. [4p Sterling today.]

The same day we find another name appearing, for the first time but not the last, in Robert Blinker who, on Passion day, had drinking in his house the persones following, viz:- Donald Stevin, Jon Stevin, Wm Mendtheplay, Jon Southerland, Donald Hendersone, alias "Cassere", John Rug, Wm Cordiner, Walter Quoyes, Issobel Rug, Christane Rug, Issobell Groat, who were all to be charged. On May 2nd they were each fined 6/8d and, if found again in the like, to pay 40 shillings each.

Seems that 40 shillings was the standard fine.

Robert Blinker, who I think lived in the Mey area of the Parish, was again convicted of selling drink on the Lord's day when he was sharply rebuked and threatened with severe punishment if repeated. One gets the impression, from other matters, that he kept a noisy house to say the least.

There is perhaps a certain repetitiveness in this drinking on Sabbath but the sheer number of names which are mentioned from some 340 years ago and which have survived with such detail, some 1,200 of them in this Parish on the Pentland Firth, make this Record unique in Caithness History, and indeed many of the names are still to be found in the several districts of the Parish, though it is not easy to trace direct descent as later records were not too good. Perhaps just as well! So on we go.

We find a smaller fine of 10d charged on Alex Liell and David Warrs, convicted of Sabbath drinking, but David Warrs was a servant to Hendrie Henderson and possibly could afford no more. Looks like *"temperance"* with mercy!

Before we leave December 1652 there is reference to poor attendance at Kirk so it was determined to keep a Roll of the names of the families each Sabbath, and those noted absent to be fined 40d each. It was further, in March 1653, the people of Stroma being poor kirkgoers, that it was enacted that any with boats should pay 13/4d Scots [a merk] and others 40d. if they stayed away, and that no passengers were to pay any fare for coming over to the Kirk. Attendance at "sermone" was not helped by the apparent selling of drink at a taverne at the Kirkstyle, and it was ordained that if any be found drinking there on the Sabbath day the sellers were to pay £4 Scots for their fault.

For the first time Ockingill features with reference to Andro Braibner drying malt on ye Sabbath, to Andro Mowat, *"ye pyper"*, convicted of straightforward drunkenness with no Sabbath connotations and, *"if he be found in the like therafter, to make public confession and to pay a dolor".* [58/- Scots.]

Donald Liell in Stroma featured again in July, 1654, as being drunk and casting down of a dyke which he alleged his neighbour built on his land. It would appear that both faults were committed on the Sabbath though that is not too clear. Donald Liell appears as a name many times, sometimes clearly as in Stroma, other times as in Cannesbey, and also as *"elder"* in Cannesbey. Where the Session Records have two names the same it was very useful to have an address being given to distinguish between the two, and that practice long survived.

In February, 1655, Donald Mursone was accused of drinking in Sandie Harrow's house on Sabbath and both were before the Session to repent and promise etc. This seems to have been private drinking sessions between friends, with some frequency, but still was a fault to be prevented at all costs.

By January, 1656, the Session publicly intimated that any found drinking in ail houses on the Sabbath would be severely punished but if any desired drink then they were to send for it in sobriety and have it in their own houses. I suppose this would keep drunken drivers off the roads, even if only with a horse and cart. The advice would still be good!

In December, 1657, Stroma people were again at odds with the Session, or should it be the Minister, and were accused of profaning the Sabbath by playing at football and dancing. Those guilty were to stand in the joggs, one in time of the lecture, one in time of the sermon. Andro Dunnet was accused of leaping and playing at pennystone on the Sabbath. I think he belonged to the Cannesbey shore, pled ignorance, and was admonished.

The same month Alex Rosie was referred to the Justice Court for going to Dunnet on the Sabbath, craving moneys, and taking Jon Owman back with him to Mey, drinking in an ailhouse, not comeing to Kirk, and carrying aqua vite with him on another Sabbath. The brousters in Mey, Adam Seaton and Jon Sinclair, charged with selling drink on the Sabbath, presumably to Alex Rosie and Jon Owman among others, enacted themselves that if ever there was drink sold in their houses on Sabbath they were to pay £5 Scots and stand in sackcloath. Shades of very recent times when Wick went *"dry"* and John O'Groats was not, that hostelry being tolerated to give drink and lodging to strangers. A traveller had to come more than three miles but I am sure there is still many a Wicker who can remember the hard and necessary and dangerous journey to John O'Groats on a Sunday, or the Portland Arms in Lybster, or Dunnet Hotel, all over the magic three mile limit!

Not much apparent change, is there?

Alex Rosie and Jon Owman's case continued, and, on 7th March, 1658, Jon Owman gave evidence that Alex Rosie came to his house in Ratter on a Sabbath craving money, and afterwards they came to Adam Seaton's house in Mey to drink. He drew three Sabbaths in sackcloth and had to make public confession of his fault. Donald Liell, the Mey one, drinking on Sabbath, was warned.

On the 25th December, 1659, being Yule day, and on the Monday after, there was great drinking and dancing, referred to further trial on the 15th January, 1660. It would appear that the 25th December, 1659, was a Sabbath day and on March 4th the following were delate for sitting in ailhouse in time of sermon, I presume referring to the above, viz:- Issobel Baine, Janet Rosie, David Simsone, Wm Smith, Malcolm Rosie, Jon Rosie, Alex Gilbertson, all of whom to be charged.

And a further group the same day, viz:- William Tenent, Margt Rosie, Margt Warrs, David Warrs, Donald Harpar, Alex Simsone, Wm Jonsone, David McFend, Wm Dunnet, Jon Mowat in Mey. These were a mixed bag but I think Wm Tenent and

Alex Simsone were Stroma men though David Warrs was Dungasbey. The two groups could have been in different ailhouses. They were all repeatedly called but seem to have ignored the charges, and eventually they pass from notice, whether dealt with or forgotten I cannot tell.

Adam Seaton had another and previous claim to fame in having drinking and masking plays for the Englishmen in his house December 30, 1655, without doubt Cromwell's soldiers, quartered on the Parish from February 1652.

Katherine Smith in Mey confessed in March, 1664, that *"Finlay McOhie and Dod Robertsone drank wt her on the Lord's day until 12 o'clock at night, also Janet McBaith and Elspet Miller, all to stand in front of the pulpit and pay 13/4d".* We will come to them again.

Finally, in October, 1664, we find drinking in Andro Baine's house in the Miltoune of Oukingill with the following behaving very scandalously in dancing and fighting, viz:- Geo Bain in Freshwick, James Bain in Oukingill, Jon Farqr, ygr. there, James Tulloch in Nybster, Jon Mowat there, Donald Bain there, Gawan Manson there. Geo Bain got his hand hurt. On 30th October Andro Baine in the Miltoune appeared and denied any such thing in his house on the Lord's day, and stated that the young men drank but a pynt apiece.

Believe that if you will.

— Chapter 3 —

Visitors to the Parish

Life in the Parish on the Pentland Firth in 1660 one would
have thought would have been quiet and peaceful and
remote and idyllic and far from the rush and bustle of
modern life, even in 1660, just as it is today! Or was it?

History points out that the long gone Picts were here, giving
their name to the Pictland Firth, that stretch of riotous sea tidally
sweeping between the Orkney Isles and the Mainland. The
Romans visited and referred to the Picts in passing, and to some
of the features of the land which will outlast us all.

The Vikings appeared and swamped the Picts, though here
and there a standing stone, a burial barrow, a Picts house, a
Pictish brough — a Norse word but a more ancient origin — a
Pictish place name not quite eradicated but much changed, still
shows evidence of their passing through. These Vikings left
their mark in many place names of the North of Scotland and
in the features of the coastal dwellers of Caithness and in particular in the Nordic features of many of those still dwelling in
the Parish on the Pentland Firth. It was folklore in my early
dancing days that if you liked them blond go to Canisbay or
Keiss, but if you liked them dark go to Bower or Spittal!
I went to Keiss!

The year 1650 brought another invasion from the North, this
time it was Montrose with an army of Danish mercenaries who
wintered in Orkney and crossed to Sannick Bay in Canisbay
on 5th April of that year, some Orkneymen keeping him
company, to be defeated disastrously at Carbisdale [Corbiesdale,

the valley of the crow] on the River Shin, and so to his death
by execution. Whether the sound of beating drums drew them
or just loyalty to the King we do not know, but a few men from
the Parish joined in. Alex Jack was one, being later called a
chased rebel by Jon Farqr in Ockingill, who also said he was a
thief but had to retract that charge before the Session and restore
to Alex Jack his good name.

Alex Southerland was another, being called a *"runneing
rebell"* by Issobel Mathesone who told him to *"goe home to his
own country as he was a sheip thief".* Presumably he was a
Sutherland man but he did not go away, and for all I know he
is still around.

Hendrie Henderson, in April, 1652, was scandalyzed by Jon
Stevin in Ockingill, alias *"Crookie",* who stated that he and all
the rest that were in the war were perjured. These were all I
noted but they are only referred to because of some uproar
being brought to the attention of the Session, and there could
have been others.

These invaders, however, brought another group of visitors
to the Parish on the Pentland Firth when, on the 29th March,
1652, the Session did not convene because there were "Inglishes"
quartered in the bounds. On the 2nd May the Session did not
meet as there was a party of English horsemen in the fields. A
goodly number crossed the Pentland Firth to be stationed in
Kirkwall in Orkney as late as 1663, after the Restoration of
Charles II by a few years. So their presence there was not just
for Cromwell's purposes but had more an international reason.
For sure the English were not in Canisbay to control the local
population and prevent further uprisings such as the futile
attempt by the now dead Montrose. So what were they doing?
And why were they there?

They were there to control access to the shores of Caithness
by invaders attempting to win back the throne for Charles II,
crowned King at Scone in January of 1651 but without a throne
to sit upon or a Crown to place upon his head or a Kingdom to
govern. The landing beaches of Caithness were controlled by
detachments of soldiers stationed at strategic points, Ackergill
to control Sinclair Bay, Freswick for Freswick Bay and Canisbay
for the bays of Sannick at Duncansbay and Gills opposite Stroma.

There is a story that they stabled their horses in the Kirk of

Canisbay but there was no reference whatever to that in the Session Records of the time, and I do not believe it. The Session met with regularity and without interruption week by week and do not appear to have shared their accommodation with any horses. When there is reference to *"quartered in the bounds"* it refers to the bounds of the Parish and not the bounds of the Church. On 8th September, 1654, the Record reads *"No session by reasone of ye trouble of ye tymes yt no elder culd remaine, ther being souldiers quartered in and about yr houses."* So service was held, then the elders went home with their wives and daughters!

Cromwell's men were in Canisbay at least into 1656, featuring in the case of the drinking and masking plays on the Sabbath at Adam Seaton's house in December, 1655. The Session Records do not refer to them in Canisbay after Adam Seaton's Xmas party, but not till 1663 did they finally leave the Orkneys, or disband, for some of them stayed on in Kirkwall.

They left trace of their stay in the Parish of Canisbay in the Bridge called Cromwell's Brig at the Mill of John O' Groats which would have given them better passage along the coast to Sannick from Canisbay, possibly for the movement of guns. They also built a gun emplacement on the Ness of Quoys controlling the entrance to Gills Bay from the East and the passage between Stroma and the Mainland. There is not much left of that emplacement but, having seen one of Cromwell's cannon still mounted at the Ness of Tankerness in Orkney, controlling the entrance to the sheltered waters of Deer Sound, I calculated that I would find the same at Canisbay to explain the presence of Cromwell's Men in that remote Parish. And when I went looking for it there it was. Locals told me it was a *"plantie crue"* for the growing of cabbages but with no soil within, and situated on the edge of the sea, not even a Canisbay man would try to grow cabbages in such an exposed and sea spray covered spot.

One must consider that there were no harbours in Caithness at that time, ships were loaded and offloaded over the beaches and would certainly have landed an invading army over them. On the 6th of June, 1944, we did the very same thing in Normandy!

Some names are in the Session Records relating to Cromwell's men, mostly as being on overfriendly terms with some of the local girls, but what else would you expect. The ones mentioned were Thomas Carre, John Clegge, Johne Gudelad, James McConile, Leut. Roy, Glengarrie and Capt Wood. I think Lt Roy and Glengarrie would have been the same person and James McConile one of Glengarrie's clan of MacDonalds, and illustrate that Scots were present in Cromwell's army. It was a Scottish Clan maxim that if father was supporting one side then his son supported the other, so that which ever side won one of them would keep the ancestral estate, giving rise to that well known phrase "The canny Scot."

Old Glengarrie was one of those who held out against Cromwell longer than all the rest. Capt Wood was at Freswick. There were payments made by the Session to several poor soldiers out of Church funds, slightly more generous than those made to locals but not greatly so.

Another *"visitor"* to the Parish on the Pentland Firth but who stayed on was John de Groot whose name is now applied to a portion of it. There is the well known folklore tale of his eight argumentative sons and his eight sided room with its eight doors and its eight windows and its eight sided table designed so that each son could have his chair at the top of the table. I think this is the Caithness equivalent of the Loch Ness Monster which you can believe if you wish. If it had any trace of truth whatever it would have been the coldest and draughtiest house that ever was, and I doubt very much if a hard Dutchman could not have controlled his offspring in a warmer manner!

There was a house shown in General Roy's map of 1747 called Johny Groat's House in the general position of the present Hotel. A few years earlier, in 1735, Aneas Bayne referred specifically to it and I think it is worth quoting in full, his spelling included.

"Two miles East of the Church of Canesbay is the most Northerly point of the whole Island of Brittain, called Duncansbay Head, or Dungsbey Head, near to which there is a house commonly called John O'Groats because possessed by men of that name in a continual succession from father to son near two centuries bygone. Strangers who visit the Shire have a strong curiosity to be here and commonly carve out their names on an old table preserved in the house, that posterity may see how far travelled they are. But it is mortifying to know, which is a matter of fact, that their names are razed out every 12 years or so, and the Table fitted for new Impressions at the desire of new visitors. But they have still one way left of doing themselves Justice to Posterity on the point of travell, and that is by carrying away with them from the Shoar a certain kind of shell which the vulgar call *"John O'Groat's Buckies"*, and these are thought rare things in the South of Scotland, as indeed they are, as well because they are rarely if at all found on any other shoar as for singularity of their figure. They are now crept into the Closets of the Curious and are lodged in the same Cabinett with Meddalls and Reliefs. Some ignorants in oyr Countreys believe this firmly to be the end of the World and that it answers Virgil's query :

"Tell me, and then my oracle shall be
Where Heavens measured but by fathoms three."

So in 1735 there was a tourist trade of visitors to John O'Groats catered for by the occupants of John O'Groats House, and nothing much over the years has changed!

Other visitors passed through, sometimes by virtue of temporary appointment to work in the Parish.

David Allardes was one, being appointed as Session Clerk on 7th August, 1659. He had been Minister in Olrig and was deposed for his support for Montrose and for Charles 2nd. He then had a struggle to live but seemed to drive a fairly hard bargain on his appointment to Canisbay, requiring some consideration from the Minister and elders more than the usual benefits. The Session Records do not tell when he left though he was still there in 1660, but I think he became re-established in the Church after the Restoration. He would certainly have been an asset as far as keeping the Session Records were concerned, and towards the end of the period Donald Beaton records that the writing had become difficult to read, presumably a new Session Clerk with David Allardes moving away.

A new teacher was appointed in May, 1653, when Hew Groat, an elder, was ordained to write to Thomas Taillour to come to teach school in Cannasbay, according to his *"ingadgement"*, without further delay. Taillour came and was a frequent witness to baptisms until at least late 1659. He was succeeded as schoolmaster in October of 1660 by Donald Reid Skinner, the only double name found in Beaton's manuscript.

I have not studied the original but suspect that Beaton misread a name, possibly a place name, and that Donald was really Donald Reid and that he came from some other place with a name close to Skinner, i.e Skinnet, or *"Skinan"* long ago, near Halkirk, where there was a chapel.

Thereafter he appears frequently enough as Donald Reid and when the Session Records closed on February 18th, 1666, he was Presenter and Reider of the Scripture, for which he got *"bot litle"*.

The Parish had another transient group of visitors on the 24th March, 1665, in 23 Hollanders who had suffered shipwreck in Orkney. They were given 2 shillings Sterling and sixpence to one to "guid" them to Dunnet. We can assume they were heading for Thurso in the hope of a passing ship to take them to Holland.

Robert Drummond appeared, Sheriff of Orkney, and married Mary, a daughter of the Rev. Mr Davidson on 15th April, 1665. Whether he was passing through on his way to Orkney when he met her I do not know. Where better to stay in Cannesbey than with the Minister while waiting a suitable crossing to Orkney? Sheriff Drummond was also a witness on 31st May, 1665, to the baptism of twins, Patrick and Helen, by Malcome Groat, ygr. in Dungsbey, so must have been visiting. Early the next year, in February, 1666, Davidson moved to Orkney to the charge of Birsay where he eventually died in 1690.

There could have been many others who came and went but again without trace as far as the Session was concerned. The Laird of Mey had a ferry in regular use carrying horses and passengers to Orkney. There was a long tradition of young horses from Strathnaver in Sutherlandshire being taken to Orkney for rearing and then sold back to Caithness farmers after a few years when fully trained. Donald Water was arraigned before the Session for crossing the Pentland on a Sunday on Mey's ferry with horses. Traffic and trade to and from Orkney was constant. And again, with the sea route Northabout passing the shores of the Parish on the Pentland Firth, there must have been many a storm bound ship waiting for a change of wind and a suitable tide to get Westwards, or even shipwrecked mariners waiting a chance to get home.

Who knows, it was all a long time ago.

— Chapter 4 —

The Case of the Suicide

The Church, and it's Session, must have had a large influence on Parish Life on the Pentland Firth, with some poor
wrongdoers coming before it almost every Sunday, which
so concerned the "Provinciall Assemblie" of the Presbytery,
meeting in THURSO, that it suggested that the Session should
be held on a week day so as not to hinder the carrying out of
"Holie Dueties".

The argument went further in stating that even dealing with
delinquents on a Sabbath was a profanation of the Holie day
and therefore should be dealt with on a week day. This was put
to the Session by the Minister on 8th August, 1656, and the
unequal struggle went on between the elders and the Minister
until the 21st December, 1656, when he finally gave up the futile
fight.

He must have been trying to get their individual agreements
because on 30th September it states that for no private dealing
could the elders be moved to keep Session on a week day for the
great hinderance to their own private affairs.

The power of the Session must have been very great and
much pressure put on people by the very public nature of
having to sit in sin before the pulpit, to wear *"sackcloath"* for
their wrongdoings, to declare before the congregation their
repentance for many Sundays in succession, to stand in the
joggs for the slightest, in our eyes, misdemeanour, or to give
their sworn oaths in Kirk that they had not transgressed.

It would appear that this pressure was too much for one poor girl because on the 14th March, 1652, in "The Case of The Suicide", it is recorded that Girsell Groate, charged for the third time with fornication with Gilbert Laird, and with Wm Caldell, and also with Thomas Groate, "*murthered herself.*"

Murder itself does not appear to have been too serious a crime and there was "The Case of The Murder" in December, 1658, when Isobell Groate in Mey was delivered of a child to her father-in-law, Donald Miller, who, upon a sudden, tried to strangle the infant with a cloth. This he could not do so his wife and daughter brought in water in which they drowned it. This rather gruesome crime was punished by them all being committed to "*waird*", [ward or prison], but not too long afterwards, in July 1660, the people of Mey were admonished not to "*recept the murtherers*", so it would appear that they had been released.

In "The Case of the Attempted Murder" Wm. Budge in Mey was delate as "*intending to murther*" a little lass but after one further passing reference the matter must have been dropped. Doubtless little lasses in Mey could be cheeky enough even then to rouse the ire of a sober Parishioner to threaten murder!

In "The Case of The Attempted Rape" Wm Barnie, coming out of Stroma with Alex Braibner's wife and going through the Moss, did cast her down and, in her words, "*wald have lyen wt her if he had gotten leave.*" Wm was ordained to stand in sackcloath and make public confession.

On 11th July, 1652, in "The Case of the Slander", Margaret Groate was before the Session having allegedly miscalled Marione McBeath in the Parish of Wattin of murder, witchcraft and theft. Mr Wm Smith, the Minister of Wattin, had sent a letter desiring that the business should be tried. Witnesses were called who stated that they did not hear any such words, neither did they know anything but honestie about Marione. The case seems to have been dropped with no further reference.

As so many cases were coming before the Session by word of mouth, "*qlk bred confusion*", it was ordained that in future all complaints had to be given in writing to the clerk, Andro Ogstoune, with the names of witnesses for proof, and a deposit given which the complainer would forfeit to the Kirk's use if failing in probation. Andro Ogstoune was Session Clerk until

David Allardes appointment in August, 1659, and appears in various references until the end of the Records. He must have been a son of Andro Ogstoune, the Minister of Canisbay from 1601, when Mowat of Bucholie introduced him to the charge, until his death on 31st March, 1650, at the age of 83 years. Previous to 1601 Ogstoune had been schoolmaster at Turriff in Aberdeenshire and our Andro would have had education enough to hold office as Session Clerk, probably from his father, though I do not know exactly how Canisbay fared for schooling in the early 1600s. His likely descendants are still in Canisbay.

Ogstoune the Minister had problems in Cannesbey in 1639 when he complained that he could get but 9 or 10 people into Church to hear sermone, the rest gathering in the Kirkyard but not coming in on the orders of Sir Wm Sinclair of Mey who appears to have been at odds either with Ogstoune or with Mowat of Bucholie who appointed him.

On a lighter note was "The Case Of The Naked Girl", which could be described as "Comedy in The Mill of Mey."

The star, if we can call her that, was a girl called Christian Harris, the other actors in order of appearance! Christian, at a Session meeting on 14th February, 1664, complained that when she was asleep in the Mill of Mey, one would suspect with drink taken but it is not referred to, a lad named Jon Geddes turned up her clothes to her breast so that her nakedness was shown to all that were there, and then she was almost burnt by straw being set on fire between her and Jon Geddes. Enter Henry McPhend who was given credit as being the instigator of the business by promising to give meal to the lad to lift up her clothes. Witnesses came on stage to give evidence that Hendry McPhend did as the girl stated, to wit John Andersone, Helen Barnetson, John Harrowe. The case was continued to the 21st February when evidence was again heard, but in more detail. Christian *"deponit"* that her clothes were shown up to her *"weastcoat"*, and that all did laugh at her. Jon Geddes admitted everything and said Henry McPhend bade him do it, and gave him meal for so doing. Dod Grott, not referred to at the first hearing, deponed he saw her *"honches bear naked"*. Jon Gills said Henrie bade shew hir clothes and all did laugh. John Andersone said her sark and all was shown, and all did laugh. Helen

Barnetsone deponit *"ut supra"* and said all did laugh. Verdict was given and Hendry McPhend was ordained to stand in sackcloath and pay a shilling to the poor. Jon Geddes, the lad, was to be put in the joggs the next day. Jon Guedes, the Miller, probably the lad's father even though the spelling differed, was admonished to keep his Mill in better order therafter, both by night and by day, and if any Miller therafter were to countenance any such wickedness in the *"milne"*, they were to pay 40s. Scots and be censured according to their guilt.

A Mill, apart from grinding meal, was to all intents a meeting house for the district and I am sure there are people still around in Scarfskerry and in Mey who can remember many a good laugh in the Mill of Mey, though possibly not such a case as has just been related! Incidentally, though I use the name Christian **Harris** above, someone has been at Beaton's copy of the Records and overwritten "Harris" on top of the name "Hame" for their own particular reasons! The original Record in Edinburgh gives "Hame". Harris never occurs again, and I am quite suspicious.

Some of the offences tell us a bit about aspects of Parish Life on the Pentland Firth of which otherwise we might not know. One of these was the growing of flax, or lint, which was used in cloth making, or linen at the upper range of quality. Not all cloth made from flax was linen, only the finer fibres being used, and the coarser fibres were woven into a cloth called *"harne"* which would be similar to a rough sackcloth. Only if the fibres were separated would we get the range of cloth which flax was capable of producing but there is no reason to doubt the ability of the Parishioners to do that work. It would have been similar in many respects to wool spinning and weaving after the initial processing. Freswick is the only place mentioned in relation to lint and it is possible that people in other parts of the Parish, tenants under the same laird, had a right to grow flax, or lint, on land in Freswick.

At the North end of the sandy beach is a strip of land still called *"Hemp Rigg"*, hemp being an old name for flax. It would have been too burdensome to grow elsewhere and take it to the pools in Freswick for retting and for further milling and processing.

Wm Cogill and his wife appeared before the Session on 17th August, 1658, charged with the appearance of evil in going on the Sabbath to Freswick to see their lint. I think it would have been still growing at that time rather than in the process of harvesting. Earlier in the Session Records in October, 1652, Andro Baine, Issobel Baine and Magnus Stevin were delate profaners of the Sabbath by binding of lint on Sunday, so the harvest would appear to have been much later than when Wm Cogill went to Freswick.

Flax had to be steeped in water pools as part of the process of extracting the fibre and there is reference to lint being stolen out of the pools at Freswick when Margaret Groat gave in a complaint that John Warrs and his wife called her a thief in stealing their lint out of the pools, that he beat her and almost strangled her with her own kerchief. John Warrs came from Dungasbey so again we find someone using Freswick for lint growing or processing.

Leather in those days would have been valuable and worth having for shoe making and saddlery and for other uses. In March of 1658 Wm Bowar and Wm Baine were convicted of skinning, on the Sabbath, a mare that came in by the sea, and were sentenced to stand in the joggs, or pay 13/4d [a merk] each. Likewise John Water and Donald Hendersone in Dungasbey were dealt with for skinning, on a Sabbath, a selkie, or seal, that came in by the sea. The bounty of the sea was important, as still it is, to the Parish on the Pentland Firth, so that even on the Sabbath parishioners were on the scrounge. Wm Mowatt was charged by Wm Deiran in Mey with taking *"lubster"* out of the ebb. He was also charged with taking in the Sheriff Officer on a Sabbath to arrest debts in his name so does not appear to have been the most popular man in Mey. Gathering seaweed for use as fertiliser on the land was for long a standard practice and led to many a case of strife on the beach, blasphemous and execrable words being exchanged between Issobel Mathewsone and Alex Southerland in the ware, old word for seaweed. Further out in the Firth than the beach of course was fishing and again the Session had wrongdoers before it. In October 1652 Malcolm Rosie was charged with going to sea on the Sabbath. Jon Gill, being at sea fishing with Andro Barnatsone and Wm. Bowar and getting none, threw over his hook saying *"If thow slay not in God's name, slay in ye Devill's name."* He was reported to the Session for taking God's name in vain and eventually had to stand in the joggs, though not finally dealt with until almost a year later.

In November 7th, 1659, David Warrs in Dungasbey and Malcome Budge, coming from the sea, fell out and were reported for curseing, Malcolm calling David a thief. Witnesses called were Adam Baine, Jon Warrs and Donald Hendersone. On 25th December David Warrs finally appeared and muddied the waters by declaring that he saw a man in a long gray coate with a woman whose plaid he took about him, and they went to the ground together. He thought that the man was Wm. Groat. This seems to have taken the heat off David with this spicier item as no punishment of David Warrs is recorded. The sea, as always, had a price to be paid, and Andro Ogstoune gave half a merk to the two men who buried the man that came in by the sea. Wm Caldell, earlier referred to with Girsell Groate and son of Issobell Groat, lost his life at the sea. The father of one of the daughters-in-law of Wm Rosie in Stroma was drowned at sea.

Other delinquencies of more minor degree were Donald Liell in Cannesbey for drying malt on the Sabbath day, as was Andro Braibner and others, Wm Budge in Mey in November, 1652, for shearing on the Sabbath, presumably harvesting corn as wool would have been plucked or pulled or *"rooed"* off the sheep's back much earlier in the year. Helene Baine in Freswick was charged for carrying corne on the Sabbath, and David Baine for being an accessory to the same, and also an absenter from Kirk, Alex Brabiner in Freswick for carrying timber on Sabbath, Margaret Water in Cannesbie for carrying of salt water on Sabbath, Wm Plowman in Mey for carrying home heather and also for going to Dunnet about his wordly business, both offences on the Sabbath day. William had been previously dealt with for winnowing corn and for mucking out his house on the Sabbath, this being so serious that he was referred to the Justice Court.

Donald Harrow in Mey was delate for watering his kale on Sabbath, James Deiran for scaling of diffets on Sabbath, Katharine Broch for walking abroad at night when others were in bed, therfore to be banished Dungasbey. Margaret Thompson, going needless errands to sundry people on Sabbath, was rebuked. Margaret Gills stated that Effie Mathewsone said she enticed her servant woman to steal her meal and bake it in her house, Effie being then convicted of slandering Margt Gills. Witnesses Jon Harrow and Margt Ham said there was no truth in the charge. Elizabeth Robsone and Margaret Skeall were convicted of baking on the Sabbath and had to make public confession of their fault. Donald Gun in Mey was charged with fighting with an unnamed man and *"stricking"* him on the Sabbath, almost suggesting that it would have been all right on a week day!

These are but a token of the variety of offences which appear in the Session Records of "Cannesbey", 1652-1666, but they do give some light, over 300 years ago, on "Parish Life on the Pentland Firth."

— Chapter 5 —

---◆---

Love and Courtship

To pass from the Session Records of Cannesbey without reference to "Adam and Eve" would be quite unfair to the work done by Donald Beaton, Free Presbyterian Minister of Wick.

Many writers quoting these Session Records used not what they saw but what they thought was expedient to their work, such as Craven who quoted the Session Records in his book "The History of the Episcopal Church in the Diocese of Caithness". published 1908, but chose to close his eyes, or his reader's eyes, to the great bulk of the material which has survived over these centuries. He must have written his book on the Caithness Church before Beaton wrote his Transcription because Beaton is not mentioned in Craven's acknowledgements. Craven does refer scathingly to a lack of co-operation from the Keepers of the Records in Edinburgh, albeit about 1908, and definitely not true today.

How to deal with the very frequent mentions of men and women, cohabitation, fornication, marriage, adultery, incest, without the appearance of being either salacious or trying to copy the worst of the Sunday papers is an exercise I must in fairness attempt, and the references used are from 350 years ago and most certainly do not refer to anyone still alive!

In this present "permissive society" the impression is given that all is new and wonderful and has never till now been discovered, really a horse laugh of high quality. In the Parish on the Pentland Firth it all happened before and many years ago. And let no other Parish get too smug about their squeaky clean records either, they just were not recorded!

Courtship in the Parish on the Pentland Firth must have been a very dangerous pursuit in the 1650s as young people, or at least some of them, were under the constant surveillance of others who then reported the slightest matter to the Session.

In these Records of the Parish on the Pentland Firth there are quite a number of small lifestories where we can almost travel through life with the young man, first noted before the Session for climbing the cliffs on the Sabbath after gulls eggs, then drinking and tulzeing [violent quarrelling] and fighting, then drinking in company with a girl, then charged with being *"under blankets"*, or *"in suspect places"*, then fornication with the girl, who then appears as *"being with chylde"*. This surprising development is followed by the baptism of a child where the name of the mother does not appear but possibly one of the witnesses to the baptism is of the same name, probably her father or brother. Time passes and we find a marriage between the two which is later followed by further baptisms but again only the name of the father, the mother's name not being used.

I would like to say that finally our young man becomes an *"Elder"* but that, I am afraid, is stretching it too far with a mere 14 years glimpse of his life. There is not actually anyone who fits ALL these requirements but some come pretty close. Spelling varies, so do not worry about it.

Such a one was Findlay McOchie who first appears on February 14th, 1664, as drinking with Janet McOhoy on the Lord's day. Janet at that time was Janet McBeath but by association she sometimes appears as McOhie though not yet properly so called. Later at the same Session Findlay McOhie was delate as *"does ordinarily goe to bed with Janet McBeath"* and is to be cited to the next day. On the 21st February, 1664, Findlay McOhie and Janet McBaith were delate as being among the customers of Katherine Smith who was charged with selling "aill" to them, probably on a Sunday and a follow on from the previous charge on the 14th. All lived in Mey.

On August 28th we again find Findlay who, after drinking in Dod Southerland's house in Mey with Jonat McBeth, lay among the corn on Martinmass night. This just HAS to be

Marymass night which is at the beginning of August and not Martinmas which is late November. A possible rare misreading by Beaton.

At the same Session Findlay confesses fornication with Margaret Omand in Mey and both are cited to the next day, the case being further continued to the 25th September, 1664, when Findlay promised to find cautioner for himself, and Jon Omand [Rattar?] stood cautioner for Margaret Omand, probably his daughter. On 30th October, 1664, Findlay is again in the wars when he has to give his oath anent an allegation made against him and Jonat McBeath by an unnamed elder. On December 30th it is delate that in May last Findla McIllhuy was found about midnight in ye house of Jonet Miller drinking with one Jonet McBeth, and that she had left her master's house. I wonder if the master in question was also the elder, and also what was a nosey elder doing going about the Parish as late as midnight.

In February of 1665 Margaret Omand payed part of her penalty to Jon Dunnet, the collector, Findlay McOhie paying his 40s. penalty on March 19th for his involvement with her. At the same Session it is recorded that he had a purpose to marry Janet McBeith which, if he failed to do, he was to pay 4 merks by way of penalty for the breach.

On April 20th, 1665, Findlay was to find caution the Sunday next for his marriage to Jonet McBeith.

On July 9th Findlay gave his oath that he was free of carnal dealing with Jonet McBeith, they must have been "just good friends". This would be in preparation for their marriage, which I assume took place, and Findlay and Janet pass into History, there being no further references.

Still in Mey, on 10th July, 1664, we have a short entry relating to William Paterson who was a gardener and could only have been employed at the Castle of Mey, charged with lying in naked bed with Elizabeth Dundas. Next Session William enacted himself that if ever he was found in suspect places behaving himself scandalously with Elspet [Elizabeth] Dundas they were to be held as fornicators and suffer accordingly at the will of the Session. He regularised the situation in December, 1664, by contracting with Elizabeth Dundas to get married, with Wm Davidson the Minister being surety for him and James Dundas surety for Elizabeth, his probable daughter.

Alex Cogill, after a brief fling as being guilty of fornication with Issobel Baine, in May of 1653, baptised an illegitimate daughter Barbara in November the same year with Alex Barnatsone and Thomas Robsone as witnesses, as usual no mother mentioned. In May of 1654 Anna Barnatsone confessed she was under a plaid with Alex Cogill, and Margaret Mowat gave evidence that Alex stayed often out of his house since Xmas last, being suspicious. On November, 1654, Alex went with Anna to St John's Chappel in Mey and on 24 July, 1655, they were married. Thereafter Alex baptises Margaret in 1656, William in 1658 and Issobel in 1660.

Alex Southerland was charged with getting Christane Laird with chylde in December, 1655, baptised twins Hew and Elizabeth in August 1656, married Christane Laird in January 1658, and baptised a daughter Marion in November 1658. These few examples are sufficient to show progressive courtships, there were many more.

There was one case of alleged adultery, among others, which had a story behind it and that was between Effie Robsone and Andro Sinclair, in November of 1660. Effie had a husband, [-] Liell, who went to Uster [Ulster?] about 1650 and it was testified that he was left weak and sick, with a presumption of death. However, it was held that there was no clear evidence of his death so, though ten years had slipped by, Effie was held to be still married, and therefore her association with Andro Sinclair was adultery by her. They had to stand in sackcloth and their bairne was to be baptized, which same was done when Andro, servand in Mey, baptized an illegitimate son William on 23rd December, 1660.

I rather think Effie was the same who, as Euphemie Robsone, was charged on 15th November, 1652, with lying in bed at night with Donald Smith in a sellar near the Minister's house in Dunnet, a *"sellar"* being the bedroom in houses of those old times. They were to purge themselves of such scandalous behaviour and Effie had to stand in sackcloth. She was also charged with being suspiciously with Walter Mendtheplay, in 1659, but denyed everything.

Cohabitation is not a new word of the 1990s, occurring often enough in our Records. There were two kinds, one straight forward such as Jon Cormack in Freswick cohabiting with

Elizabeth Baine in July, 1654, to which they confessed and had to evidence their obedience, and another kind of cohabitation where the two concerned were living in the same house and therefore were much at risk. Such was the case of Walter Robsone and Helene Barnatsone, being both employed by Jon Simson, their master, or employer in today's terminology. In June, 1659, Walter Robsone was charged with lying severall nights in bed with Helene Barnatsone to which he confessed, but denied that he knew her carnally. The self restraint of those times must have been quite something.

However, seeing they both lived in the same house, the Session ordained their master, Jon Simson, to remove one of them for prevention of further possible filthieness. Jon Simson appeared the next Sunday and Walter Robson, having drawn the short straw, had been put away according to the Session's requirement.

Gilbert Dunnet was another, accused in June, 1659, of falling with Elizabeth Durham, which he denied, but she, being charged, confessed that since Christmas last he had known her. Upon consideration of their ignorance paines were to be taken to instruct them to better behaviour, and meantime Elizabeth to be warned to remain from Gilbert, both living in the same house. In August they were ordained to give their obedience.

John Liell in Stroma married Jonet Cowie in December, 1663, with John Kennedy, eldr and ygr, as Cautioners. In March, 1664, they were before the Session as having been guilty of ante-nuptial fornication as she was found to be with child shortly after they were married, for which they had to express repentance.

Paternity was a problem and Elizabeth Gills was charged on 22.11.1654 with being with child to William Geddes. On December 11th both were charged and confessed. On January 29th, 1655, Wm Geddes appeared concerneing the bairne fathered upon him by Elizabeth Gills and declaired plainly that it was not his as she had passed a month of his time. It was referred to further advysement. This came up again on 15th March, 1655, and William denied the bairne could be his. Further, the bairne had the look of Paul Dunbar, who Elizabeth at first stiffly denied, but under pressure she confessed, and

Paul Dunbar was ordained to be charged to the next day. There is no further reference to him.

To illustrate the ability of the Parishioners to identify parenthood I would quote a few short lines from the Island of Stroma where a lad, in more modern times, came visiting an old lady's house to be greeted with :

"Fa's 'at, Ah think Ah ken yer face,
Doun't tell me – chist gaes a bit o grace,
Airs a bit o' auld Dave in ye, so weel Ah mind his grin,
An airs a look o' ae Bremners, ye've got their pointed chin.
Yer eye is lek auld Mowid's, as lek's Ah've ever sawed,
Bit air again, weel, they all were lantern jawed.
Ah see lekness till ae Nicolsins, bit at's no fa ye are,
Noo ae Taits aa were bonnie, ah can see yer no film star.
Fit aboot ae Bankses, aye, yer no at straight in ae back,
And they ah were carpenters, ye widna hev the knack,
Yer teeth aa are gappan, some Warses hed at is weel
Bit yer no one oh em, Och, on at Ah jist can feel.
Yer sort ah lek ae Smiths, boot most o' them were small,
Noo fit aboot ae Simsons, aye, they were beeg and tall,
Boot look at yat long Sinclair nose, Mercy, Ah'll niver learn,
Ah hev ye noo, ye rascal, fa else bit Chrissie's bairn."

With that keen eyed observation what chance had wrongdoers!

Catharin Barnatsone was delate as being carnall with soldiers, to wit Thomas Barr and James McConile, but purged herself on oath as being free of them. Suspicion must still have been there because it was enacted that if ever any woman be found under blankets with any man they were to make public repentance and pay a penalty. So they were warned!

There are in the Records many other variations of the "Adam and Eve" theme, some less printable than others. These few will suffice for the present.

There is moreover no suggestion whatsoever that the Parish on the Pentland Firth was the original "Garden of Eden", though some would have it so!

— Chapter 6 —

Who was Who in the Parish

What of the old Cannesbay Records we have delved into, and what has been missed. Not a lot really, apart from numbers and scale, though there are many small incidents we have not referred to. But before we round off this small glimpse of this part of Parish Life on the Pentland Firth so long ago perhaps the office bearers of the Parish circa 1660 may desire to be remembered.

We began with William Davidson, Minister for the period of the Records. Bernard Barnatsone was Church Officer, mostly just called "*Barnie*". John Dunnet was the Collector and was succeeded in that office by John McBeath in June, 1652. However, John Dunnet was Collector again in January, 1664, when he gave half a merk to the men who buried the body of the man who came in by the sea. Shortly after his appointment in 1652 John McBeath was authorised "*to by a spade and a schovle for the Kirk's use.*"

The office of Clerk to the Session was held by Andro Ogstoune until David Allardes appointment in August, 1659, but when Allardes left and who succeeded him is not detailed. Elders chosen on 11th October, 1652, owing to the weakness of the Session, were Hendrie Miller, James Banks in Holomey, Donald McBeath in ye Fields of Braibstermyre, Jon Mansone in Stroma. Hew Groat was already an elder. Elders who were detailed on the 3rd July, 1659, to go to Stroma with the Minister to look into some serious allegations in the little Island were

Donald Groate, Andro Ogstoune, John Dunnett, Donald McBeath and John Mansone, who was already in the Isle. Those who were present in Stroma on the 9th July, 1659, were Donald Groat, Jon Dunnet, Donald McBeath and Jon Mansone. On the 24th July when the Stroma matters were finally dealt with, presumably back on the Mainland, the elders were Sir William Sinclair of Mey, Magnus Mowat of Freswick, Donald Groat, Hugh Groat, Andro Ogstoune, etc.

Elders chosen on 15th October, 1659, were :

For the Bounds of Mey:- The Laird of Mey, the Laird of Dunbeath, James Dundas, elders, George Rosie, deacone.

For Holomey:- Gilbert Banks, elder, James Banks, deacone.

For Cannasbey:- Donald Groat, Jon Dunnett, elders, Andro Dunnet, deacone.

For Freswick:- the Laird of Freswick [Mowat], the Laird of Balwhollie, [Mowat], Andro Ogstone, elders, Magnus Stevin, deacone.

For Dungasbey:- Hew Groat, Jasper Flett, Wm. Moresone, elders, Hutcheon Harpur, deacone.

For Stroma:- Jon Kennedie, eldr., of Kermuck, elder, Jon Mansone, deacone.

For Braibster:- Donald McBeath, elder.

This would, I think, be the full list of elders.

Thomas Taillour, who was the first schoolteacher we come across, was asked by Hew Groat, elder, by letter of the 30th May, 1653, to fulfill his *"ingadgement"* to come to teach school in Cannasbey. Taillour was there until at least late 1659 and probably into 1660, when succeeded by Donald Reid. He was a frequent witness to baptisms and as a cautioner.

Education and schooling must have been taken very seriously by the leaders of the Parish and Taillour complained, on March 7th, 1658, that many people did not put their children to school at all, and many that did took them away in the middle of the quarter, or before the Elders and the Minister had tryed them to see if they had "profitted" from their instruction. It was enacted that any that did not put their children to school, or took them away before they were presented to the Minister and elders to see if they had profitted from instruction, were to pay 40s. for contravening the order. There was also the matter of the quarter's pay to the Schoolmaster. Jon Water, in Dungasbey, June, 1664, badly abused an elder about the paying of the Schoolmaster, saying that those who appointed him were false and full of tricks.

On 28th October, 1660, Donald Reid agreed to be Schoolmaster at Cannasbey to teach the young children that should be sent to him, and for his paines got 5 bolls of victuall – oat meal or beremeal – at today's weights 700 lbs or 320 kgs per annum, or about two lbs a day. Not a lot for his porridge!

The Schoolmaster was getting 16 bolls meal in 1760, more like a salary. In 1660 the 5 Bolls would have been mere subsistence. A farm worker in 1750 got 6 bolls, 3 of oatmeal and 3 of beremeal, and I would think that the Schoolmaster would probably need a bit more in the year than 5 bolls. He was still schoolmaster at the end of the Record on 18th February, 1666.

The Stroma children must have been taken across to Huna to attend school in Canisbay because in March, 1658, Jon Mansone in Stroma was charged by Wm Liell with taking *"buds"* [bribes, a private reward for services rendered] from sundry in the Isle, including Jon Caldell's *"bud"* and six pynts of aille, and that he gained 10 merks from *"ye bairnes of ye school".* A bit vague but it would appear that Jon Mansone must have provided some kind of service between Stroma and the Mainland, by boat obviously, carrying goods and people, and also that in some way he could get 10 merks in relation to the schoolchildren, which could only be by ferrying them across. Did he overcharge, or was he supposed to take the bairnes across free, as attenders at Church were supposed to be taken. Anyway, to keep up the good name of Jon Mansone, the charge was dismissed. Was he the elder, whom it looks like, and how had he got up Wm Liell's nose?

In July, 1652, Wm Anderson was admitted to the vacant bursarie, did this mean he got a bursarie to go to University from the Parish? or had it some other meaning? It was £4.40d for the half year, compare with the £20 Andro Ogstoune got as clerk for a year. I think University the likeliest and indicates that our Parish was not totally out of touch with higher education.

In 1760 in the Parish the following were the valuations charged towards the school. B.F.P.L. stands for Bolls, Firlots, Pecks, Lippies, the measures used for meal and for grain, in this case meal. A Boll in my earliest recollection was 140 lbs or about 65 kgs but it did have a heavier weight of about 160 lbs in days gone by. In either case it was 10 stones but the old Dutch stone was of 16 lbs. The other elements above divide by 4 each time, so we get 1 Boll = 4 Firlots = 16 Pecks = 64 Lippies, making a Lippie close on a kilogram.

CANNISBAY PAROCH. [1760]

Schoolmaster's Sallary £ 20. [Scots] and 16 bolls meal.
School & Schoolhouse £120.

	Valuation	Sch.Mstrs Sallary		School & Sch . House
	£ . s . d.	£ . s . d.	B:F:P:L.	£ . s . d.
Sir J.Sinclair of Mey	1148.11.06	6.03.04	4 :3 :3:0	37.03.00
Freswick for Mey's Lands				
and Freswick	1030.14.06			
Oukingill,	235.05.10			
both sides Stroma	372.12.00	10.03.00	8:0 :1:3	60.15.00
Warse .	351.19.04	1.16.00	1:1 :3:0	10.16.00
Mlm. Groats part Duncansby	35.00.00	3.06	2.1	1.01.00
West Cannisby	145.10.00	14.02	2 :1:0	4.05.00
Brabstermyre	197.08.08	1.00.00	3 :1:0	6.00.00
Totals	3855.03.06	20.00.00	16:0 :0:0	120.00.00

Andro Ogstoune, who was at one time clerk to the Session, succeeded by David Allardes in August 1659, appears frequently as cautioner to marriages and as witness to baptisms. He signed the accounts of John McBeath, collector, in December 1652, was an elder and an apparent pillar of the Parish Society of his day.

Millers mentioned were John Geddes in Mey and Andrew Baine in the Milltoun of Oukingill. The Lairds of the Parish were mostly Sinclairs of the Estates of Mey, Cannesbey, Brabster, Mowat of Bucholie, his son Magnus of Freswick, sold in 1661 to Wm Sinclair of Rattar, Groat of Warse. Sir William Sinclair of Dunbeath and Sinclair of Rattar were both mentioned. The Mowats were non-Sinclairs and had about run their course as landowners, their Estates being sold bit by bit, mostly to the Sinclairs. However, they were all so interlinked by marriage it was almost a case of musical chairs with the Estates. The Kennedys of Kermuck and Stroma appeared during the time of our Session Records and on 15th January, 1660, the Laird, John Kennedy, was given permission to *"plant"* a seat in the Church on the South side of the *"queere"* under the Westmost window, between the door and the wall dividing the church and the *"queere"*. There were two Kennedys in Stroma called John, father and son, and another called Patrick in Okingill who christened a child Catharine in April 1654. There were Ministers, William Smith who was Minister in Watten and who died in Dunnet in 1655, to whose burial William Davidson went, and John Smairt, Minister in Wick Parish Church and who preached on a number of occasions when Davidson was unwell and *"bedfast"*. A messenger must have been sent, presumably by horse from Cannesbey to Wick, to request his assistance on these occasions as the telephone had not yet reached Cannesbey in 1660!

William Davidson himself preached, by appointment of the Presbyterie, at a number of locations in Caithness, Thurso, Halkirk, Bowar, Olrick quite a number of times from where David Allardes had been deposed, Dunnet, Keiss, Stroma in his own Parish on the 15th July, 1660, and it is of interest that he had been expected to be in the Island the previous Sunday and that no persones were therefore charged to the Session that day.

He attended Synods in Dornoch, Thurso, Kirkwall, and at each Synod was attended by a leading elder from his Kirk, nominated and then chosen by *"plurality of votes"*, democracy at work even then, Hew Groat or the Laird of Dunbeath usually.

Surnames were universally used in the Parish on the Pentland Firth, the only exception being *"Graycoate"* who was an apparent witch. Some names had an alias and some a nickname. Johne Stevin alias *"Crookie"*, probably a bit of a cripple as I am unaware of any place name of *"Crook"* in Canisbay even though it occurs in many locations in Caithness, the nearest being Crooks of Howe in Lyth. Donald Henderson was alias *"Cassere"*, a meaning escapes me. Janet Sutherland was alias *"Wanton"* which apart from it's more usual meaning also meant jovial, waggish, free from care. As she had, in November, 1658, a testimonial from Mr Alex Clerk, presumably a Minister, she was promised similar at her removal out of the Parish, according to her deportment. In August of 1664 Janet Sutherland, spous to [-] McIntagger living as a vagabond away from her husband and having no testimonial, was ordained to remove herself out of the Parish, and any who gave her lodging should be fined a merk for each night she stayed, unless she gave a sufficient testimonial. It looks rather like the same person, irrespective of Alex Clerk's testimonial, and on 4th September, 1664, she left Dungasbey. There was another Janet Sutherland referred to in December, 1654, with one of Glengarrie's soldiers, then accused in December, 1655, of fornication with Hendrie Geddes, but they marry in August of 1656 and all's well.

It is of interest to find surnames so well established and that they are much the same as today's, minor differences in spelling to be ignored. Place name surnames were used such as Bowar in Stroma, Stroma on the mainland, Swanny from Swona, or Swina as it was once called, Broch, Cogill from Cogill in Watten, and as they still like to remind you, the only name in Caithness which is "*of*" a place name. Other place names used were Banks, Deiran, Dunnet, Gills, Harrowe, Hame, Quoyes, Warres. Some names were recorded which I personally would have associated with the Orkneys but were in our Parish in 1660, such as Irving, Flett, Mueur, Stout, Tulloch, Yeill, Wylyman [Wylie]. Many names were common to both the Orkneys and Caithness, too many to be worth mentioning, but they indicate the closeness of the two. There were a few names from the Highlands such as McBeath, McCloud, MacFend, McKenzie, McLeane, McOchie, Southerland. Watsones were there, did they all stem from John Watsone, alias Wobster, who became Minister in 1572.

Mendtheplay occurs, eventually to vanish, though there was one in Thurso in 1701. Williamsone and Water, Tenant and Thompsone, Swansone, Stevin and Smithe, Omand, Rosie and Rugg, Mathesone, Miller and Mowat, Kennedy, Liell and Laird, Jack and Hendersone, Groate and Geddes, Dunnet and Davidsone, Cormack and Couper, Clyne and Caldell, Budge and Bruice, Brabner and Begg, Barnatsone, Bayne and Baikye, Angus and Andro, Alexandersone and Allan. All appear in number while other names I have not detailed are also there, though those above were the most common.

Who knows, perhaps your name was there too!

— Chapter 7 —

Cost of Living and Inflation

Everybody today is overfamiliar with the phrases "Cost of Living" and "Inflation", but in our Parish on the Pentland Firth long ago just what did that mean, particularly to the common people as distinct from the Lairds whose living was better documented in lists of shopping requirements still surviving, dealt with particularly by John Donaldson in his "Mey Letters" and in his "Caithness in the 18th Century."

Leaving our Session Records slightly behind we can have a look at the Expense of Husbandry which was essentially the cost of clothes and of food in the years 1750, 1790, 1798, and this applied to the cost to a farmer of employing both men and women on an annual basis and on short term hiring. In money terms we are still looking at pounds Scots, of which 12 to a £1 Sterl. A man servant had **annual** wages of £1 Scots in 1750 which rose to £3 in 1790 and then to £5 in 1798, while a woman had 6/8d rising to £1 and then to £1.12.00. When engaged for the harvest, which lasted about 8 weeks a man had his *"victuals"* and 5/- in 1750, 15/- in 1790 and £1.10.00 by 1798, while if on a daily basis he had 6d, 8d and 1/- without his food, and 4d, 6d. and 8d if *"with victuals"* in these respective years. When you divide by 12 to get Pounds Sterling the mind boggles, and in the last year quoted, 1798, we were in the age of the great Agricultural Improvers who included in Caithness such luminaries as Sir John Sinclair of Ulbster and James Traill of Castlehill and Rattar in Caithness and Hobbister in Sanday in Orkney.

Such moneys are beyond comment and little more than tokens for the reward of a year's work, as close to slavery as we can get. There was in addition of course their *"cost"* which was mainly meal and over these 48 years a man servant received per annum 3 bolls of oatmeal and 3 bolls of beremeal, about 420 lbs or 190 kgs. of each at today's weights of a Boll, but I think slightly more at that time. Women servants received half that, 1.5 bolls of each, presumably they were single with no family to feed. Besides getting their meal menservants were stated as being *"unwilling to ingage"* without also getting pasturage for a cow and ground on which to plant 3 or 4 pecks of potatoes, in quantity about 4 buckets of seed potatoes and enough to plant a small garden or yard, not a lot. Even in my time in farming a man often had a cow, which gave him milk for his house and a calf to sell, and 60 chains of drills for potatoes which was nearly a fifth of an acre. The farmer was further encouraged to insist on the labourer planting his potatoes in uncultivated soil so that in a few years time he could eventually enlarge his farm at the expense of his servant's unpaid hard labour in breaking in new ground. By practices such as these the arable land of Caithness was increased but incredibly slowly and laboriously.

In addition to their meagre wages and *"cost"* both men and women had two pairs of shoes. The TOTAL cost of employing a man for a **year**, meal and clothes, was £3.06.08d Scots in 1750; £6.11.06d in 1790 and £9.11.00d in 1798, and a woman servant cost £1.10.04d; £2.17.00d and £4.00.00d in these respective years As a cow and calf was worth £5 in 1798 a man servant's worth was about 2 cows which at today's prices would be about £2,000 or £40 per week, but a woman would cost a poor farmer less than a cow, or under £20 per week. These were the bare costs itemised by the Parochial Schoolmaster for his own interest in 1798, but in addition were listed a detailed account of the Daily Habit and Dress Habit [Clothes] of both men and women for these years of 1750/90/98.

It would appear that the farmer provided everything needed by his servants as far as food and clothing was concerned, and with their money wage at the levels itemised I doubt if they could have bought the clothes we will come across.

In 1750 we begin, for a man servant, with 3 yards black Kelt for a coat, Kelt being a kind of homespun black or grey cloth used for outer garments, priced at 10d a yard. The amount was reduced to 2¹/₂yds by 1790 but the price had risen to 3/9d, and by 1798 he was tastefully turned out in blue cloth at 5/6d a yd. Next was a yard of blue stuff for a waistcoat at 7d. a yd., rising to 1/3d and then only ³/₄ yd. at 5/6d in 1798. Breeches followed at a yard of Kelt again, quite neat I would have thought at only a yard, same again in 1790 but by 1798 he needed 2.25 yds of Mankey, a glossy, almost waterproof, woollen material, for the same breeches at a cost of 6/3d., a huge increase in the amount of cloth needed. A shirt needed 3 yds of coarse linen and the price rose from 1/- to 3/- to 5/-. A pair of stockings at 9d., 1/ 3d., 1/6d. A bonnet at 10d., 1.6d., 3/-. A pair of shoes, working ones, at 10d., 2/9d., 5/-. A napkin at 10d., 1/6d., 4/6d. completed the ensemble. Additionally there were some small charges to a tailor for making the clothes, 8d., 1/4d., 3/-.

Now to the Dress Habit, or Clothes, and here we are indeed putting on the style! The dress coat in 1750 required 4 yards of Camlit costing 4/8d. By 1790 2 yards was enough but it was of English cloth making inroads on the Scottish market, costing 16/- and then £1 in 1798. Black Mankey was still acceptable for a waistcoat in 1750 but by 1790 was replaced by velvet at 4/6d. and then to a swansdown vest at 5/-. Breeches used Mankey in 1750 but by 1790 corduroy was the order of the day, while a shirt needed linen probably of a better quality than for a working shirt. Dress stockings, bonnet, napkin, shoes were of better quality or at least were dearer than those pertaining to Daily Habit. And before we think of these bygone farm labourers daintily touching their lips with a napkin, let us go back to the original name of *"napekin"* and visualise it around the nape of the neck of the labourer to keep out cold, chaff, rain or dust, much as a coalman even today. Bonnets sported trimmings by 1790 and 1798 and the napkin escalated in price from 1/- to 4/6d to 5/-. I wonder though if every farm servant got his velvet or swansdown vest as per the above list.

The total cost of a man's daily habit over the years was 9.01d., 18.04d., £2.06.09¹/₂, while the dress habit was 16/09d., £2.08.05d., £3.04.00d. Compare with the cost of woman's clothes.

Now to the more interesting list of woman servant clothes, both daily and dress habit, which of course is of greater length. I wonder why! They were also more expensive. I wonder why!

Starting with Daily Habit, the woman had 5 yds "stuff" cloth for her gown, at 2/11d in 1750, rising to 6/03d to 7/06d. It became blue stuff in 1790 and 1798. She then had an outer petticoat needing 4 yds of cloth, an inner petticoat needing 3 yards of coarse flannel, a shift needing $2^1/_2$ yards of coarse linen at 5d., 8d., and 1/4d a yard in the years mentioned.

This adds up to $14^1/_2$ yards of cloth she was carrying around at her daily work, and if she wore it all at the same time on a hot summer day the mind boggles. It makes quite a contrast with a miniskirt! In addition to these she had an apron of stuff, a mutch [headdress like a hood], a napkin, a pair of stockings and a pair of shoes. The daily habit remained constant in the items over the period of 1750 to 1790 to 1798, the total cost therof being 12.00d, £1.05.06d., £1.14.03d.

Turning to the woman's servant's Dress Clothes, the gown began in 1750 with 5 yds of fine stuff at 5/- but by 1790 had changed to 6 yds of Calicoat [cotton cloth] at 18/- and then to £1 in 1798. The outer petticoat required 4 yds and then 6 yds and then 8 yds of English Mankey while the inner petticoat was of Flannel in 1750 but of white cotton in 1790 and 1798. This is an indication of the effect that American cotton was having on British cloth manufacturer which in 1750 was entirely of wool and linen produced at home, but by 1810 cotton had effected a considerable lowering of the costs of women's dress, though men were much as before. Style was creeping in because the fripperies such as napkin for dress in 1750 became elevated to a silk napkin in 1790 and to a necklace and breast knot in 1798. Here we have again the original usage of necklace as a nap(e)kin made of lace. In 1790 gloves appear for the first time, a pocket handkerchief and a pair of pockets, no doubt fastened to a belt, also a cloak. The hair was now adorned with a ribband. The costs of women's dress wear was £1.06.09, rising to £4.15.06 and then to £6.06.04 in 1798.

This occasioned the author to write:

"N.B. The Dress Clothes generally last five years but so strong is the desire for Braws that some new thing is added annually to ye flock." [Braws – old Scots word for fancy clothes.]

Thus a woman servant by 1798 required twice as much to clothe as her husband, and that's nothing new!

There was a final comment by our researcher on the changing times in 1798. This was the introduction of Spinning Factory which was not the new building we today would expect but the factoring or giving out of lint by merchants to young women to spin into linen thread in their own homes, the origin of the name *"spinster"* to denote a young unmarried woman. Murdoch Campbell, factor in Freswick in the late 1700s, gave out lint to 90 girls to be spun and sent South for weaving. Much of this lint came from the Baltic or Russia and undercut the growing of flax in Freswick referred to in a previous article. It was stated that this trade was so *"inticing"* that the women seldom *"ingage"* as servants except during harvest when they demanded as much wages as they could have got for a half year's service. He went on to describe this as a pernicious system which must prove highly damaging to the interest of the Farmer unless regulated, but how he did not say.

What of the cost of living, though, and what prices did the *"poor farmer"* get for the produce his Servants produced for him? There was a table produced showing the prices of various commodities for the years 1750, '90, '98, and we can bear in mind that Britain was at war with France and with Napoleon in 1798, one result of which was the blockade of supplies of lint from the Baltic and a corresponding explosion of trade in cotton with our very recent and newly independent colonies of the American States. This trade eventually hit the linen trade very hard though it did struggle on for a long time, linen being a better cloth than cotton though more expensive.

The farmer's produce in the years mentioned was, for a cow with a calf 15/-, £3.10/-, £5.05/-, and without a calf 12/-, £2.08/, £4.

A horse fit for ploughing was respectively £1.10/-, £3.07/, £7.

A wedder [sheep] in season 2/6d., 7/6d., 12/- while a lamb could be got for 6d., 2/6d., 4/-.

A hog [pig] or a sow made 2/6d., 10/6d., 15/-.

A goose was 6½d., 1/2d., 1/8d. while a hen made 2d., 4d., 6d., her eggs being a 1d. per doz of 18, then a 1½d. a doz of 12, and 2d. in 1798.

A stone of butter of 24lbs, called a double stone, [11kg.] was 5/-, 15/- and 18/-, and was a commodity used to pay rent, especially in Parishes such as Latheron where they kept large numbers of small black cattle in the interior of that Parish which was fit only for grazing. Cheese likewise was used for rental purposes and made 2/6d per stone, then 4/- and 6/- in 1798, again 24 lbs. a stone. Fed or fattened beef sold per lb at $1^1/_2$d., $2^1/_2$d., $4^1/_2$d. and by 1810 had risen to 6d. These were the prices received by farmers in the time of the Agricultural Revolution and the Improvements of Sir John Sinclair of Ulbster, James Traill of Castlehill and Hobbister, and many others in the County. Against the money wage of the farm servant they were academic.

These costs show the economic circumstances of the times which shortly led to the clearances in poorer areas and the spread of sheepfarming, while better areas were resumed by the landlords at the end of the lease and amalgamated into the larger farms we see today.

The commons were enclosed and apportioned among the riparian landowners, usually in proportion to the rental of their estates. There was little incentive to the worker to live on, or exist, in his native land, and it is not to be wondered that so many migrated to the South or emigrated to other lands, leaving formerly populated areas to the naturalist and the Conservationist. Indeed may I quote a paragraph from the 1841 Census in Halkirk Parish which stated:- "*A considerable number of families have of late years been removed from this District by the introduction of sheep farming. The houses in general are of so fragile a construction that, if left unoccupied for a few years, they crumble into dust and soon disappear, which may account for so few being marked as uninhabited in the schedule.*"

Against that background it is not really surprising that there are more Scots outwith Scotland than there are living in their native land.

— Chapter 8 —

The Pentland Firth itself

To conclude this Canisbay portion of "Parish Life on the Pentland Firth" we pick up a few remaining aspects from 1652 to 1666, and perhaps add a few more from other sources which may give a glimmer of light on the darkness of the past.

What of the Pentland Firth itself, that must have so influenced the lives of those living in the Parish on it's Southern shore, and on the Island standing sentinel in the path of the streaming tides, watching impassively the Picts on their migrant way North to Orkney to build Skarabrae, and vanish, the Druids to set up their Standing Stones, if it were they who did so, the Priests to build their isolated chapels and dwellings on Eynhallow, Papa Stronsay, Papa Westray and the other Holy Isles of the Orkneys, the Viking Norse with Longships passing on their summer raiding, and then to settle on both sides of the Pentland Firth and scatter their place names and their red blood and their fair descendants over the North. The linking of Caithness and Orkney under the Norse Earls must have occasioned many a passage of people either way.

Until 1468 the Pentland Firth was the actual frontier of Scotland with Norway/Denmark, Orkney being then pledged to the Scottish Crown against the dowry of Margaret of Denmark, irrecoverably as it turned out.

In 1527, the Caithness Sinclairs and their Caithness men sailed from Huna over the Pentland to Houton in Orkney to

Summerdale to be massacred by Orkney Sinclairs and their Orkney men. The ships of the Spanish Armada passed East and West of the Pentland though I do not think any attempted it's passage, going Northabout to skirt the Orkneys and not all with success.

Orkney men crossed the Pentland at various times to fight in Scottish battles, including Bannockburn and Flodden, sometimes a one way ticket. Montrose crossed the Pentland Firth Southwards in 1650. Cromwell's men crossed Northwards in 1652. Englishmen came North again to build the Martello Towers at Lyness in Hoy as defence against the French under Napoleon, again in 1914 - 1918 to turn Orkney into a fortress and a naval base at Scapa Flow. Their sons and daughters crossed once more in 1939 - 1945 to do the same job all over again. In 1919 the German Grand Fleet steamed through the eastern end of the Pentland Firth and into Scapa Flow and their eventual interment under water, only for many to be raised and towed to Rosyth for breaking up, many still upside down.

In 1815 James Tait from Caithness crossed the Pentland Firth with cattle bought in Orkney, droving them to Carlisle to Thomas Morton at Brough in Cumberland, a husbandman who was in Caithness on the 15th April, 1815, there witnessing the baptism of James's daughter Janet in Lyth. She was the mother of William Tait, founding partner of J. & W. Tait of Kirkwall. Until the days of steam Orkney cattle moved South in considerable numbers by the Pentland Firth route through Canisbay Parish, landing over open beaches on the Canisbay shore at Sannick and at Huna and at Freswick, according to wind and tide. Young horses from Strathnaver in Sutherlandshire crossed to Orkney, some returning as mature and trained horses later in life. Our Session Records mentioned Donald Water crossing with horses from Orkney on the Laird of Mey's boat on a Sabbath in 1663.

James Tait crossed the Pentland Firth many times from Caithness pursuing cattle dealing, staying the Census night of the 6th June, 1841, in the Ferry Inn in St Mary's in Holm with two other Taits and two Swansons, all termed "cattle dealers". And it was from St Mary's that Italian prisoners of war, having made the crossing of the Pentland Firth, began to build a lasting memorial to themselves in the Churchill Barriers, linking South

Ronaldsay to the Mainland of Orkney and leading to the recent illstarred idea that the Pentland Firth was but a ditch to be crossed easily and quickly by a "Short Sea Crossing". Perhaps, someday, but not today!

And from the Parish on the Pentland Firth crossings are still being made by Thomas and Bews ferry from John O'Groats, carrying on the tradition of Jan de Groot himself, nor must we overlook the other crossing at the western end of the Firth from Scrabster to Stromness by the St Ola, the fourth of the series, coming a very long way from the first crossing by steam in 1856 by the "Royal Mail", a paddle steamer of 103 tons, about the size of a medium seine netter.

I suppose I date myself by stating that I have crossed the Pentland on all four St Olas! The prewar sailing was from Stromness to Scapa and then on through Scapa Flow, sometimes touching at Lyness, before the reach across the Pentland Firth past Cantick Head in Hoy and on past Dunnet Head and into Scrabster, my own introduction to Caithness. Later, during the War, the St Ola had to sail westward of Hoy, omitting the pre-war call at Scapa Pier, and that is the present route, as it was the first.

It is of interest, with the Short Sea Crossing controversy of recent date, to quote from *The Orcadian* of 7/6/1851 a report of the dispute of **that** day:

"All agreed that Scrabster should be the point of departure on the other side but on this side three places, none of them with piers, found their champions – Scapa, Holm, and especially Houton, but as might be expected an indignant Stromness protested. Eventually it won the day, for it was from there that the first steam packet carrying passengers, freight and mails, made the crossing of the Firth in 1856."

Of the water of the Firth itself we have this description taken from Aneas Bayne's comments on Canisbay Parish in his "A Short Geographical Survey of Caithness, 1735."

"The Pictland Firth which bounds this Shire to the North is one of the most rapid seas in Europe. North from Dungsbey Head is what they call "The Boar of Dungsbey" where, during the flood tide, the Sea rages with prodigious high surges which form a ridge of about 4 leagues reaching to South Ronaldsay in Orkney. It falls with the Ebb, at which time raises, about 4 miles West, an equally long Ridge of Raging Seas called "The Men of Mey", which reaches from St John's Head in the Parish of Canesbay to Walls in Orkney, or very near. The former swells most when the wind is at East, the latter when the wind is at West.

"Many ships and boats are wrecked here, for it requires great skill to know the Tides in this Firth, which the Picts found to their sad Experience, whose overthrow here made it to be called "The Pictland Firth" as it was ordinary among the ancients to call their Seas by the names of any notable persons to whom they had been fatall.

"Icarus Icarys nomina fecit aquis".

"In the Firth, North East of Stroma about a league, is Swina, an Island of Orkney, South West of which are two dreadful whirlpools very terrible to passengers, wheeling round with great rapidity during the first three hours of the flood, when, if a boat chance to fall into them, it is carried round in the vortex and not easily freed. These are commonly called "The Wells of Swina." They very much resemble the vortex between Jura and Isla, two of the Western Isles of Scotland, or rather the Scylla and Charybdis in the Straits of Messina as described by Virgill [Aenid.]

Translation:- Latin omitted,

"Mishapen Scylla on the Right abides,
Cruel Charybdis on the left resides,
Thrice in her Gulfs devours her waves and then,
Thrice to the Starrs, she Spoutts them up again.

Lauderdale. "

On Stroma, and again from Bayne's comments on Canisbay Parish:

"In the Pictland Firth 2 miles North of Canesbay is Stroma, the only Island belonging to this Shyre, in Circumference about three miles, holding of William Sinclair of Freswick. It contains 40 families who maintain themselves by corns and fishing, which are indeed the main commodities of this Parish, for they have some Cattle but yet they are of the smallest size and none of the best of their kind."

On the land of Stroma itself the following comes from the Caithness Valuations of 1701:

"The whole land of the Island of Stroma belonging once to the Earle of Caithness and to Kermunks [Kennedy] was 9 P/1d and 5 octos and yt conform to the Contract of Wadset therupon wherof in the Overtoun of Stroma Ratter has five P/1d, every P/1d pays yearly of Martinmass Debt £15/4/-d. Scots in money and of ferme 6 bolls, with the Teind Sheaff which cannot be rentalled nor exactly valued by reason some years, and yt very ordinar, with the blasting of the sea and drift of the salt water, they will have hardly any oats to be got and not a peck of oatmeal. And the bear likewise will not be anything worth. Wherby in communibus annis the teind in the strictest cannot be rentalled or valued to more than 3 bolls vituall for the teind of each P/ld. Qch with the boll of ferme, is nine bolls for each P/land for ferme and teind. The sd nine P/ld and five octos pays 8 bolls vict. to the Minister of Canesby, Qrof. Ratter, owner of the said Overtoun of Stroma, pays 4 bolls."

So farming in Stroma was not without risk.

[P/1d = pennyland, about 18 acres, octo= one eighth thereof. A Boll of meal was 140 lbs [64kg.] but 160lbs long ago. A £ Scots equalled 1/8d Sterling, now 8.33p.!!]

And taken from the Census of 1841, some comments made by Davidson, Canisbay Schoolmaster, the enumerator.

CANISBAY PARISH. Census of 1841.
"CANISBAY DISTRICT.

"There is a considerable decrease in this District since 1831, the cause appears to be the partial introduction of Sheep and converting severall farms into larger ones which occasion the removal of severall families. It may be also mentioned that very few Marriages have taken place in this District for a number of years past as compared with the other districts of the Parish. The Decrease upon the whole Parish since 1831 is 71. In this District there are more inhabited houses than Families, this arises from where a part of the same family slept in an Outhouse or detached building, the said Outhouse or detached building is enumerated as a separate dwelling house as directed by Article 5 of Enumerators Instructions.

This will also occur in other districts of the Parish."

and on STROMA DISTRICT of CANISBAY.

"There is a considerable decrease in this Distict, the inhabitants being at and previous to 1831 much addicted to smuggling, but now, smuggling being completely suppressed, severall families have left the Island and removed to the Orkneys to follow more lawful pursuits."

and on **DUNCANSBAY DISTRICT,**

"Several families have removed at the Whitsunday term to the Orkneys."

and on **BRABSTER DISTRICT.**

"There is a small increase in this Distict since 1831. One family consisting of 3 males and 4 females Emigrated from this District to Pictou, Nova Scotia, in the week ending 5th June, inst., being the only persons Emigrated from this Parish to the Colonies or Foreign Countries during the last six months."

and on **KEISS DISTRICT. [North.]**

"There is a considerable increase in this District." [This must reflect the growth of herring fishing at that time.]

For what it is worth, a tabulation of the various districts of the Parish on the Pentland Firth in 1841, ending with a plus or minus according to increase or decrease in population since the previous census of 1831.

Houses	Inhab.	Empty	Bldg.	Male.	Female.	Total.	Families.	
Stroma	42	4	-	87	99	186	42	-
Huna etc.	63	2	-	128	153	281	62	+
Canisbay Gills	59	-	-	122	143	265	55	-
Duncansbay	63	3	-	129	173	302	60	-
Freswick	97	4	-	185	216	414*	92	+
Brabster	37	-	7	76	44	170	36	+
Mey	96	2	3	223	244	467	92	+
Keiss North	49	-	- 1	13	108	221	47	+

* 13 extra in anchored boats lying off Skirza.

These paragraphs are somewhat statistical and to many are dry, they are however a record of the past.

From our Session Records we have already mentioned some aspects of the Firth, including, in November, 1652, William Liell not staying to hear sermone, and going over the ferrie with Alex Begge, Alex Liell and Donald Watsone. There were a number of occasions when an entry states that no preaching was held by reasone of a storm of snow and drift, or of tempestuous weather. So they had their storms then as now. Though Stroma was not mentioned by name it had to be the *"ferrie"* to Stroma, these were all Stroma men, and it could easily have been deteriorating weather that caused them to head home while the sea was still passable.

After all, they lived by the sea.

Sometimes they died by the sea.

— Chapter 9 —

⟫◆⟪

Kathren Creak, thief

Stretching Parish Life on the Pentland Firth round Duncansbay Head on the North East corner of Caithness and on to the south, we come to the Parish of Wick and, continuing our interest in the Caithness of the 1600s, there we find the "Counsell Book of Wick", of which the earliest surviving copy covers the years from 1660 to 1711. It is in reasonable shape for being over 300 years old but quite unreadable for most people as well as being very tender. At present it is in the care of the North Highland Archives in the Wick Library Building, already becoming a collecting centre for old manuscripts, maps, plans, and other records of the Caithness of long ago and of the North of Sutherland, too many of which records have in the past ended on a bonfire! Incidentally the Wick Counsell Book is the earliest written record in the Caithness Archives up to the present, 1997, though earlier records such as some scattered Sheriff Court ones are available in The Scottish Record Office in Edinburgh.

As I had already done some work on this old style of writing, mostly on old Orkney Records of Kirkwall as far back as 1612, it seemed that, with a bit of patience, an infinity of time, and not a little luck, I might be able to do a transcription of these old records so that in time coming those interested could read easily that which is almost impossible now, certainly impossible on a short visit to the Library. Apart from that, these tender old manuscript books will not stand any great deal of handling

and modern transcriptions should and ought to be a requirement of any archives. The work entailed is enormous and can
only be done by interested hobbyists working patiently on their
own and preferably from photocopies. A word processor is
essential, the work being done at home and NOT on a quick
visit to Wick.

The Counsell Book of Wick has been delved into before and
many a story has been quoted from it, so some of what I might
write in this book of "Parish Life on the Pentland Firth" may
well be familiar to some readers. The transcription will allow any
student of the Old Record to compare side by side with the old
writing mirrored by typewritten copy. It might even help
someone in the reading of other ancient records of that period.
Copies of the Transcription are available in the Libraries of
Wick, Thurso, Kirkwall, Inverness and in the Scottish Record
Office in Edinburgh.

Perhaps a little historical background would be helpful and,
though I am not by any means an out and out monarchist, the
reigns of the sovereigns of that time are relevant. The year 1660
saw the Restoration, after Cromwell's Commonwealth, of
Charles the 2nd who was King until 1685, being succeeded by
his brother James the 2nd. Flirtation with Roman Catholicism by
that monarch, and the tendency of the Stewarts to adhere to
"The Divine Right of Kings", resulted in his rejection and replacement by William III of Orange [Holland] grandson of Charles
1st through his daughter Mary, and William's wife, also Mary,
daughter of James 2nd., and who ruled jointly with William.

Mary died in 1694 of small pox and William died in 1702,
the result of a fall by his horse tripping on a mole heap which
led to the Jacobite drinking toast to "The gentleman in the black
velvet coat!" William was succeeded by Queen Anne in 1702,
younger sister of his wife Mary, and whose reign lasted until
1714 when she was succeeded by the first of the Hanoverians,
George 1st, second cousin of Anne if I remember my History,
and a Stewart on the maternal side. Such was the monarchy
during the period of the first Counsell Book of Wick, 1660 to
1711, and I mention them as they are now and again referred
to.

The Counsell Book itself runs to 118 pages, some very
detailed, some very scanty, being but one short paragraph.

Certain matters run right through, the election each autumn of a "Provest, Bailyies and Toun Counsell for the nixt Inshewing yeir", the annual setting by public roup of the Customes and other dues. Sometimes these are the only entries for a twelve month, and there was a period when no entry was made at all, particularly 1687 to 1706, whether another book was in use, fairly unlikely, or some other reason of which I do not know. I did wonder if the Battle of Altimarlich in 1680 just outside Wick with John Campbell of Glenorchy had any effect but found no reference to it and no evidence of some of the main men of Wick vanishing from the scene after that skirmish. Other portions are quite detailed, in particular the first portion after 1660 and the latter portion after 1707 to the end of the book in 1711, giving some partial insight to the life and times of the "Burgh Toun" of long ago, of the fights which were endemic to Wick, then!!, of interactions with Central Government, with acts of Parliament percolating down to local level, even an Act of Parliament of the 6th year of the minority of Mary, Queen of Scots, passed by the Scottish Parliament under the Regency of her mother, Mary of Guise. This related to the appointment of Deacons of Crafts for the better arrangement of local affairs, the act being quoted verbatim.

In the period of the first Counsell Book Wick Burgh had a landward interest which extended South to Berridale, North to Keiss, West to Watten, while we find passing mention of Henrie Sinclair of Isauld, David Murray of Thurso, Wm Sinclair of Hoy, other names and other places scattered around. Mostly though it is of Burgh affairs we find note and of Burgh people. For example, what was Baillie George Bruce doing fighting with James Doull, shoemaker, why and over what did John Donaldson draw blood from James Dunbar, glover, why was Willie Calder, merchant in Wick, striking James Forbes in Field, how did John Sutherland get into so many scrapes?

These chapters were done in the main as the transcription progressed and are not supposed to be in any particular chronological order, being written on a more "happen chance" manner.

I think some keen genealogist just might, with some luck, jump the gaps in the Old Parish Records of Wick which began in 1701, and find that they are related to one or other of our "heroes". I hope any reference they might find is taken with pride even if the incident is somewhat shady. After all, not everyone can claim a hanging among their forebears! And the story that I find the most sad and touching revolves around Kathren Creak.

Kathren first appears on the 24th of January, 1669, when she was *"Indytit and acused"* for the stealing of twentie pounds of goose fethers from William Sinclair, merchant in Wick. She was a "srvetr" of William and had taken the twentie *"pund"* of goose feathers out of his *"nether loft"*, putting them in a wallet, which was at that time just a large bag. Goose feathers were very much a commodity of those times and rents were sometimes paid to include a quantity of feathers.

She was *"apprehendit"* taking the feathers out of the loft and giving them to Thomas Yonge, a Chapman or travelling merchant, who had *"trysted"* with her to apparently steal the feathers, and he promised he would give her a "Snood" for the feathers. The crime was compounded by being committed on the Sabbath day, whether Sinclair was at the Kirk or not we cannot tell.

Both Kathren and Thomas Yonge, with their respective procurators Wm Caldell and Johne Mursone, denied the charges and Frances Mansonne, fiscall of the Court, undertook to prove the Indytment, asking for another court day to be provided for proof, the 28th January being fixed. The procurator was bound over to produce the said Kathren and Jon Mursone to produce Thomas Yonge in Court on that day, under pain of £20 Scots for failure.

At the Court on the 28th January Kathren confessed that she had indeed put the feathers in the wallet and for the promise of the Snood, and Thomas Yonge confessed he gave her the Snood for the feathers. The crime was considered to be "frivolous" by the Bailyies, Frances Sinclair of Stirkok, Allexr Cormok and Allexr Mansonne of Wick, and I take it that "frivolous" meant that Judgement on small matters could be dealt with by the Bailyie Court without referring to an Assize Court which doubtless dealt with more serious crimes, probably under the Sheriff. Sentence was then pronounced on Kathren who was to be put in the Joges at the *"Marcatt Croie of the Burghe"*, there to stand for an half hour with a paper hat upon her head setting out why she was there. No doubt being in the Joges made one a target for whatever rubbish bystanders could throw and was not a soft option.

The Judges referred the punishment of Thomas Yonge, the apparent instigator of the mischief, to his father, Andrew Yonge, that *"he cmit nocht the Lyik falt in Tyme Cmg."*

Kathren was not to be forgotten though and on 27th July, 1669, she was again in trouble, this time more serious. Described as being in Keiss, north of Wick, she was "Indytit and acused" of breaking the locks and stealing sums of money from an "almere" in the hall of William Sinclair, merchant, and his spous [wife] Margrat Oswald. Use of the word *"Hall"* makes me ask if that could be the old Keiss Castle still partially standing on the cliff edge of the sea, as in all other cases a dwelling is referred to as *"Hous"* or *"Duelling"* rather than *"Hall"*. William Sinclair was described as a "merchant thair" which I read as in Keiss as there is no reference in this particular Indytment to being in Wick. In the incident about the feathers William was described as merchant in Wick but many of the landowners of estates great or small had a house in either Wick or Thurso, of which the Thurso valuations of 1702 give ample evidence. So William could have been of both Keiss and Wick.

Kathren was Indytit with stealling and *"awaytaking out yrof the numbir of thretie dollires of Silver, or thairby".*

She then, rather foolishly I suppose, immediately spent some of the money in buying a *"tartane plaid, some small linen, some stuff [a type of cloth] and a certane quantitie of Silk Ribbons and uther necessares for her awin use."* She was "apprehendit" with the remainder of the money still in her possession and this money was produced as evidence at her trial. The law took a certain style of correct procedure and Kathren was represented by a *"procurator"*, Johne Mursone. She was described as *"ane Comone and notorius theiff"* and a little later as "of *evill report, off Comone Broot & open fame"*. So her previous conviction was held against her, if not others of which we have no record.

She *"compeired"* and confessed that she did take out of the *"almeire"* sums of money but oddly her amounts did not tally with William Sinclair's account of what had been taken. The fiscall protested that the matter be put to an *"Assysis"*, which was fixed for the last day of July, not wasting any time apparently.

The nominated assessors were 15 in number, admitted by the panell, Kathren Creak, and her procurator. The accused was lawfully sworne in Judgement. The Indyttment was then read to her and her procurator. Kathren confessed to her purchases being with the stolen money, and further confessed to the stealling of 14 dollires and forty shillings Scots money, divide by 12 to get Sterling, therefor 3/4d. I suppose a great deal for the times. The Assysis, sitting in the Tolbooth of Wick, elected David Caldell as Chanceller of the Assysis and James Doull as their clerk, *pro tempere*, and in one voice found Kathren Creak guilty of stealing the money and buying the articles she had, but absolved her of comone broot as there was nothing proven to that end.

The Judges, taking the verdict to consideration and wasting no time, then ordained Kathren Creak to be taken within half an hour to the Joges at the Croie, where she had been before, and there her left ear to be *"nailed therto"*, to be *"scurgit"* [whipped] until she *"Ryved"* [tore] out the grip of the nail, and then to be further *"scurgit"* from the Market Cross of the Burgh to the Churchyard and past, which presumably must have been at the Parish Church. Further to that she was warned that if ever she stole more than 3/4d Scots money in future she would die the death, but an Assysis would have to be called against that. The amount of 40d Scots as the point at which hanging would be imposed was apparently not for the first offence but was a part of Scots law. I have read of two cases in Orkney of that period where warnings of the peril of stealing more than 40d. would be death, and in the Wick Records there is a reference in another incident of a man being called a "40d. man", suggesting that he was a thief who kept his marauding below the magic and relatively safe figure of 40d. It was used in that case as an insult.

I found no further reference to Kathren Creak, hopefully she lived a long and happy life afterwards, or perhaps not. The poor girl obviously hankered after a bit of finery to grace herself, she had worked in the Hall of William Sinclair and his wife Margrat Oswald where finery and fripperies were the privilege of her master and mistress, her attempt to emulate them came close to her own destruction.

— Chapter 10 —

Trouble at sea off the coast of Wick

Wick without the sea would be quite unthinkable and the Counsell Book of 1660 to 1711 has its fair share of references to that Eastern Boundary of the Burgh. Fishing, trading, warfare, shipwreck, all mentioned, and fishing would seem to have pride of place and importance if for no other reason than the recent history of the Burgh as a herring fishing port in the 1800's and the earlier part of this century, unfortunately now but a memory. In 1660 the landing places of Staxigoe, Papigo and Wick itself were not harbours as now we know them but landing beaches down which boats were launched by manpower alone, and up which boats were hauled to safety.

And fish were as important then as now.

There was a complaint made to the Counsell on the 17th March, 1707, about the selling of fish to local people, and it might be of interest to quote it in full, spellings included, to illustrate the English usage of the time. So many have asked me was it in Broad Scots or what? but in actuality the usage of "*English*", and I use that word advisedly, was little different from today, surprisingly similar at times, legal phrasing being even more so. Abbreviations were fairly common but should be self-evidently understandable.

*"At the Burgh of Wick the 17 of march, 1707, The Provest and
Bailyies upon Complaint given in to ym be the Inhabitants of the sd
Burgh Anent ane act formerlie made be the preceeding Provest and
Bailyies anent the Buying & Inlanding of fish be any persone or persones wtin the sd Burgh for yr own behoof, In not giveing ane equall
shair or so much for yr own moey in buying as pnt necessitie qn the
samen comes to the Shoar of Wick. Therfor the pnt Provest & Bailyies
homologats [approves] any former act made yranent. And yt all psones
wtin the sd Burgh sall have libertie to buy for yr own use qt may con-
venientlie Srve ym, the fish being equallie proportioned & Divydit,
good and badd. And ilk contraveener to be lyable in Ten pounds Scots,
toties quoties, qron act."*   CHA: SINCLAR [Provest]
                                            WILL MURRAY [Bailyie]"

So fair shares for all, if you had some money with which to
buy, and presumably the other half of the catch could be disposed of as the owners of the boats wished and to whom they
preferred. It would appear that a corner must have been made
in the market some time in the past and that local people were
being frozen out either by the Capitalist fish merchants of the
time, or sheer unwillingness by owners to sell on personal
grounds to some one or other. The act previously made must
have been getting ignored, hence the complaint.

Moving just round the coast to the North at Staxigoe there
was an incident dealt with by the Court on the 21 May, 1708,
when Alexr Mullikine was charged with taking a boat to sea
without permission, a boat owned by Sir James Dunbar. Again
I will quote the old entry as it is self explanatory. He did seem
to have a VERY poor memory about the incident, and who his
helpers were, but even today's Sheriff Courts sometimes throw
up a similar and very odd loss of recall! It appears to be genet-
ically transmissible in most areas.

*"Alexr Mullikine, Schoemaker in Wick, you ar Indytit & acused
for takeing doun & makeing use of ane fishing boat belonging to Sr
James Dunbar at yor own hand wtout consent of the Skipper or Crue
in the harbor of Staxigoe, And yrby reced great damnadge qrfor you
ought & should be lyable not only for ye Damnadge the boat hes sus-
tained but also for ane amerciement of lawe And for the loss of the use
of the boat since the sd Dountaking, now & in tyme comeing, being
uncapbable to goe to sea.*

"21 may, 1708. cmpeires Alexr Mullikine & confest the making use of the boat & knowes not qhither the men yt helped doun the boat wer any of the crue belonging to her or not. Therfor appoynts twa skilfull seamen to visit the damnadge of the boat & make report wtin eight dayes & the peneltie taken to advisandy.
ALEXR DOULL. "

The boat in question, though not stated, would almost certainly have been a four oar boat, similar to the Shetland *"Fourareen"* as opposed to the *"Sixareen"*, light enough to be manhandled and hauled up the beach, and whether Alexr Mullikin went to sea only himself with the boat, very unlikely, or did he have some helpers in his enterprise whose names he conveniently *"forgot"*, the record does not state. It is just possible that with drink taken he and a few of his friends thought that an evening spent fishing would be a good idea, and taking the boat of a local laird, who at that time was very much on the make, met with approval. I am quite sure it would not have been the only evening in which a few Wickers were at sea!

No further reference was found so I cannot tell what the damages came to. The records are not by any means totally complete and do leave one wondering what the outcome of some particular affair or other was, having had ones appetite whetted by the original reference to the case in Court. Other cases are concluded at a later entry and sentence dealt with and recorded.

Further out on the water there was an incident concerning two boats, both crewed by four men, probably the size of boat for the times with four oars each, as referred to above. The men in the first boat were William Suyrland, seaman in Wick, Michael Lamb there, John Gune there, Hendrie Mckurchie, and the boat with which they had the set to was skippered by William Garrow. According to the Indytment and charge Wm Garrow's boat and crew were pursued at sea to the danger of their lives, and had to run ashore for their safety. They must have come to hand to hand fighting on the water as Sutherland and his crew were charged in Court on the 21st May, 1708, with:

"the violent beating blooding & blaeing of William Garrow, yongr, and persueing him & his crue at sea to the hazard of yr lives, qll they wer forced to run ashoar for yr defence."

They were charged to the next Court on the 26th, but did not appear, being described as defenders. The Burghe officer, George Mansonne, had personally cited them to this "*Dyet*" and they were accordingly fined 50/- each for non appearance and "*summondit*" to appear the Fryday next.

William Garrow was also Indyted along with his crew of David Suyrland, Alstr J'sson & Jon Tailyor, charged with the same violent beating, blooding and blaeing of Wm Suyrland and his crew, sauce for the goose being also available for the gander. They were additionally charged with provoking and abusing the other crew, "*ilk ane of ym in yr good name & reputation.*"

What words passed between the crews out at sea is not stated but I doubt if words in the wind off Wick would have damaged any of their reputations! Not until the 10th August does anyone appear in Court when Wm Garrow and Alstr J'sonne "compeired", the rest being absent, and were each fined in 50/- Scots, as also were the first crew.

The terms "*beating, blooding and blaeing*" appear frequently in the Wick Records, beating being self explanatory, blooding being treated as a serious matter which in those days of swords, or whatever came handy, and, in the absence of modern medical aid, might well have been serious if infection set in. Blaeing was blue bruising with the use of the word "*blae*" still with us in the well known Scottish moorland delicacy, the "*blaeberry*".

The incident then seems to have been forgotten as I found no further mention of any of them. The Bailyies sitting in charge of this episode were Alex. Doull and Rob: Calder, an interesting change of "*Calder*" to the more modern and continuing spelling of the name as, very shortly before in the Records, he had been called "*Robert Caldell*", along with Wm Caldell and Johne Caldell.

Further out to sea in April of 1665 there was the threat of attack by Dutchmen as Charles II and the United Kingdom was at war with Holland. On the 11th of that month the Counsell, under Bailyies Frances Mansonne and Andrew Baine, considered the keeping of a watch "*within the Toune and alonge untill St Ninianes Heid, ordainit to be keipitt be the Earle of Caithness.*"

The Counsell, following instructions, ordained that the persons within the Burgh who had not got sufficient guns or muskets for keeping the watch had to provide themselves with the same within the four days to Tuesday next. These were Johne Cormok & Allxr Doull, veaveres, David Mowatt, James Printoche, Wm Simsonne, Wm Petrie, Donald Malcome, Johne Murson, schomaker, and there is the appearance of some urgency. Failure to obey the ordinance was to be penalised by a fyne of ten punds Scots. Added at the end of the entry were the names of Johne Gedes, Thomas Hossack, and Johne Rorison, veaver, who also had to provide themselves with arms.

St Niniane's Head also featured in a challenge to a duel between two of the upright citizens of Wick. On the ninth of September, 1663, the Court considered the case of Allexr Pruntoche, merchant in Wick, and William Beike, yonger, tailor there, *"who bothe being drunk in the hous of Johne Naughtie, mchant, the said personnes undertook a partie combatt to have mett withe thair Seconds at St Niniane's Head below the said Burghe."*

Pruntoche chose John Gedes as his second while Beike chose Allexr Mansonne. While the challenge had been *"concludit"*, no reference to *"swords or pistols"* was made, nor whether at dawn or whenever. Both parties *"confest"* in Court to the *"combatt"* having been arranged but the record stated that no meeting took place. However, Wm Beike confessed that he had turned up at the appointed time and place with *"ane sword"* and therefore, being obviously regarded as the more aggressive of the two, was fined £5 Scots. Allexr Pruntoche, probably having sobered up, wisely did not appear at St Niniane's Head, and was fined the lesser sum of 50/-. [£2.50 for the decimal currency addict.]

They both were further warned that if they did the *"Lyck heirefter"* they would suffer a penalty of £100 Scots and imprisonment, so it was dealt with as potentially serious.

The location is of interest, and is mentioned in Donald Beaton's "Ecclesiatical History of Caithness." He held in that book of 1907 that St Niniane's Head was situated about the Camps or just to seaward of the North end of the old Service Bridge of which the present one is a replacement. A duel, or *"partie combat"*, was an affair to be held away from onlookers so I am of opinion that we have to go much further out than the Camps to the point of the present North Head where, unfortunately, the ground is so messed about that there is little or no chance of finding any trace of old settlement. After all, St Ninian was reputed to have been here in the mid A.D.500s, establishing Christianity and a Chapel at Wick, but little would have remained anyway after so long a space of years. I am referring to the Chapel of course, not Christianity.

That apart, and I have the greatest respect for Donald Beaton and the infinity of work he did on Caithness History, any watch for Dutch shipping trying to approach the coast to raid or bombard Wick would have been done from much further out than the Camps from where you cannot see the coast line North or South, while from the present "North Head" there is a good lookout in either direction to spot any coastwise creeping by enemy ship.

Bear in mind that shipping i.e. Dutch Men of War, progressed by sail alone in those days and that it was not too easy to creep up unsuspected to any point. I suppose that some anglised cartographer in a fit of post Reformation zeal decided that the Saints were OUT and that the two Heads on either side of Wick Bay were better described by the unimaginative if more geographically correct descriptions of North and South, on a par with that old and historic street in Thurso, the "Coogate", Nordic in its connotation and very much part of the old Viking History and Heritage of Caithness when it was owned by the Norse Earls of Orkney, with Coo being self explanatory and "gate" meaning road, which, being no longer suitable for the modern and highly sophisticated Atomic Age, required changing by Thurso Town Council to "Riverside Place"!

Ye Gods!, even Edinburgh has not committed such Historical vandalism.

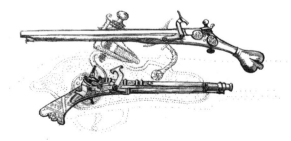

— Chapter 11 —

⟞⊸⟝

Claim and counter-claim over a stricken ship

M any a ship has been wrecked around Wick over the centuries, all too often with tragic loss of life on an unforgiving coast with little enough shelter even today with a modern harbour, spectacular with a hard South Easterly gale blowing and looked at from the safety of the land. What it looked like when afloat must have been daunting for small fishing boats trying to get in, and my own personal memory is of coming back to Wick with Nettie in the teeth of a South Easterly gale from a day trip to Orkney on the last of the St Olas before the Roll-on Roll-off era, possibly the maiden trip by that vessel and certainly her maiden trip day from Wick. We got in, eventually and late, and I will never forget the sight of the pilot boat soaring and swooping beside us in the gathering gloom before the pilot got safely on board. We came very close to turning away and heading for the shelter of Scrabster.

This episode out of the Old Counsell Book was not, however, of tragedy or of a day trip to Orkney but of a vessel which was *"cast away"* on the 13th of March, 1661, within the *"Road of the said Burghe and the water mouthe thairof."* With no stone piers or harbour at Wick ships must have "rode" at anchor in the bay for loading and unloading by small boats, and were at considerable risk if the weather came in from the East, being quite unable to beat out of Wick Bay against a gale. A dragging anchor or a broken cable and the shore beckoned. But a vessel ashore was a bounty not to be ignored, and this stranding reminded me of the tale about the low lying Start Point at the treacherous East end of the Island of Sanday in the North Isles of Orkney, whose Minister, offering up a prayer for the safety at sea of mariners, concluded with the phrase "And if it be God's will that a ship should come ashore, please do not forget your poor Island of Sanday."

So we come to this rather lengthy report in the Counsell Book of the "*cast away veshel*", and of the machinations of some Wickers about the spoils from the wreck, with claim and counterclaim. The Court met on the 29th of March, a fortnight after the stranding, to consider a "*humble petition*" submitted by the Bailyies and Toune Counsell of Weik to My Lord Earl of Caithnes, contra Allexr Sinclair of Telstane and Wm Bailye of Mylntonn.

Telstane, or Tachingall in the 1666 valuation of Caithness, Telstane or Toftingall in the 1667 and 1683 copies, was a small property in Bower Parish which I found referred to in these Valuations valued at £13.03.04d Scots, a very low figure and therefore a very small property. In the 1683 Valuation it is a half pennyland, approx. 9 acres, lying at the Kirk of Bower and formerly owned by Toftingall, but it was included in Wick Parish in 1683 for Valuation purposes.

The vessel was described as . . ."*having within hir 300 Timber or thairby, qlk was bocht be Johne Muirsonne, Bailyie, Wm Sinclair and Hew Blair, for themselffes and the Remanentt Inhabitantes of the said Burghe, Reservand ane hundreth Timber for my Lordes use.*" This was confirmed by a letter from Wm Bailyie of Mylnetonn which was before the Court.

Secondly the record stated that the "*holl*" of the vessel was bought by John Muirsonne for the "skiper and owner" for the sowme of twentie fyve Rex dollores, going on to state that the owner was content to take the rigging to himself, excepting the anchor and the best cable which was by right and title the property of the admiral, a fancy name for a receiver of wrecks. This buying of the vessel "FOR" the owner and skiper when I would have expected "FROM" I find obscure but the writing is clear. Could it be that the "admiral" had prior claim as receiver of wrecks and that even the owner had to buy back the hull. The owner bought a boat from James Watersonne, yonger, of Wick, intending to convey the rigging to Aberdeen or some other place where he could best sell it.

Immediately Francis Mansonne, Bailyie, heard of the owner's intention to transport the rigging South he went to the owner and made a bargain to buy the same at four score dollores, "qlk should be payitt uponn the morrow efter completing of the said Bargaine", reserving that the 25 dollores paid before by Johne Muirsonne for the broken hull was to stand at the first end of the payment. It does appear as if the Bailyies were acting together for the good of the Burgh.

Enter Alexr Sinclair of Telstane.

The record states "*In the meantyme, the nicht befoir, the forsaid Alexr Sinclair of Telstane did quyetlie convein the said owner and skiper over the water of Weik and at the Bankhead yrof, and payit their the said monies greid upon befoir, under Cloud and Silence of nicht,*" *qrby the said owner and skiper was pre-empted, nowayes knowing the same."*

So it looks as if the jurisdiction of the Counsell of the Burghe stopped short at the Wick River and that Alexr Sinclair rather craftily conveyed the owner and skiper over the water, possibly, though not stated, with drink taken, and there concluded the bargain to his own satisfaction. It also appears that if the two were *"nowayes knowing the same"* they were either very drunk or were foreigners with no great knowledge of the language, even if money talked.

Be that as may be, next morning being come as the particular time for payment by Francis Mansonne and his *"Compertener"* Burgesses of the Burghe, the money being *"numerat & told & consigned"* in the hands of James Doull, schomaker, the owner and skiper refused to accept the same, saying that Alexr Sinclair had pre-empted the Bargain befoir. This brought about the protest by Francis Mansonne and the Remaining Burgesses for the unlawful dealing by Alexr Sinclair, contrary to the acts of Parliament and the Liberties of the Borrowes. And of course the Baillie Court found against Alexr. Sinclair, stating that he had no lawful right to buy the wreck, quite apart from intruding onto a transaction already completed except for payment. Again, in Orkney there is many a tale of the admiral coming too late to an Island to get his share of a wreck, only to find the cargo mysteriously *"washed away."* The first 25 dollores was to be offset against the four score so the owner and skiper had a total of 80 dollores offered from the Burgh and its officers against the 100 dollores from Alexr. Sinclair. So an appeal to My Lord of Caithness was not without some self interest for My Lord.

Even though the record states that the 25 dollores had been produced in Judgement and thereafter paid in Johne Muirsonne's house to the owner and skiper, he may have thought he was at liberty to make another and better deal. The Burgh Counsell, however, had other ideas and were not letting Alexr. Sinclair and Wm. Bailyie put one over on them, so action was taken and Allexr. Sinclair removed from the deal.

This reference to *"Rex or Rix Dollires"* is interesting as it refers to currency more usually applicable to Holland and to Norway though it had an occasional Scottish usage. In a document of

1649 in Orkney there was a payment made to Wm Pottinger in Bergen in Norraway for a ratification of a sale of land called Greinwall, in Holme in Orkney, to Edward Pottinger in Hobbister, Kirkwall, a merchant, skiper and landowner, and the money was stated as 32 dollrs at 58/per peice. Sorry about the name. This does give us a clue, however, to the value of the monies we are dealing with in the Wick transaction referring to the cast away vessel, so the 100 Rex dollores from Alexr Sinclair would be £290 Scots or about £25 Sterling. While I am not looking at the subject of dollores I do think it was a maritime currency as I have found it used in relation to sea faring and cargo and ships, and I think it was a recognised coinage, probably Dutch, accepted in Norway and in Holland and by other North Sea traders, an early example of common currency, or the "Eurodollar.!" This does suggest that the wrecked vessel was either Norwegian loaded with timber, one of the exports of that country, and coming to Caithness to trade timber for grain, tallow, salt beef, malt, feathers, or possibly a Dutch ship doing the same. I will plump for the Norwegian source and, as no names were itemised in the Counsell Book, I do think it must have been a foreign vessel.

The case of the cast away vessel was not yet concluded though the sale had been regularised, and on the tenth of August, 1661, David Murray, merchant in Thurso and admiral deput within the Shyre of Caithness, put in his claim for the best anchor. The Bailyies condescended that he should have the anchor as entitled but upon condition that he should give a bond with security to the Bailyies and Town Counsell, that if their advocat, Mr Wm Hoge, and David Murray's advocat, name not given, should agree that the anchor and best cable should rightly belong to the Burghe, then these items were to be restored to Wick. If they agreed that the anchor and cable lawfully belonged to David Murray as admiralitie, then the bond was to be null and void as if it had never been granted. David Murray's cautioner in security was Wm Sinclair, merchant in Wick. Whether he was of the Murrays of Pennyland or of Clairden I do not know but probably one or the other.

The rights of the owner of a ship driven ashore seem to have been singularly small or almost non existent. The cargo was bought by the Bailyies, probably at knock down price, the hull made very small money though no doubt it was beyond salvage other than as timber, the rigging, sails and ropes appear to have remained the property of the owner and he could transport them away or sell them as standing as he wished. The rights of the "admiral" were paramount if he could get to the wreck in time, were laid down in law and enforced with enthusiasm. Any foreign ship would fare even worse if language was any barrier though I think the North Sea was but a small pond to these men and communication by language was probably not too great a problem.

Little else remains of reference to the sea in these records. There was trading to the Murray coast, the Dunbars and the Inneses had family connections there. There is a passing reference to anchorage dues and shoar dues at the ports of Wick and Staxigo and these were rouped as one annually. One reference to the Customs was on the 2nd February, 1706, in the presence of Alexr Doull and William Murray, Bailyies, and the Toun Counsell, when the dues were rouped. The successful bidder was Anthony Doull, joyner in Wick, who, after *"fair roup"*, obtained the right to collect the anchorage and shore dues plus the Customes and other public dues belonging to the Burghe. Rouping was referred to in another entry where it stated *"efter twa half houre glasses"* which suggests that the roup remained open for an hour for offers, being timed by a sand glass.

There was an upset price of £90 Scots at first offer below which the dues were to remain in the hands of the Counsell for disposal as they thought fit. Anthony Doull offered £91.10.00d Scots so from the 2nd February, 1706, to the time of Candlemas, 1707, he would collect whatever was due. He had to find Securitie for that but his cautioner is not named. There was an addendum to the effect that Hemprigs was "excempted", special treatment for Dunbar. By this date he had acquired Telstain's landholdings, purchased around 1691, rolling the lands of Telstain and Oldwick, Miltoune and Campster, along with another purchase of the lands of Ackergill, Noss, Reiss and pendicles, into his Hempriggs estate, previously valued in Latherone Parish. This exemption meant that a fairly large portion of the land around Wick would not be contributing to local taxation and suggests an element of exploitation creeping in to Dunbar's benefit.

It would not be the only instance of that in the affairs of Wick.

A final look at the sea, or almost, was in one of the perpetual fights which must have been popular in Wick at that time. I only include it here in this "sea scape" as it included reference to two men whose names and calling were not of Caithness, and the details of the interesting fight may well be left to another time. The men were Walter Dalrymple and Thomas Hall who were described as "*tydwaiter*" in Wick and Thurso respectively, and in a later entry as "*tydsmen*". To the best of my knowledge, though I am not laying down the law on this one, a tydwaiter or tydsman was an officer of the Crown who would be today probably a Customs Officer. If so, then the tydewaiter or tydsman would have boarded ships coming in to Wick or Thurso and examined them for any contraband such as brandy, tobacco, arms, etc. or for any other purpose related to the Crown. They were stated as "Mr" at one point, which was a cut above the common herd, and at one dyet of court Dalrymple was absent as he was in "*Edr.*" on business as one of Her Majesties servants, the dyet being continued to a later date. Although we assume that ships lay at anchor in the "Rodes" it was quite in order for small trading vessels to come in on the high tide and beach themselves in the River mouths of Thurso and Wick, so the title Tydsman or even Tydewaiter may have been a very accurate description of their office.

— Chapter 12 —

The Old Men of Wick – 1660

"In The Name of the Father the Sone and the Holie Ghost. At the Burghe of Weik the sext day of January, 1660 yeires".

"Th . . . . . e quhilk day, the said Burghe being destitut of Bailyies The Two previous yeires, for Remedie wharof, The Burgesses, Counsell and Tounesmen of the said Burghe, having given ane Certane petitionn to Walter Innes of Orvin, Bailyie prnll To ane Noble Erle George, Erle of Caithnes, Provest of the said Burghe, anent the choosing of Bailyies and Counsell thairin."

So begins the first page of the Counsell Book of Wick, 1660 to 1711. Why the Burgh had been without Baillies for the previous two years I do not know. It was the last two years of the Commonwealth under Oliver Cromwell and, after his death in 1658, under his son Richard. The affairs of state nationally were drifting into some disarray and eventually the United Kingdom went back to the Monarchy under Charles II. However, it could well have been the Earl of Caithness who was dilatory in the execution of his duties and it was that Earl George who eventually borrowed extensively from John Campbell of Glenorchy, wadsetting his Caithness Earldom estates in security, and finally mortgaging his Earldom itself to Campbell, which he had no legal right to do. George died in 1676 at Thurso East and the eventual outcome was John Campbell marrying George's widow, the Countess of Caithness, who was a daughter of the Marquis of Argyle and a Campbell herself. John Campbell assumed the title of Earl of Caithness, temporarily, leading to a fair amount of strife with the inhabitants of the County and to the Battle of Altimarlich in 1680.

In any event the people in 1660 gave in a petition to George, Earl of Caithness, through Walter Innes of Orvin, seeking to reinstate the lapsed order of affairs and again have Baillies and possibly Counsellers as well, though that was not stated. Orvin I am not sure of but it has been suggested that it was in Morayshire where the Innes family were also located. Democracy of course held sway, then as now, so a list of names was put forward from whom to choose Bailyies. Bear in mind that many a Wicker must trace back to these persons even if evidence is lacking on their connection. The record continues:-

"Comperitt the said Walter Innes, In name & beheff of the said Noble Erle, and efter Lall fensing of the Court as use is be William Patton, notr public, Clerk of the said Burghe, George Mansonne being officer.

The particular Names who were uponn Leitt to be choisen Bailyies followes heirefter in Ordr, To witt:-

Wm Bailye of Mylnetoun	*Johne Clyne in Weik*
James Doull in Blakmyre	*Hew Blair thair*
Allexr Mullikin in Papego	*Johne Muirsonn thair*
Francis Ma'sonn in Weik	*Wm Caldell thair*
Allexr Cormok thair	-

Out of that list James Doull and Allexr Cormok were nominated and chosen as Bailyies to hold office for the next year, Wm Patton to continue as Toun Clerk and George Mansonne as Toun Officer. They all gave their oathes of fidelity for administration of Justice According to their power and knowledge.

The record continues:

"Heirefter followes the particular names of the Counselleres of the said Burghe, choisen and admitted, to witt:-

Johne Cormok, weaver	*Johne Muirsonn*
Hew Blair, mchantt	*Wm Doull*
James Watersonn, yonger	*Johne Printoche*
Wm Caldell, mchant	*George Bruce*
George Annand	*James Doull, Schomaker*

At the first Court held by Bailyies James Doull and Allexr Cormok after their election the Customs of Wick were rouped and were taken by Patrick Sinclair for £55 Scots for the *"space of ane year"* , the Customs being described as *"great and small"*, and being rouped for *"the Runing out of twa heff hour glasses"*.

The whole Counsell and Tounsmen were present so it must have been a great event, or at least it had its own little exitement. Nothing much has changed if you go to any furniture auction in Wick to this day, onlookers being times more numerous than buyers!

Similarly the Snuff making for 1660 was taken by Johne Muirsonne and Wm Caldell, mchants, for the space of a year from the 10th January, for the payment of fortie mrks Scots money and the said Two persons being *"bound conjointlie & severallie for the same."*

There then followed an entry about the unfree men of the Burghe who were warned to the Court for the purpose of making them freemen and Burgesses of the Toun, no doubt collecting fees for that privilege. There was a certain tightness about who could trade in and enjoy the privileges of the Toun, jealously guarded and fairly obviously not to the interests of the country dweller.

Meantime, as we look at those who lived in Wick, there was a list of trades and persons which gives a glimpse of what people were doing at that time. Some of the names carry on for years but as this entry was the first tabulation of their names, it may interest present possible descendents. I do not think the list included all the tradesmen of the Toun, rather those who had not paid their dues and were being taken to the mark. If Burgh affairs had been slipping for the two previous years, as it appeared, then it is understandable.

Marchantes:

George Bruce, elder, Patrick Sinclair, Frances Innes, Walter Bruce yonger, George Mullikin, Allexr Mansonne, Wm Simsonne, James Doull, schomaker, Allexr Printoche, Johne Ross.

Tailyours:

Allexr Doull, Allexr Beike, Johne Hamilton, Wm Beik, yonger, Allexander Gilbertsonn, James Watersonn, yonger.

Schomakers:
Allexander Lamb, George Sinclair, Williame Petrie, Allexr J'sonne, Allexr Abernethie.

Weavers:
James Doull, Donald Malcome, Johne Gune, Allexr Cordeiner, Johne Rorisone.

Smithes & Couperes:
Allexr Ranie, Johne Dodsonn, wright, Allexr Shand, couper, Wm Evirach, smith.

From further entries on other matters it is apparent that other occupations were carried on in the Toun, such as skippers, seamen, fishermen, masons, joiners, glovers. At the end of the year 1660, 18th October, the Record continues with a new election for the next year, and gives us some more names of the "Tounesmen of Wick.":

"*The qlk day anent the Choosing of New Bailyies becaus the former wold nocht on nowayes cntenew Langer in the said office, Williame Bailye off Mylnetoun, whom the Earle of Caithnes had nominat befoir to be his deput as Provest, being presentt, togider withe James Doull in Blakmyre as ane of the former Bailyies, Anent the Choossing and Electing of New Bailyies.*
"*Ane list of theis wha ar uponn the leitt as Bailyies. To witt*:

"*Frances Mansonne, Allexr Cormok, Johne Muirsonne, Wm Caldell, James Murray Watersonn, Hew Blair.*
[The above list has to be those from whom Bailyies were to be chosen and not a list of actual Bailyies.]
Names of the Tounsmen and Burgesses cnveined for the nominating & choising of the saide Bailyies, be vottes as followes, To witt:

"Johne Cormok, veaver	vottes to James Murray Watersonne, ygr
Wm Doull	vottes to Allexr Cormok
George Annand	vottes to Frances Mansonne
James Doull, schomaker	vottes to James Murray Watersonne
James Blair	votes to Frances Mansone
Andrew Lamb	vottes to the said Frances Mansonne
Johne Gune	vottes to the said Frances Mansonne
Johne Innes, Schomaker	vottes to James Murray Watersonne.

Arthur Wrightt, Dyer	*vottes to Frances Mansonne*
Allexr Mansonne, mchant	*vottes to the said Frances*
Allexr Cordeiner	*vottes to the said Frances*
Johne Hamiltonn, Tailyer	*vottes to Johne Muirsonne*
Allexr Lambe, Schomaker	*vottes to the said Johne Muirsonne*
Allexr Rorisonn	*vottes to Frances Mansonne*
Jsonne Cordeiner	*votes to Johne Muirsonne*
Walter Bruce, Elder	*votes to Frances Mansonne*

["votes" was spelt both ways, not my doing!]

"*The qlk day be maniest vottes of the personnes pticularlie above nominatt, Frances Mansonne and Johne Muirsonne ar admitted as Bailyies untill the tyme of Michaelmes, 1661 yeires. Mr Williame Gedes, Minister at the said Burghe being pntt, and heiring the saids Bailyies admitted & Sworne for Lall administration of Justice, Williame Pattone, notr public thair cntenewed Clerk being pntt also, And qruponn the said Bailyies & Clerk gave thair oathes of fidelitie uponn the Lall execution of thair offices*".

The various crafts and trades of Wick were referred to when, on the 27 December, 1660, there was considered an act of Parliament made many years before under the Regency of Mary of Guise, Queen of King James 5th and mother of Mary, Queen of Scots, in the sixth year of her reign. As Mary became Queen of Scotland in 1542 six days after her birth, the act was some long time existing. This act must have been brought to the attention of the Toun and meant to regularise a probable disarray among tradesmen, or at least to bring them under some nominal control of the Provost, Bailyies and Counsell.

"*Actt of Parliament anent Deacones, 6 yar of quein marrie*"

"*Item becaus It hes bein Leatlie understand be the quein Regent and thrie estates that the Choossing of Deacones and men of Craft within Burghes hes bein richt Dangerous, and as they have used themselffes in Tymes Bygonne hes causit great Troubles in Borowes, Comotion and Raising of the queanes Leidges in Dyvers part(i)es and the making of liges [leagues] and Bandes amonges them selffes & betwixt Burghe and Burghe, qlk Deserves great punishmet, Thairfor the queines grand Regentt, withe advyis of the thrie estates forsaides, hes statit & Ordainit that thair be no Deacones choisen in Tyme Cming within Burghes Bot the Provost, Bailyies and Counsell of the Burghe, To chois the most honest men of Craft of good Confidance and of everie Craft, To viseitt thair Craft that they Labor Sufficientlie and that ther sall be sufficient Stuff and wark, and thir persones to be callit Visitores of thair Craft and to be Elected and choisen yeirlie at Michaelmes be Provest, Bailyies and Counsell of the Burghe, and that they thairefter give thair aithe in Judgement, To visitt laullie and Trewlie the said Craft without any power of gathering or assembling of them to ane privat conventionn or making of any actes or statutes, bott all Craftesmen in Tyme Cmg To be under the Provest Bailyies & Counsell and thir visitores, choisen, Sworne and Admitted to have voiting in choising of officers as utheres thinges as the Decones voiting of befoir, and that no Craftesmen brook office within Burghes in Tyme Cmg except Twa of the most famous honest men to be choisen yeirlie upon the Counsell, and they Twa to be ane partt of the Auditores yeirlie to the compt of the Comone goode, Acording to the acts of pliament maid thairuponn befoir.*

A. . .nd whosoever Ctinues in the cntrair of this act to be punished be warding [imprisonment] of thair personnes be the space of ane yeir and Tinsell (forfeiture) of thair freidom within Burghe, and never to be receivitt thair efter as friemen untill the Tyme they obtein the favor and benevolence of the provest, Bailyies and Counsell qr the falt is cmitit, And the Thrid part of their goodes To be esheitt and applyed to our Soverane Lord's use for thair Contemptoun."

And that Act of Parliament from 450 years ago!

— Chapter 13 —

Public Health

I have a map of Wick of 1802, or rather the South side of the Water of Wick, with the proposed future developments laid out upon it which eventually became the new town of Pulteney. Not really relevant to our present interest in the 1660 - 1711 period but Wick itself was but one street on the North side of the river from the Parish Kirk [a much nicer name than Church] to the Water Mouth, the Camps as it is now called. This High Street, the King's or Common Calsay, really was the centre of the Record of the Counsell of Wick, contained the Mercat Croie, the Mercat Place, the very important Tolbooth which was the centre of civic affairs, the houses, premises, shops and booths, of the Tounsmen. If any map of that Street at that time exists I have not seen it, but would very much like to. Off that main street were the lanes and small courts of which little now remains other than a name here or there.

Before 1800 Wick was but a small place, possibly little more than two hundred people, not yet swamped with the eventual influx of country folk who in the early 1800's made their way to Wick to build a new town and a new industry centred around herring curing. I came across one example of that influx in the ancestry of Deborah Wares of New York, a fifth generation emigrant from Wick, whose paternal forebear had been in Howe in Lyth, marrying a Bruce from Aucorn, Keiss, and back from that to Donald Warse in Canisbay. So people moved into Wick in the 1800s. And in 1660 public health was a very important subject then as now.

On the 6th of September, 1661, James Watersone, younger, Isobel Bruce, widow, and George Mullikin, merchant, were accused of breaking the various acts made previously against middens being placed upon the Comone Calsay. Each was convicted in 50/- Scots money except the widow who was let off with a fine of 30/-, no doubt poverty tempering justice with some mercy. They were given 48 hours to remove their *"midings"*, under a further penalty of £5 Scots if they did not comply.

The problem must have continued as, early in the next year on the 21 Day of January, 1662 yeires, by common consent of the Counsell, it was *"ordainit"* that every person who had their *"miding"* upon the Comone Calsay should remove the same within the 25th instant, being four days grace. *"Ilk personne Contraveiner under the paine of £5 Scots money, and that no miding be found uponn the Comon Calsay heirefter under the paine forsaid Toties quoties, and the Same to be published by the officer and by tuck of Drume wherby no person might pretend Ignorance."*

There were other references to *"the gutter"* in the High Street, usually someone being thrown into it, which suggests that the middle of the so called *"High Street"* was little more than an open drain, if not a sewer.

So you were warned. What the High Street must have smelt like on a warm summer evening I will leave to imagination, but perhaps the old name of *"High"* Street was more accurate than we now appreciate.

Education was not neglected by the Toune Counsell in 1660 though who went to school we can but guess. Many of the entries in the Record carry the phrase *"with my hand touching the pen led by the notar public becaus I canot wryt myself"* so there was an obvious need for a school and a schoolmaster.

On 20th March, 1683, the Bailyies, with the consent of the Toune Counsell, ordained that four quartermasters be chosen for overseeing the building of a school at the Shore of Wick. Each inhabitant had to furnish a servant as required by the quartermasters appointed for that building under the penalty of 6/8d per day for failure to so provide, to be paid by either the servant or the master. The sum of 6/8d was actually half a merk, an old Scottish coin. It is interesting that it was every *"inhabitant"* who had to provide a labourer which makes it look as if their servants were not included as *"inhabitants"* of Wick, rather they were an underclass. A considerable number of servants had the same surname as their "master" but whether they were of his family or a near relation is not stated. Whether there was a school in Wick previously I do not know but we can guess that such a facility was lacking in the Old Toun.

Later, on the 6th January, 1710, there was a record relating to Andrew Sutherland, schoolmaster, who had been embroiled in a fight of a kind with Allexr Dunbar, merchant in Wick. Dunbar was accused and indited for beating and blooding Andrew Sutherland by hitting him on the mouth with his hand to *"the great effusion of his blood."* The Pser [pursuer, Andrew Sutherland] being solemnlie sworne, deponed that he *"receaved ane strock from the Defer [defender] with his hand upon the mouth & that he loused on(e) of his tooth and the blood issued out & [he] fell down upon his back. This he declaires to be of truth as he sall. ansr to God.   AND. SUTHERLAND "*

His signature was well written as a schoolmaster's should be. The Bailyie, Allexr Doull, found Dunbar guilty and fined him ten punds Scots, to be paid before Dunbar removed out of prison, which was the Tolbooth. There was an upstairs and downstairs in the Tolbooth, though the downstairs could well have been a cellar and contained whatever lockup there was.

In the manner of the times Dunbar had also charged Sutherland with an offence and gave evidence that the schoolmaster had violently abused him with bad discourse and several aggravating speeches, and offered to strike him with his staff and bloodwyte [a penalty for drawing blood which could extend right up to a payment to relatives in settlement for a murder.] The use in the text of *"bloodwyte"* is slightly obscure as written but it's meaning is clear. It was paid in the sum of 500 merks by James Finlayson for Magnus Pottinger, merchant in Kirkwall, slain by him in 1627, to his widow and three children. No doubt it settled the matter for cash, and no hard feelings!

In his own defence Andrew Sutherland denied the charges. Dunbar then, under oath, swore that Sutherland came up to him on the loan of Wick and said he must have the bear due to him, and wagged his staff in his face, and said *"I must have it".* [The *"bear"* could have been beremeal or possibly whole grain which had a very important use in malting to brew ale or beer.]

The Bailyie thought the provocation light and therefor assoylied the schoolmaster from any crime. The loan of Wick could have been the green now called the Riverside, or more likely the grassy roadway leading up from the Toun through the arable lands for the passage of cattle to the common grazings, now the Airfield and area around. Bear in mind that many of the tounsmen would have had a cow or two kept within the Toun, and that until not too long ago.

What part Dunbar had in this provision of meal I can only guess but from other Caithness records existing from 1760 each landholder was liable to pay a certain amount to the schoolmaster, and also to the minister, according to his assessed rentall. In 1760 no less than 12 lairds in Wick Parish, great and small, were apportioned the "*sallary*" of the schoolmaster, no doubt each being responsible for his own apportionment and for the paying thereof. Perhaps Sutherland was only trying to get out of Dunbar that which was due to him.

Donald Reid, schoolmaster in Canisbay Parish at the same time, made his bargain to come to Canisbay to teach the school and was to be paid 5 bolls meal, which he said was too small an amount, but he would still come. He was to have 3 of peats as well for his fire, whatever "3" was, though it would be reasonable to assume that it was an amount sufficient for a year's firing. I have no doubt the "*sallary*" of Wick school-masters would be little different from Canisbay but a quite common "*wage*" around that time was 3 bolls of oatmeal and 3 bolls of bere meal, with peats for a fire. By 1760 the schoolmaster's "*sallary*" for Wick Parish was 24 bolls so things had moved on from 100 years previous, enough meal for some to be sold on by the schoolmaster and converted to money.

Weights and measures were obviously of acute interest to the Counsell and on 28th January, 1669, Francis Sinclair of Stirkok, deput provost, instructed that the Standard Measures of Linlithgow were to be adopted "*by the Burgh of Weik and the wholl parochin thairof*". The order to so do was subscrived by My Lord the Earl of Caithness and was dated the 3rd March, 1668, at Thurso, where the Earl of Caithness had his home at Thurso East. It seems to have taken a long time to travel to Wick!

The measure was for a firlot but meal and bere had different measures, a meal firlot and a bear firlot. The firlot for meal was to contain "*twentie ane poynts, 3 mutchkines*" and that for "*bear*" to contain "*thretie ane poynts, ane mutchkin*". The "*poynts*" would have been the old Scotch pint and held nearly a quart, twice our present day pints with which a few modern beer drinkers might have some slight knowledge. Meal would have been already ground from oats and was an exportable commodity of Caithness, in considerable quantities at one time, much of it being shipped from Staxigoe to as far away as Norway, and more locally around the coast and through the Pentland Firth to Strathnaver, a good cattle country but a poor grain one, leading eventually to ample justification for the "*clearances*" in some minds, and even further in 1735 to Glasgow. "*Bear*" was another matter and had a multiple use. It could be ground into beremeal or malted for brewing ale and for the production of "*aqua vitie*" as other entries in the Record refers. Our school-master certainly had an interest. It would have made sense to have it measured in a larger measure if it was the whole grain that was being traded. Malt was also being traded at that time, some of that product going to Norway in exchange for timber and iron, brandy and tar, and measureing it was a monopoly for the traders of Wick. The phrase "*metes and measures*" was used, the word "*mete*" being the now largely forgotten. To "*meet ones just deserts*" would have meant only to get measured out one's share, probably of meal. To mete out justice is a phrase well enough known but who now knows that the word "mete" is to measure. The old words linger on though the meaning and usage gets changed from the original.

The Royal Croie was to be put on a Burne Irone to be used to mark the firlots which were to be made under this order. The Counsell ordered all measures to be subject to testing and measuring with a penalty of £10 Scots for "*Ilk contraveiner that will nocht compeir and presentt his measure, and Ilk landward persone £5.*" Apparently the Country folk were another class, which some would hold they still are!

To finalise the weights equation Frances Sinclair, the bailyies being present, in the name of my lord Erle of Caithnes, ordered Allxr Baine & Allxr Schand, Couperes in Wick, to make the said firlot measures and that the Irone Gadge of Linlithgow should be burnt thairuponn. These were then to be the stan-dard measures for the Burgh and the Landward parts of

Caithness, and Wm Caldell, Johne Nachtie and Allexr Mullikin, all merchants in Wick, were appointed to oversee the measureing and the putting of the "*gadge*" upon the correct measures.

In November 1665 a complaint was made to the Counsell by Johne Gedes and Alexr Mansonne, merchants in Wick, that certain country folk were coming to town to the public market and that they were weighing their commodites other than with the certified weights of the toun merchants, no doubt themselves! These commodities were butter, cheese, tallow, feathers and other commodities, and they were getting them weighed at the houses of weavers, possibly in Wick. It appears that at least some weavers had weights, though it is an odd thing for weavers who would have sold their product by measure rather than by weight. Still, that is what the Record book states. The Counsell ordained that no weaver weigh any of the said commodities to any person until they came to the merchants booths where the just weights were. The penalty was a fine of £5 Scots.

So the Toun Counsell was on occasion looking after local affairs and trying to keep some semblance of order. Vested interest shows up from time to time but why not. Various people were charged with not being freemen or burgesses, some from far away places such as Dundee and trying to trade in Wick.

Two such persons were George Ruthven and Gilbert Christie from Dundee, and the next chapter deals with them and their particular commodity, salt.

— Chapter 14 —

Salt, Salt and ever more Salt

George Ruthven and Gilbert Christie, both merchants from Dundee, on the 4th June, 1660, were accused before the Burgh Court for keeping an open Boothe or *"chope"* within the Burgh, their crime being unfreemen of Wick and contrary to the Acts of Parliament and Acts of Borrowes [Burghs]. Christie placed himself at the reverence of the Judges, sucking up to them I suppose. Ruthven had been warned to that day but did not *"compeir"*. The Judges therefore ordained the officer, George Mansonne, *"to arrest the said George Ruthven his Boothe Dore, that it be no wayes open to nather sell anie goods or merchandise thairin untill Suche tyme as he sall give agreement to the forsaid Judges"*.

George was again before the Court on 26th March, 1661, for breaking an arrestment laid upon his Salt and other merchandise, and for breaking the law by selling the same to unfreemen in Wick. He *"compeired"* and denied the charge of breaking the arrestment, so the *"fiscall"*, Johne Muirsonne, undertook to prove the same. I think the *"pror. fiscall"* was not a permanent office but could be undertaken by whoever fancied his chances, usually a Counseller. Nothing changes! Over the years different names for that office appeared and it was never a formal appointment as were the town clerk or the officer. Muirsonne was prepared to undertake the proof on the *"morrow"*, the 27th March, and *"the said George was personnallie chargit at the Bar to that effect"*. Came the next day, the *"morrow"*, and *"the said George Ruthven, being thryis Lallie Callit at the Dore and windo of the Tolbooth as use is, efter Lall fensing [conveining] of the Court, and nocht Compeirand to heir the forsaid actionn, Lallie qualifeit and proven in Judgementt be the said pror. fiscall as was Lallie Done, Thairfor the forsaides Judges decernit & ordainit the said George To pay the soum of £40 Scots money conform to the actt of parliament, and that suche personnes as ar Restand him any money for Salt within the said Burghe is arrestit in thair hands, and decreits of furthcuming to be promult against them proportionallie In favoure of the Theasaurer of the said Burghe. [Furthcuming:- a legal action brought by the arrester of a debt against the arrestee to make goods available for arrestment. i.e. forth coming].*

"*Names of theis persones Resteres of the said Salt, viz:*

James Muirsonne, yonger - 3 bolls; relict of Wm Doull - 2 bolls; George Mullikin - 2 bolls; George Annand - 2 bolls; Thomas Hossack - 2 bolls".

A boll was a measure of quantity, not weight, but over the years the boll became standardised for different commodities according to their weight and density. A boll of oats and a boll of barley and a boll of meal of either were all of different weights. In my own younger days, prewar, the married farm men received 4 bolls of oatmeal as part of their wages, one boll per calender quarter. The boll of meal of these latter years was of ten stones at 14 lb. per stone, 140 lbs, which converted to kgs, comes to 63.6 kg, a modern measure that has never filled me with any great pleasure. The boll of meal of the 1600s was ten stones of 16 lbs per stone, called a Dutch stone, and a boll at that rate would be 72.7 kg. So the persons abovenamed had a fair stock of salt in hand. And the possession of such quantities of salt is really the matter of interest in this reference to George Ruthven.

Now George was but a small actor in this glimpse of life in Wick in the 1600s. Other merchants or traders from outside the Burgh and outside of Caithness appeared in the Records from time to time. What is of interest is the commodity "Salt" which George was selling and the quantities bought by the parties above mentioned, and for which they owed money to George Ruthven, an opportunity for the Burgh to get their hands upon the cash, arresting the debt against payment of penalty or fine. There was another reference to salt in July of 1665 when the Court sat under Bailyies Frances Mansonne and Andrew Baine to consider a complaint made against Allex Abernethie, schomaker in Weik, Thomas Sutherland & Allexr Mouatt in Telstane, who were accused of breaking up a barrel of salt beef belonging to Wm Sinclair, merchant in Weik. They were alleged to have taken seven or eight salted ox tails out of the barrel which was within the boat of Walter Bruce, Skiper, besides some tobacco.

"*Comperit the said Allexr Abernethie and Allexr Mowatt, Thomas Sutherland absentt, and the first twa Confest the taking of ane litle peice of the said Salt Beiff, and Thomas Sutherland airt and pairt withe them. Thairfor the forsaids Bailyies withe advyse of the Toune Counsell cnveined for the Tyme, fynes & Convicts the said thrie persones as followes viz:- Allexr Abernethie and Thomas Sutherland, Ilk ane of them in £5 Scots, and the said Allexr Mowatt in L./- [50/-] qruponn act.*" There is the predictable difference between what the owner said was stolen and what the culprits admitted. Surprise!

Allexr Mowatt was fined only 50/- so he was either a poor soul or more likely but a lad in bad company late at night in Weik. Certainly Alexr Abernethie was well established as a "*cordeiner*" in Weik, a "*cordeiner*" being a maker of ropes out of hemp or leather, very necessary in the days of sailing ships. The word "*cordage*" referred to a ship's rigging. Leather was available locally and hemp was the rougher fibre from flax, grown in Freswick in 1658 by William Cogill and his wife from Mey, among others, and there is no doubting the name of "*Hempriggs*" had real meaning. Flax or hemp required good soil. The ploy with the oxtails looks like a bit of midnight nonsense.

Later, on the 16th May,1710, Marie Grant, brine bearer in Weik, was before the Court accused for comeing to "Gate, Dores and Windoes" of Hugh Harrow, merchant in Weik, and his wife Anna Calder, and getting into a right good going row miscalling Anna. Shortly after that row, on the 25th April, she was accused of coming to the house of Patrick Sinclair, toun clerk, and again miscalling Anna Calder. The details of this episode we should leave to later. What is of interest is the reference to "*brine bearer*", almost as a profession in itself.

These references to "*Salt*" and brine and salted ox tails, and to a barrel of "*small salt*" in the Tolbuth broken and scattered on the floor by Alex Abernethie when a prisoner there (11th August, 1665) were a timely reminder to me of just how impor-

tant a commodity salt must have been to the Wick of 1660, a
prime essential of life then, a great and much used essential of
life into my own boyhood years, and the very basis of the
development of Wick and my native island of Stronsay as
herring fishing ports. It is salutory that an element of life which
most people now associate casually with their fish and chips
was at one time so important to their very existence. Reflecting
on the part salt must have played in the lives of our heroes of
the Counsell Book of Weik, 1660, I remembered my boyhood
in Stronsay in Orkney and the part salt played in our lives. O.K.,
this is not strictly a reference to Wick of the 1600s, this is recent
history, just pre-1939, but then I myself had almost forgotten
many if not all of the things in which salt played full part in the
days of my youth. I will not be alone in that respect.

The paramount use of salt, both in 1660, and in 1939, was in
preserving food for use out of season in the days of no
freezers, no fridges, no dried fruit or food, no tinned lobster or
leeks, no canned mackerel or herring. And Wick without salt
would never have been other than a wee village with a wee
harbour struggling to make its voice heard, another Lybster of
the North.

I most certainly will not pontificate on Wick and the herring
fishing, what Ian Sutherland in Wick has not dealt with in that
regard is not worth mentioning.

But before the herring came South off Wick they schoaled
east of Stronsay on their way south from Shetland, and Stronsay
was as much of a herring fishing port as ever Wick was, and,
as now, that is but a memory. My father farmed at Whitehall in
Stronsay and the village of Whitehall lay in the arms of the land,
a beach, a road, a single line of houses facing the water and the
harbour of two piers, the "Auld" and the "New". And the curing
yards. And the coopers' sheds. And the storehouses. And the fish
market. And Davie Chalmer's coal business, married to a
Caithness lass, and the shops, the bakers, the butchers. And the
pub.

My father had horses and carts and low loading four wheel
lorries with a turn table front axle and a farm to feed the horses.
All farm equipment but from early July to mid August fully
occupied in servicing the herring curing. Today we call it
diversification. And it was a great personal honour a few years

ago for me to get into conversation with a Wicker chance met watching a rugby match at the Harmsworth Park, only to find out quite fortuitously that he had carted herring and barrels and herring guts and herring nets and salt for my father many a bygone year.

So back to salt. It was one of the first cargoes into Stronsay in anticipation of the coming season and was carted loose and by the cartload from ship to shed, being thrown roof high in the stores by shovel and sweat. Coarse salt from the Baltic. Then the ships with barrels stacked mast high, unwieldy cargo in a gale, light and bulky. Carted also to the yards and pyramided high as many an old photograph of Wick Harbour well illustrates. So I have always had a sympathy with the "Toun of Weik" which was the next port south when the fish and the boats and the season deserted Stronsay, and where my mother's mother gutted her fair share of herring in her younger days.

Leave the herring fishing, not yet a part of the History of Wick in 1660. But salt was. And I am drawing upon my own memory when I think of the myriad uses of that most common of substances.

In summer the cows milked too well, if that were possible, and much cheese and butter was made. Mother salted down a portion of the butter into earthenware jars of considerable dimensions, and that for the winter. Pretty salty, but we ate it. Then there was the pig, salted as strait pork or cured as ham with saltpetre and brown sugar and spices and a touch of smoke in a large barrel. Some ham was cured dry and hung from the rafters. Some was put into the pickle barrel and brine, prepared from salt, poured over it, covering the ham. Mutton was salted down and another pickle barrel came into service. I quite liked it. Beef also went the same way but we did not do much of that, preferring the butcher's fresh meat.

Even on the farm salt came into use and many a haystack had its layers of salt which helped to keep damp hay fresh and cool and free from mould and palatable. The quantities used were enormous. And of course there was the fish.

Most households on Stronsay had a boat, or access to one, and many a summer evening sped by on the water fishing for haddock, cod, ling, caithes, or cuddin to the Caithnessman. Sillocks – young caithes – were taken out of the water by a pock net, fishing from the rocks or off the pier. Even a skate or two or a dogfish came aboard. And salt again. Most of these fish were split, salted, piled in layers, turned daily, dried by air and sun. A crack over the head with a dried salt cod was a memorable experience, the old stock fish of the Vikings. In the midst of our Pentland Firth was Stroma whose very existence centred around dried salt cod for many a year. Wick long ago would have had at least its fair share of fish, having its own bylaws to allow the inhabitants to purchase a portion of a landing, and the boat borrowed without permission and damaged at Staxigoe by Alexr Mullikin, not to forget mention of the fight at sea between two fishing boats.

Of herring there is no specific mention in the Counsell Book but they were mentioned by Aneas Bayne in 1735 along with white fish. These would have been undoubtedly salted down in large quantities for winter consumption and for selling on.

At summer's end there was another and very large requirement for salt, the killing of the "mert". This was a cattle beast fattened all summer on grass and killed at the onset of winter at Martinmas, or Mertinmes, and the very name "mert" suggesting that time at the end of November. This was a very necessary killing as winter fodder, mostly hay, was all needed to keep the cows and young stock alive. The beef was salted down and barreled in pickle, or brine. It was sold in Kirkwall in the 1600s by William Laughten, merchant, to the King's Navy, and in large quantities. No doubt another tradeable commodity, exported abroad as well as for home consumption, provisioning passing sailing ships, whalers to the Arctic, to Northern Canada by the Hudson's Bay Company as they sailed from Stromness. And no doctors telling people to cut down on their salt intake, it was quite unavoidable. Even eggs could be preserved in a pickling mixture for winter use. And there was the salting down of young sea birds, not a personal experience but St Kilda, Lewis, Foula, Fair Isle, Copinsay carried on this practice to within recent times. The Chinese were doing the same 3,000 years ago. So George Ruthven, who no doubt conveyed his salt to Wick by ship, even if not a freeman of the Burgh, was at least filling a very much needed requirement of the Toun and probably had stood on the toes of some vested interest of the Burgess merchants of Weik.

Marie Grant, brine bearer, must have carried brine prepared by some Wick merchant, if she did not prepare it herself, to any customer thereof, no doubt in the old style of two buckets carried by suspending them from a wooden yoke balanced over her shoulders, a knack I never quite mastered, spilling most of the water over my legs. The recipe for commercial brine I do not have, but I do remember my mother making brine, water saturated with salt until a fresh egg would float in it, using it for ham and mutton pickling. I do not suppose there is any great recipe for making ordinary brine but there were and still are recipes for some salted delicacy using brine well spiced with one thing or another.

Perhaps in that trade Wick could restart it's tradition of curing, if fish are scarce there is plenty of good beef available.

— Chapter 15 —

The Pentland Rascals of 1660

The near distance view of Orkney lying to the North from the Parish on the Pentland Firth did not mean that those Islands were out of touch with either Canisbay or Wick Parishes, or that the Pentland Firth was an impassable barrier. Far from it. Every now and then in the Counsell Book of Weik there was reference to some Orkneyman or other, and Orkney women are not to be ignored either, then or now!

One Orkneyman, Magnus Flett, was involved in the Bailyie Court in Weik with George Annand, merchant, on the last day of July, 1662. Annand was accused for taking the rudder off a boat belonging to Magnus, this in respect of the nonpayment of Customs Dues owed by Flett to George Annand, who held the rights of collection of the Customs of Weik. These Customs, annually rouped, were taken on the 17th January, 1662, for the sum of £46 Scots, in the first instance by Wm Cormok, schomaker. Annand had taken the snuff making rights for £34 Scots at the same roup. However, Cormok thought better of his deal, or took cold feet, and four days later passed on the Customes to George Annand at the same price.

Magnus was in Weik with his boat carrying *"victuall"* from Orkney as cargo, normally grain or meal or malt, but most food-stuffs were *"victual"*. Annand was also accused for *"dinging, blooding and aboosing of Thomas Robson, srvetor to the said Magnus Flett"*.

The dinging took the form of beating Robson about the head with a *"trie"*, just what size we cannot tell, but the most usual use of the word *"trie"* in those times referred to a roof trie, now no doubt a couple leg, if not an even more modern word. Whatever the size of the trie, even if only a club, it would not be a recommended cure for a sore head. The Court of Francis Mansonne and Allexr Cormok fined Annand in £10 Scots for the beating of Robson, ordered Annand to restore the "ruther" to Flett, and to receive the Customs Dues which Flett should have paid to Annand in the first place.

Another Flett from Orkney appears on the 8th day of July 1663, but only as a witness. The case related to Wm Abernethie, servitor to William Sinclair of Hoy [Caithness], and he was accused for *"the perturbation and aboosing of Mgratt Aikin, spous to Johne Printoche, throwing hir to the ground in hir awin hous"*. No reason for the offence was given. Allexr Flett, in Ronaldsay in Orkney, was one witness, the other was Jaspert Flett, carpenter in Haubster, probably another Orkneyman settled in Caithness, and most likely related to Alexr. Both must have been together in Johne Pruntoche's house. The place name of "Haubster" was in transition from "Haubister" to "Haubster" to "Hauster" to "Haster", moving from the old Norse "Hau" – a low lying piece of ground, and "bister" – farm stead, to the abbreviated Caithness pronunciation of the "Haster" of today.

Another Orkneyman, James Wares, appeares on 22nd November, 1664, when Margaratt Schand in Weik was accused for the:

"Recepting of ane Kist lock, withe a certane quantitie of tobaco found in hir hous, and Stollin be James Wares, ane Orkney boy. Comperit the said Margratt Schand and Confest the having of the Lock & Tobaco, bott alledgitt she did nocht know that the same was Stollin. Bot she, being ane Comone Brouster, did Acept of the Same as ane price for Drink Drunkin be the said James Wares."

"The quhilk being Takin to the Intlognitur of the Judges and Counsell, they have decerned and ordainit the said Margratt Schand to pay £5 Scots money within tyme of law, and iff ever she shalbe found in the Lyck in Tyme Cmg, to underly the Lawes Criminallie and to be Censured yrfra Acordinglie, qruponn act."

A *"Brouster"* was a brewer, and no doubt a pub keeper as well.

The name "Wares" was also found at that time in Canisbay Parish and there is ongoing debate as to it's origin, Orkney or Canisbay. There is a place name "Warse" or "Wass" or "Walls" on both sides of the Firth, so it looks like a stand off.

But possibly the most interesting Orkney reference I came across was on 22nd July, 1663, with a complex series of entries concerning property belonging to James Dunbar, merchant. Unfortunately though James Dunbar is called merchant in . . . . , the name of the place is blank. Now the Dunbars were an involved family with several side connections which it is not my task to unravel, thankfully. Henderson's Caithness Families gives some run down on the genealogy of that family but does not clearly identify James even if he did belong to it.

The entry in the Counsell Book of Weik suggests that James belonged to Wick and to the Dunbar family, who by that time had estates in Latheron prior to acquiring their eventually extensive holdings throughout Caithness. James was stated as *"goeing for the Barbadoes Island"*, that same West Indian Island being acquired and settled by the British Crown, though stated in 1627 as *"English"*! Among other parishes in Barbadoes is St Andrews, possibly a Scottish connection.

The entry reads:

"The 22 Day of July, 1663, In pnce of James Doull & Allexr Cormok, Bailyies. The qlk day anentt Certane Lining [linen] and Clothes [cloths] withe Sundrie Stuffs, Sundrie wobes [webs] thairof appertening to James Dunbar, mchant in ...?... going for the Barbadoes Island, Stollin and awaytakin furthe of his Storhous in Cairsten [Stromness] in Orkney, in this pntt month of July. Stollen and awaytakin be his Srvantes under nominatt, his bound Servantes, and transporting the same fron Orkney to Caithness in ane Certane yooll [yawl] boatt, stollin also and awaytakin be the personnes undernominatt in Lyikmaner, and efter thair Landing at Dungasbey, they did put the said Boatt Emptie to the Sea , yt [that] she was found thairefter be the sands in Dungasbey. And thairefter the personnes, Comone notorious theiffes, being thrie in number, did Cume to the Burghe of Weik, and did sell the forsaides wobes and Stuffes to the personnes undernomatt, nather did they reveill thair names, bot Immediatelie wentt away but [without] the knowledge of any personnes, and thairfor the byeres of the said wobes and Stuffes aucht & sould underly the Lawes for the same, Ilk ane for thair awin pairtes as followes, To witt:

"*George Mullikin, mchant in Weik, Acused for the bying of twentie four elnes of Lining Clothe, withe ten elnes of Swazinges, Compeirit the said George Mullikin and Confest the Claime. [An Elne was 37 inches, near enough a yard.]*

"*Jeane Ballenden, Spous to George Annand, Compeirit & Confest seven elnes of the said Swazinges.*

"*Patrick Dunbar, glover, Compeirit and Confest four elnes of the said Stuff.*

"*Johne Mansonne, Schomaker in the Bankhead, for bying of certane of the forsaid Clothes, being Lallie warned & nocht Compeirand, cnvict in cntumacy L./- [50/-]*

"*Adam Sutherland in Mospalme, for bying of Certane of the said Clothes, being Lallie warned & nocht Compeirand, cnvict in cntumacy - 50/-.*

"*And efter Consideration of the former Confessionn be the pties byeres of the Clothes and Stuffes, the Judges ordaines the wholl thairof to be Inbrocht To the Tolboothe the morrow, being the 23 of July Instant, and the pryces yrof To be estimatt be honest men.*

"*The quhilk 23 of July, Compeirit George Mullikin and producet so muche Lining & plaiding as was left unsold be him, and the pryces yrof estimatt be Johne Clyne, Johne Cormok, weaver, & Andrew Baine, the plaiding being bocht at 4/8d Ilk elne, and now declared to be worthe 9/- Scots Ilk elne, and the Lining Clothe qlk wes bocht at 6/- Scots the elne, is declared & estimatt to X/- the elne.*

"*Sicklyck the plaiding bocht be Jeane Bellenden at 4/8d the elne, estimatt at 9/- Ilk elne yroff. Sicklyck it is ordainit that the morrow being the 24 July, the wholl pties concerned who bocht the said lining, plaiding, & Stuffes, nocht brocht in as yt, To bring the Remanentt, Ilk personne for yr awin partes, withe thair awin personall presence, Ilk personne under the paine of 40/- Scots money, and to this effect Wm Sinclair, mchant, Caur. for Jeanne Ballenden, and James Doull, Schomaker, Caur. for George Mullikin.*

"*The 24 July, 1663. The qlk day the forsaid personnes Comperit and producet the Clothes as followes, To witt:*

"*Adam Sutherland in Mospalme & Jon Masonn, Schomaker in the Bankhead, and producet twelff elnes of plaiding, withe Sevin elnes off Stuff.*

"*Johne Leithe in Keiss producitt ten elnes of Lining qrof George Mullikin was chairgitt. [bought from Mullikin]*

"*And thairefter the complener James Dunbar, craving Justice cnform to the Lawes of this Kingdome, and the Clothes and Stuff being producet in Judgement, and efter matur deliberonn of Wm Balye, provest deput, and the Balyies and Toune Counsell, have decernit and declared the Clothes and uthers abovespeitt to be restored back againe to the said James Dunbar, Just owner of the Samyne, and for the aboos done be the pties Complained uponn In bying of unLall goodes, from personnes nocht knowen nather themselffes, nor thair pticular names, Thairfor the saids Judges fynes & cnvictes:*

"*George Mullikin, befor named, for the recept of the Stollin clothes and Stuffes mentioned on the former pages of this Book, fynes & cvictes him in ane unlaw of £10 Scots.*

"*Jeane Ballenden, for the Lyck recept, cnvict in ane unlaw of Xmkes Scots.* [unlaw - old term for a legal penalty or fine.]

Adam Sutherland in Mospalme and John Mansonne in the Bankhead did not dwell in the Burghe, and therefore were outwith the Jurisdiction of the Counsell Court. Not, however, beyond reach of punishment. Their cases were referred to the determination of my Lord's [the Earl] Barone Bailyie, who was Wm Balye of Mylnton. No doubt a Burgess of Weik himself, he fyned each of the "*twa*" in an unlaw of 5 merks Scots, to be "*uptakin and applyed to the weill of the Burghe.*"

So we pass from James Dunbar and those Orkney rascals, or were they Caithness rascals. The laws obviously held that merchants should not and could not trade with persons unknown to them who did not give their names, but who immediately took off out of reach of the Burghe Court or the Law. Their names were not recorded even if the early portion of the entry suggests they would be. They were bound servants of James Dunbar, a state in which many a rebel from Jacobite times found themselves in the new colonies, from where very few ever returned. People in debt sometimes got out of their problems, probably only temporarily, by becoming bound servants, and this carried on for many a year after our Counsell Book, well into the 1800s. Many an emigrant, some from the Clearances, indentured themselves as bound servants to some landowner in the colonies in return for their passage abroad. It is unlikely that the Baronetcy of Nova Scotia of Sir William Dunbar of Hempriggs, created in 1698, was an empty title, he could have had interests abroad to justify the use of "Nova Scotia" in his title. Having no son, his brother and successor was Sir Robert Dunbar of Northfield, the Nova Scotia baronetcy continuing down that line. A few years later a new Baronetcy was created, "Dunbar of Hempriggs", by James Sutherland, 2nd son of Lord Duffus. He had become the second husband of Sir William Dunbar's daughter Elizabeth, whose first husband was Sir Robert Gordon of Gordonstoun, who died in 1701. The estates of Hempriggs had been entailed on Elizabeth by her father, Sir William. In 1706 James Sutherland became Sir James Dunbar of Hempriggs, adopting the surname of Dunbar. He would not be the first or the last to whom the expedient of adopting his wife's surname was attractive when an estate was also on offer.

Trading was the name of the game for those on the make, the ownership of land gave access to rents paid as grain and other agricultural products, including cloth, to be carried abroad for trading. Tobacco, a product of the New World, has already been mentioned. Rum and sugar will be. Outfitting a vessel to trade with the West Indies or the American Colonies would have been one route to fortune, if successful. Our James Dunbar of 1663 was obviously taking that path from his store house in Cairsten, now Stromness.

The name James Dunbar appears later in the Counsell Book when Sir James Dunbar was elected Provost of Weik in September, 1707, an office he held for two years, being succeeded by Capt. Robert Sutherland of Langwall, but most improbable to be the same James from 1663 in Cairsten.

Sir James Dunbar we have already mentioned as the owner of the fishing boat in Staxigoe taken without leave and damaged by George Mullikin, merchant in Weik. Dunbar also owned the Barnyards of Papigoe in 1708, mentioned in another incident of theft we have not yet referred to. In both cases he was called Sir James Dunbar of Hempriggs, yonr. Though I do not think so, is it just possible that he was the same person as had the goods stolen from Cairsten in 1663? Did James Sutherland also have a claim to the name Dunbar? or use it as an alias or other name. Forty or so years had gone by, but not an impossible span from a young man going abroad seeking his fortune in Barbadoes in 1663 to an older man in 1707 content to fill the office of Provost.

— Chapter 16 —

Swords and Pistolls, Bows and Arrows

By all accounts Weik must have been a pretty dangerous place to live in during the 1600s, according to the Counsell Book. There are references to such weaponry as swords, pistols, knives, shooting bows, as well as the much more apparently normal uses of battens of wood, tries of the same, rungs such as we would now associate with ladders but in those distant days were a bit heftier, preasts which now only have significance for an angler about to dispatch a salmon undoubtedly lawfully caught with rod and line on the Water of Weik.

May as well complete the list with reference to feet and fists, pewter plates and pynt stoups of ail, a quart stoup on one occasion, stones and sand, oars then called skulls, perhaps a well chosen name at that, though we cannot include all the above in this present chapter.

On the seventh of April, 1662, Alex Printoche, merchant, came to the house of Johne Printoche, who was his brother, and drew a sword to Alex Cordeiner, a weaver in Weik who happened to be in the house. There he threatened to take his life but settled for beating him with his hands. Cordeiner swore on oath to the truth of that, and accordingly Printoche was fined in £6/13/4d., which was the round figure of ten merks Scots.

On the 16th April, 1662, Hew Blair, merchant in Weik, and Patrick Dunbar in Akergill, were accused for blooding of "*uthers*", and in the context of the Counsell Book "*uthers*" means "*each other*", not other persons. Patrick Dunbar especially was accused for the drawing of a sword and of a "*preast*", the preast being at that time a cudgel much loved and used by sailors, pirates and others for despatching someone into the next world. Many a landsman woke up with a sore head on board a ship far out at sea after a clout on the skull with a preast by the Press Gang.

Dunbar's aim must have been clouded as the witnesses:- "*deponed uponn oathe that Patrick Dunbar did draw ane Sword and preast to Strick at Hew Blair, bot did him no harme, except that blood whiche he gave to Johne Sutherland, who was Reding betwixt them*". So much for trying to make peace between friends. Sutherland should have known better. "*Reding*" is an old Caithness word for sorting out. Nevertheless, the record went on "*and it being proven that Hew Blair did cast ane Stone at the said Patrick Dunbar, qlk bred the first motionn. Thairfor the Judges decernes Blair in £5 and Dunbar in 50/- , qruponn act.*" So both were duly fined, and as Blair seems to have started the fracas he paid the more.

We are not finished with Hew Blair, not by long shot. He appears on another occasion, being fined £10 Scots for the beating of Thomas Hossack, merchant in Weik. For this exercise he used a small rod or trie betwixt the shoulders of Hossack. As there was usually two sides to every story, Hossack was also indited for "*the Casting of Sand down uponn the said Hew Blair, they being Casting the nets [in the] Water of Weik, the said being refered to the oathe of Hew Blair, he maid faithe in Judgement upon the Caus and yrfor Hossack cnvict in £5.*"

Small episode in itself, but the reference to "*casting the nets*" can only refer to salmon fishing on the River where the two must have been competing one with the other, probably for the best stance or pool.

Knives were another useful means of mayhem, and on the 19th May, 1662, William Johnsone, merchant, was accused for blooding and blaeing [bruising] of Neill Baine, servitor to George Bruce, skipper.

"*Comperit bothe pties and the said Neill Baine maid faithe in Judgement that the said Wm Jsone did cut his doublett Sleive withe*

ane Drawin Knyff to the verie Skine & had most Strakin him throche
the arme withe the said knyff, exept providence, and thairfor the said
Wm J'sonne cnvict in £5."

"Providence" came to the aid of many a Wicker in the Counsell
Record Book, and maybe still does, even in modern times.

In 1663, on Sept the 9th., George Sinclair, shoemaker, was
accused for the "beiting and aboosing of Johne Donaldson,
wricht." I thought we would reach the Donaldsons sooner or
later! It was not too serious a matter, however. Donaldson had
been visiting George Sinclair in George's house and the affray
was no more than Sinclair giving him a push in the breast with
the horn of a shooting bow, for which Sinclair was fined 50/-.
Donaldson must have been somewhat touchy and brought it
to Court. Of interest is the reference to bows and no doubt
arrows as late as 1663, perhaps by that time but a sport. Probably
a good quiet poaching weapon at that. After all, the Queen still
has her bodyguard of the Right Worshipful Company of Archers
in Edinburgh!

Perhaps George Sinclair had the measure of Johne
Donaldson, wricht, because Johne again appears in August
25th, 1665, *"acused for the Scandalous and most vyle Speiches, uttered*
be him against Jeanne Bellenden, spous To George Annand, Threatning
withe ane Drawen Sword of Allxr Mansonne, mchant, for the
Reproveing of the said Johne Ddsonne anent the forsaid misbehavur.

"Comperit bothe the parties and the Claime being refered to the
aithe of the said Johne Dodsonne, he refoosed to give the same , being
guyltie of the Indytment. And thairfor the Judges, withe advyis of
the Counsell, fynes & cnvictes him in ane unlaw of £5 Scots
money.

You cannot, however, keep a good man down. Came a month
later on the 15th September and our friend Donaldson features
once more *"Acused for the blooding of Jon Sutherland, tounes officer,*
Throwing of him over the Tolboothe stair in Seiking and demandinge
payment for the unlaw abovespeitt, [the £5 fine for Jeanne Bellenden]
conforme to the Bailyies orderes, the said Johne being Lallie warned to
the effect forsaid. Thryis called and Compeirand, he is ordainit to be
Somondit the 22 day of the forsaid monthe, to underly the Lawes for
the Lybell."

"Compeirit the said Johne Ddsonne, and being guyltie, putes him-
selff in the Judges will, And thairfor In respect of many former faltes

cmited be him, and his povertie being Considerit, thairfor the said Judges, withe advyis & Consentt of the Toune Counsell, fynes & cnvicts the said Jon Ddsonne in ane unlaw of £10."

"*Povertie*" comes into the reckoning a number of times in the Counsell Book when fines were pitched lower than usual, and in some cases where money obviously could not be extracted the culprit was dealt with by spending so many hours in the stokes at the Croie.

Harder weaponry was not to be by any means overlooked in Weik. On the 22nd Apryll 1666:- "*The qlk day in presence of the said Bailyies , Allxr Cormok, mcht thair, Indyted and acused for the Drawing of ane pistoll from his Syd, aboosing and beating of Wm Caldell, mcht thair, over the heid withe the said pistoll To the effusion of his Blood.*

"*Comperit Wm Caldell persewer. Allxr Cormok absent, being Lallie chargit as the officer affirmed in Judgement and nocht compeirand, thairfor cnvict in L./- Scots as contumacy. [50/-.]*

The Court had the practice of making someone else responsible for the appearance of an accused, a form of bail, so :

"*A...nd Sicklyck George Annand, James Oswald, James Doull, Schomaker, for the nocht Inbringing of the forsaid Allxr Cormok, they being ordered for that effect and Disobeying the said order, Ilk ane of the said personnes cnvict in L./- Scots, Inde £7-10/-.*

Next day, the 23rd Apryll:

"*The qlk day Comperit the said Allxr Cormok & Wm Caldell who being Acused upon the ptulares Lybellit, the said Allxr Cormok Confest the Drawing of ane pistoll and qt prejudice he receavitt thairby Iff it was Thocht worth his evill Speiches desrved the same, qlk being referred to the oathe of the said Wm Caldell, he maid faithe in Judgement that the said Allxr Cormok did give him ane Blea [bruise] withe the said pistoll upon the face, and thairfor the said Judges fynes & convictes the said Allxr Cormok in ane unlaw of £20 Scots.*

"*Sicklyck the said Wm Caldell Acused for the blooding of the said Allexander Cormok, the said being refered Simple to his awin oathe, he maid faithe in Judgement that he never receivitt any blood from the said Wm Caldell, and thairfor the Judges assoilyies him thairof in all Tyme Cming, qruponn act.*

"*A.... nd Sicklyck upon the said Twentie thrie day of the said monethe of apryll , the said Wm Caldell having obeyed the Order of the forsaid Bailyies barring himselff in prisonne and finding Caution to persew the Indytment as he did, and to that effect he was inacted for the Sowme of ane hundrethe punds Scots money, qruponn act.*

But later on that day Caldell, obviously not in prison- *"In the efternoone of the forsaid day the said Wm Caldell in most humble form going in to the hous of Johne Nachtie, mchant, withe certane honest men to do his Lall Bussines and effares, having no mynd of evill or any Suche Lyk Intention, The said Allxr Cormok Acompanyed withe James Doull, schomaker, Wm Cormok and utheres, did Cum in to the said Johne Nachtie his hous qr they did know that the said Wm Caldell was Onlie to forge ane new girnell as is alledgit, and thairfor and for eschewing of farder Trouble betwixt the said pties, Andrew Baine, Balyie, did Cum in to the said Johne Nachtie his hous in most quyet maner, and desyred the said Allxr Cormok To go home to his awin hous, or then to bind himselff be ane act of Courtt as the said Wm Caldell had done, utherwayes to go to prisonne within the Tolboothe as he did. Nevertheless the said Allxr Cormok withe his forsaids Assosiates did Thretain & menass the said Andrew Baine, Balyie, and in Specall the said Allxr Cormok for Drawing out of ane pistoll to the said Bailyie, Contrair to all actes and in Manifest Contempt yrof."*

Next day, the 24th April *"The qlk day Comperit the said Allxr Cormok and denyed the wholl Claime Lybellit formerlie gainst him be the said Andrew Baine, Balyie, who Takes him to prove the Same be the witnesses undernomatt, To witt: Wm Cormok, Schomaker, James Oswald & James Doull, Schomaker. Comperit Wm Cormok and deponed, upon oathe, that the said Allxr Cormok Denyed to obey the ordor of the said forsaid Balyie And also the said Allxr Cormok cnfest himself the Lyik bot allegit the forsaid Bailyie had no reason to do the liak as he ordered. James Doull, Schomaker, & James Oswald, uther twa of the witnesses, being Lallie warned & nocht Compeirand, Ilk personne cnvict in L./- as Contumacy."*

"And as anent the offering & Drawing of the forsaid pistoll to the said Bailyie, he refered the Same to the said Allxr Cormok his aithe, qlk he refoosed to give, And thairfor and Inrespect and for vilipending the Order of the said Andrew Baine, Balyie, Frances Mansonne, the uther Balyie, fyned & Convicted the said Allxr Cormok in ane unlaw of Twentie fyve punds Scots money, qruponn act.

Things got more serious for Wm Caldell on the 29 June, 1666, when *"The qlk day Allxr Mansone, mchant, Indyted & Acused for the Crewell hurting, wounding and Blooding withe ane chargit pistoll of the heid of Wm Caldell, mchant thair, being under Cloud & Silence of night and as apperit to be fortnocht fellonie, Contrair to the Lawes & practigne of this Kingdome.*

"*The said Allxr Mansonne being warned at his dwelling hous To have Comperit the said day as the officer affirmed in Judgement, and being thrys Called at the Tolboothe windo as use is and nocht Compeirand, thairfor he was cnvict in Contumacy 50/-.* [contumacy – ignoring the command of Court by non appearance.]

On the second of July he was "*chargit de nova at his dwelling hous as the officer affirmed, being thryis callit & nocht Compeirand, cnvict in Cntumacy £5*". So he had again ignored the lawful summons, and had to pay the more. On to the fifth day of July, 1666, when he finally appeared: "*Comperit the said Alex Mansonne, being Acused for Comiting of the said blooding & wounding of the abovewretin Wm Caldell, and for the braking of Twa Severall arestes, the ane yrof laid upon hes boothe dore and the uther upon his awin personne, being wtin his hous, for the qlk haill Judgements he Refered him to be in the will of the Judges & Toune Counsell, c'nvened for the Tyme.*"

"*The quhilk day anent the Indytment persewed be Wm Caldell, mchant, against Allxr Mansonne, mchant, Sett dune in the former page of this book and the said Allxr, cmitting himselff in the will of the said Balyies & Counsell as said is. A. ..nd efter matur deliberation, for the wounding & blooding of Wm Caldell, and Braking of the Twa arrestes verified as said is, he is fyned & cnvict in the Sowme of £50 Scots money - qruponn act.*" The "*chargit pistoll*" must have been fired, otherwise why refer to "*chargit*". "*Forethocht fellonie*" is near enough our "*premeditated*" and "*under Cloud and Silence of nicht*" is self explanatory. Not one sided, of course, it seldom was.

"*The said day Wm Caldell, Acused for the giveing of ane blow to the said Allxr Mansonne efter many evil] Speiches given be him to the said Wm and to the Balyies, the said Blow Cnfest in Judgement, thairfor Wm Caldell cnvict in £10 Scots, qruponn act.*

"*A . . . . . nd for eleiding and awaytaking of anie farder Trowble betwixt the said Wm Caldell & Allxr Mansonne, They have found the Caures underwretin for Surtie and Lawborrowes, Ilk ane to utheres as followes:*

We then find two entries that same day when, in obedience to his maiesties lawes for keiping of the peace and finding lawborrowes, Wm Caldell found George Sinclair, schomaker in Weik, as cautioner for him that - "*the said Allexr Mansonn shalbe harmles & skaithles in his body, guides & geir or anie uthers wharin he may slope or let efter the dait heirof utherwayes be ordor of law & Justice, under the paine of ane hundrethe pounds Scots money, and the said Wm Caldell binds him and his to relieve his said cautioner of all Cost, Skaithe and dampage qlk he may Incur heirthrow in all tyme Cming. Qrupon act.*

This was then initialed by Wm Caldell with the initials W.C. and signed by George Sinclair by name. Similarly Allexr Mansonne found George Bruce, Skipper, as cautioner in the same terms for the same amount of ane hundrethe punds Scots and signed by J. Mansonne and George Bruce, both able to write it seems. And they remained good friends ever after!

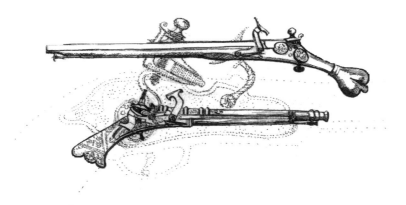

— Chapter 17 —

———⟫◆⟪———

Agnes Roull, another thief

The case of Agnes Roull, alias Suyrland, is entered in the
Counsell Book of Weik on the 6th January, 1710, and the
many thieving offences laid at her door, if indeed she had
one. As with Kathrein Creak, there appears to be a receiver of
the stollen goods who put this poor girl up to her thieving,
namely a certain girl called Marsell Baine, indited and accused
for being a common receiver of stolen goods, a corresponder
and conniver *"airt and pairt"* with Agnes Roull, alias Suyrland,
in receiving from her the gold money, linnen, etc. of which she
stood accused of stealing. Marsell Baine had been in trouble
before.

The first offence in the list refers to Agnes coming several
times to the house of John Forsyth in Smallquoys, *"under silence
of night"*, breaking through the roof of the *"chamber"*, which roof
had to be of thatch, and *"stealing and awaytaking meal, gold money,
linen and several other things belonging to Jon Forsyth and his
brother-in-law, Donald Sutherland."* Either Agnes was
exceedingly light on her feet or the victims were very heavy
sleepers. The chamber of these houses of olden times was the
inner room used for sleeping, the outer room very often being
for the cattle and other livestock.

Part of the stolen property was found in her possession. The
"several times" Agnes came to Smallquoys is odd, one would
have thought the residents would have been more on guard
after the first break in.

Offence number two for Agnes was at the house of Allex Mearns in Papigo, again under *"silence of night"*, where she *"did steall and awaytake ane green apron, wool, linnen & seall oyr things"*. She was apprehended with these items and *"bound in the said hous qll the nixt morning"*. How she could *"awaytake"* the items and still be apprehended and bound in the house, as if caught in the act, I cannot work out, neither can I understand how Agnes was not dealt with at the time. Still, that is the old record.

She was next accused of coming to the house of Mr James Oliphant, the Minister of Wick Parish at that time, on one or other of the nights of the previous November, two months before her Court appearance, and stealing out of his britches *"ane genyie and some silver qn he wes asleep"*. For those out of touch with old money a *"genyie"* was a guinea worth 21 shillings, or £1.05. Oliphant must have been enjoying the sleep of the just, and who better than the Minister.

The list continued with Agnes breaking into the house of Donald Sutherland, a merchant in Weik, *"under silence of night, stealling several ells of linen and woollens, peices of headclothes, napkins, laces and three half crowns out of Donald's pocket while he was asleep"*. Was this Donald the same Donald as the brother-in-law of John Forsyth in Smallquoys but living in a different house? An ell or eln was just over a yard, just short of a metre.

The record does not refer to more than the one occurrence and, with the amount of material taken, it is certain that Agnes had an accomplice outside the house, probably Marsell Bain, to help her carry away the booty. There was just too much for one girl to tuck under her arm.

Agnes continued her depredations with the house of Alex. Dunbar, another merchant in Weik. There she took, several times, some quantities of meal and some money out of the pocket of the *"mistris"*. *"Silence of night"* is repetitive, also references to *"several times"*.

A *"pocket"* would be more a modern handbag, but in those days probably attached to her belt. So we are already getting some idea of the possessions of 1710, green aprons, lace, linen, woollens, headclothes. A half crown was 2/6d., decimal 12½p. Meal was a necessity of life itself and at times there was little enough of it with starvation often just around the corner.

Her adventures continued at the dwelling house of Alexr Doull, one of the Toune Bailies, and her booty became slightly more upmarket. From him Agnes stole *"se'all tymes, ane silver tumler of twa unces weight, ane pynt & chopin Botle full of Rumm, nyne table napkins, ane long muslin gravat and certain qtities of meall & oyr things, qch you cannot deny."*

Silver objects nearly always had the weight mentioned, probably as a measure of value, and old wills and testaments seen in Kirkwall of even earlier times [1643] had such things as silver spoons, mazers [drinking vessels], candlesticks and chandleirs, all itemised with their weight in silver *"unces."* And had the *"Rumm"* come from Barbadoes? [James Dunbar]

Next stop for Agnes was *"the hous of Jon Nauchtie, ygr, schoemaker yr, under silence of night, and stealing furth yrof ten pound Scots or yrby, & se'all uyr small things qch you cannot deny. And yrfor ought and should be punished to the teirer & example of oyrs, conform to lawe."*

Sir James Dunbar owned Papigoe by this time, and Agnes was accused of *"stealling furth of the byckes & barne & Barneyardes of Papigo, certane qtities of bear and oats qlk you cannot deny."* Jon Forsyth, who comes into this matter, was either the tacksman or the tenant of the lands of Papigo, and appears later on in the trial of Agnes, stateing his loss.

"Bear" was the old name for the Northern equivalent of barley, sometimes spelt *"bere"*, and significantly close to the word *"Beer"*. It was a very important commodity for trading, probably the most important grain grown in Caithness, then and now, and in it's modern equivalent of *"barley"*still used for brewing and whisky distilling, being in 1660 often converted into malt before export abroad or used for home brewing of ale or beer. A *"byke"* was a small stack made of straw well wrapped with "simmans" and thatched, in which threshed grain could be kept dry for long periods. The name could also be used for the stacks of unthreshed sheaves both of bear and oats, still, if rarely in these modern days of combine harvesters, to be seen around Latheron. So to trial, and Agnes pretty well confessed to all the charges, specifying more clearly the exact objects she took.

"Wick, 6th Jany, 1710, as to the first article, confess, as to the 2d article, cnfess wooll & yearne. As to the 3d article, confess the genyie

and ane shilling sterling. As to the 4th article confess the taking of some linnen out of the chist & moey out of Donald Suyrlands pocket two se'all tymes But knowes not the qtitie qt shee took at se'all tymes. As to the fyft article, confess the taking ane sex pence of money out of the mistress pocket and about three lippies of meall at se'all tymes. As to the sexth article, confess. As to the seventh article, confess.

As to the last article, confess She onlie took it on(e) tyme out of ane Byck in Papigo, ane litle qtitie of oats. And confess & declairs shee delyvered the two genyies stollen from Mr Oliphant and Robert Calder & the moey they wantit to Marsell Baine, And also delyvered certane ells of linnen & ane pinner stollen fra Marjorie Murray & delyvered her the moey shee did steall from Donald Suyrland, merd, & Jon Nauchtie, ygr., And to the sd Marsell shee delyvered ane chopin Botle wt Rumm & ane muslen gravat stollen fra Alexr Doull, also cnfess shee gave the Silver tumler and ane pynt bottle wt Rumm to Elspet Manson, daur of Mark Henderson in Wick. The abovenamit pannell Declaires shee cannot wryt.

ALEX DOULL / P. SINCLAIR, Clerk."

Robert Calder above had not been mentioned in the listed indictments though Agnes admitted stealing a guinea from him.

Marsell Baine in Wick was also before the court for her part as a receiver and probable instigator of the stealing spree. Part of the stolen goods or booty, in 1710 sometimes called *"fangs"*, had been found in her possession. She was also *"of oppen bruit and comon fame"*, meaning other well known past convictions.

"Marsell Baine in Wick, you ar Indytit and accused as a Comon recepter of thift, Corresponder & conniver, airt & part, wt Agnes Roall, alias Suyrland, in receaving from her the gold, moey, linnen & oyrs shee stands Indytit for, qch you cannot deny, and a part found in yor posession. Yrfor you ought & should be punished conforme to lawe & also under oppen bruit & comon fame, conforme to former sentences contained in the toune Books of Wick.

6th Jany, 1710. Compeirs Henderson wt the defer & denyes the Indytment. Compeirs Mullikin, fiscall, & produces a fang cnfest be the panell. And takes him to prove the heall Indytment agt tuesday nixt, the 13 instant, & remittes her to prisone, qron act, qr all pties ar to appeir.

ALEX DOULL"

Wick 13 June, 1710. Rob Henderson appeared for the defender, Marsell Bain, and proposed that he be freed of his bond of caution, which bond was delivered up judicially.

The fiscall produced several *"fangs"* in evidence, found in the possession of Marsell Bain. The fiscall proves ane act of Banishment against her passed by the *"majestrats of the Burgh"* in the yeir 1693, dated the 17 June, yeir forsaid, by Alexr Mansone & Wm Mullikin, Bailyies, for stealling of [from] Slanders Kaithnes, *"lint, linnen yearn, several hesps [lengths] of hardn, [a very coarse cloth or thread made from the rougher fibre from flax, linen being made from the finer] wooll & some driggie [Probably rubbish of cloth and allied to dregs], qrupon the sd Bailyies past the act of Banishment agt the sd Marsell wt reservation that if shee wes to be foynd wtin the liberties of the sd Burghe yreftr, to be Imprisoned till scourging yrfor & the receptor yr efter to be liable"*.

"Receptor" meant any person who received her or gave her any help or accomodation or any other assistance, and who would also be punished, in what manner is not stated.

The Record continued :

"Elspet Mansone, daur to umqll [deceased] William Mansone in Wick, you ar Indytitt and accused for recepting and receaveing a part of the goods stollen be the sd Agnes Roull, for qch shee stands wtin Indytit, for qch you sould be punished as airt & part & comon recepter, under oppen bruit & comon fame, qch you cannot deny.

Wick 6th June, 1710. Compeirs Henderson for the defr & denyes the heall Indytment. Compeirs Mullikin, fiscall, & offers to prove agt twelf or the 13th instant, qr all pties ar to appear, qron act.
ALEX DOULL."

"Wick 13 June, 1710. efter the fiscall ordered three witnesses, viz:- George Mullikin in Bilbster, David Farqr in Tannoch, & James Doull in Haustr, to prove agt the pson indytit, they refused to depon, qrupon the fiscall named ane new day to adduce ym or oyr witness for proveing the Indytment above qch the Judge grants. The bailyies considering the above Indytments & the Indytments on the oyr page [the next page] agt Isobell Baine, ordaines the three above, Marsell & Isobell Baines & Elizabeth Manson, to remaine in prisone or find surtie to underly the lawe as they may be found guiltie befor the provest or oyr magestrats of the sd Burgh, betwixt & the first of augst nixt qn called, under the paine of two hundreth pounds Scots, qron act".

And onto the next page :

"*Issobell Baine in Wick, you ar Indytit & accused for recepting &
receaveing from the sd Agnes Roull, certain qtitiies of aits & bear at
seall tymes qrof a part is found in yor custodie, qrfor you ought &
should be punished as ane comon recepter airt & part. As also you ar
Indytit and accused for stealling ane certane qtitie of aquavitie in ane
ston Bottle fra Marjorie Murray, spous to Dod Suyrland, merd in
Wick, qch you cannot deny. And yrfor ought & should be punished
conform to lawe.*

"*Wick 6th Jany, 1710. Compeirs Issobel Baine & confess the last
article & denyes the first Indytment. Compeirs the fiscall & offers to
prove tuesday nixt the 13 instant qr all pties Ar to appeir, qron act, &
to be remittit to prisone. Wick 13 Jany, 1710: Compeirs Jon Forsyth
with the fiscall ALEX DOULL and declairs he wantit vict: out of the
Barnes of Papigo, and efter search found ane shift full of bear & oats
In her custodie & hes non growing her, & Jon Forsyth knowes not
qhither it was his or not. Therfor the bailyies ordaines Isobell Baine to
instruct the psones from qm shee reced the same*".

And after a gap of half a blank page, the following:

"*X- In fourtie pound Scots toties quoties as the act of the Date
forsd bears Compeires the fisc all & craves sentence.*"

No other comment entered.

What of Marsell Bain's previous record? Unfortunately, there
are no entries for the year of 1693 when an act of banishment was
passed against her for stealling various articles, as referred
above. Perhaps that is why Agnes Roull was brought into the
actual stealling as, with previous convictions, Marsell Bain
would have been under the possibilty of hanging if caught
again. Nonetheless there is another separate entry against her
in June of 1708 when she, with Elspet Calder and Kathren Doull,
wife of Robert Calder, one of the Bailies, was accused of lying
in wait for David Duncan, Chopman, and assaulting him on
"*the Queen's High Rod*" as he travelled about his lawful business. Reference to "*uyr yr associats*" would indicate more than
the named persons above.

They were accused of "*beating, blooding and abusing of him in
calling him Sheating Knave & rascall, And yrfor ought & should be
punished to the terror & example of uyrs to comit the lyik in tyme
comeing.*" The case was continued to the 2nd July, 1708. On the
6th July, 1708, Robert Calder appeared for his spous & for
Marsell Baine & "*craved absolviter becaus David Duncan did not put*

in his appearance". Donald Sutherland did appear for the pursuer, Duncan, and asked for another day to present Duncan personally, which request was granted by the Baillies, to Friday the 16th, when all parties were to be summond.

"Wick 17 Sepr, 1708. Compeires Rob: Calder for himself & his spous & for Marsall Baine & reffers the heall Indytment to proba'ne of witnesses viz:-"

Here we come again to Walter Dalrymple, tydwaiter in Wick, an officer of the Crown. He gave evidence of seeing Kathren Doull, Elspet Calder & Marsell Baine standing in the highway with rungs in yr hands, ready to assault & wrong the sd David Duncan, and he was positive that he saw Kathren Doull & Marsell Bain with rungs in each of their hands, but not Elspet Calder. When Duncan came along Kathren endeavored to assault & strike him with the rungs. Dalrymple tried to hinder her but his wig and hat were carried away, he was not sure if thrown by Kathren or did the Wick wind carry them over a dyke into a yard. He had to leave the affray to retrieve his prized possessions and did not see the end of it. Meantime Kathren Doull, along with Marsell Baine and Elspet Calder, *"fell upon the said David Duncan & beat him to the ground & yrby he received blood & his hair torne & if the deponent hade not taken ym off him he had received much more prejudice. And this he declaires to be of truth as he sall ansr to God . WALTER DALRYMPLE."*

The rest of the depositiones & the sentence which followed were in a paper apart but the paper is missing. Therefore we do not know what penalty was imposed on Marsell Bain and her friends. It is characteristic of the Counsell Book of Wick of 1660 that an entry is sometimes made with detail of the offence and leaving a space below on the page for the eventual outcome and sentence to be entered later. Sometimes, as in this case, this was not completed. Sometimes, as in this case, there is a succession of entries and not always following the date set out for the next hearing but some time later. It has nothing to do with the availability of the odd space, rather a quite sensible method of holding all the information about one case in one place or one page, even if it does give a scrappy appearance to a casual reader.

As for Agnes Roull, we can unfortunately but guess at her fate.

— Chapter 18 —

Tales of the Tollbooth

The Tollbooth of Weik was the central point around which the whole Toun business revolved, particlarly that of the *"Counsell"*, where the Counsell meetings were held, where the Court sat in Judgement , where the *"ward"* or prison was located. So where was it? I do not know the ancient geography of Weik, I have not seen any old map or copy which can help. Kirkwall in Orkney has the advantage over Weik in having town maps of the 1600s with houses set out, streets, tenements and their named occupiers. I am not saying such does not exist for Weik, but if they do I am unaware of them. Not a serious problem. The Tollbooth Lane at the West side of Woolworths must have been beside or on the site thereof, facing what is still the Market Square, and Woolworths is a better choice than any other. The building itself must have been of two stories, quite imposing for the Weik of 1660, for there is reference to the *"heicht"* Tollbuthe and the *"lower"* Tollbuthe, and to the stairs going from one to the other. It also held the *"wardhous"* where were *"inprissoned"* various persons for various problems, and they could be *"inprissoned"* either in the Lower or Heicht Tolboothe. I would have thought the *"Heicht"* would have been the better choice.

Elections for the Counsell of Weik were held each year in the Tollbooth, generally at the end of September or early October. The very first one referred to seems to have been held as a re-establishment of regular affairs after being in some disarray during the final two years of the Commonwealth of Cromwell, and was held on the 6th January, 1660. Another Court was held on 4th June, 1660, and the entry has an interesting addendum inserted at the side, possibly an afterthought, stating *"THIS COURT FENSIT IN KING CHARLES THE SECOND HIS ROYAEL NAME. GOD SAVE THE KING."* *"FENSIT"* was an old term used in law to open the proceedings of a Court by uttering a formula forbidding interruption. This marked the Restoration of Charles II.

While the face of democracy was upheld, the tradition was still *"The ould toon coonsell chooses the new toon coonsell"*, and George, Earl of Caithness, heritable provost of Weik, had the privilege of nominating one of the Baillies. I do not suppose the machinations regarding nominations and elections have changed much with *"coonsells"* to this present day.

One particular election held in Weik on the 29th September, 1710, did not go quite according to plan. The provestship of Weik was no longer the previous heritable right of the Earl of Caithness but much in the grasp of the Dunbars, by now owners of most of the ground around Weik. Capt Robert Sutherland of Langwell had been Provest for the preceeding year, 1709, and the retiring baillies were Alexr Doull and Jon Calder. They both demitted their office of magestracie in favour of those who were to be chosen.

And of course they were *"re choisen."*

"Therefor the sd day the wholl inhabitants of the sd Burgh Choyses & nominats Sir James Dunbar, yongr of Hempriggs, Provest. And lykwayes the sd Alexr Doull & Jon Calder, Bailyies from the dait heirof to the 29 Sepr. 1711 yeirs, qho acceptit & took the oath de fideli & qualified in the tymes of Lawe."

The next day, the 30th September, 1710, Alexr Doull and Jon Calder, the newly re-elected bailyies for the Burgh of Weik for the next year, nominated the following for Counsellers :

Alexr Dunbar, Alexr Suyrland, Wm Murray, Alexr Horne, Alexr Mullikin, Hugh Harrow and Wm Hendersone.

Came the 18th of October, 1710, and Sir James Dunbar entered the lists. He, the newly elected Provost of Weik only on the 29th September, had been obviously absent from the meeting of that day, and from that of the next day when the above Counsellers were nominated and *"choisen".*

They apparently did not meet with his approval so , quite democratically I suppose as Provosts were wont to do, he threw them all out on the grounds of procedural incompetence, with the exception of Hugh Harrow, merchant, and imposed his own list of Counsellers upon the toon. They were Capt Robert Sutherland, late Provost, who in the manner of retiring Counsellers and Provosts no doubt thought he would be automatically re-elected, and was in fact thrown out, Alexr Doull, weaver, Anton Doull, joyner, Wm Andersone, merchant, Donald Suyrland, merchant, James Mullikine, who was to be threasurer, and Hugh Harrow, merchant [and survivor.] Hugh Harrow actually came previously from the House of Mey to Wick to set up as a merchant there. He, along with Donald Suyrland, Wm Andersone, Anton Doull and Alexr Doull, were members of the Counsell of September 1709 who had met with Sir James Dunbar's approval, and it looks like a move against Capt Robert Suyrland of Langwell, retiring Provost, carried out in the absence of Sir James Dunbar, and to which Sir James came the heavy hand. More of a *"Tollbooth"* coup than a *"Palace"* coup.

I am quite sure Capt. Robert Sutherland was a relative of Sir James Dunbar, who had been a Sutherland until he became Elizabeth Dunbar's second husband. At times blood is thicker than water. I have still not worked out why James Dunbar was called *"yongr. "*

It seems to have been of some importance that Counsellers attended meetings so there was an:

"Actt anent conveining of the toun counsell of the Burghe at any neidful tyme. It is stated & ordained that they being lallie warned be the officer To compeir within the Tolbuthe yrof for advyssing & Consulting about the effaires of the said Burghe, that the absentes shall pay the soume of fyftie shillings Scots money, qruponn act."

It would appear that Counsell members were expected to contribute to any proceedings and give of their wisdom, if any, and if absent still to contribute to the Counsell out of their pockets!

When meeting the Counsell took the affairs of Weik to heart and made various enactments to do with the *"Weal of the Burghe.",* some of which we have already mentioned.

On the 16th January, 1685, the Counsell considered several

complaints which had been given in about the *"intoumen who will not work for peyt to any persone wtin the said Burghe."* I think *"intoumen"* might well have been a slight misspelling of *"intounmen"* and, though I am guessing, they were probably workmen of a labouring class rather than craftsmen or tradesmen who had their own priviledges. As such they would have been *"on call"* to anyone who wanted their services, and it appears that some of them were fussy who they worked for. Accordingly the Counsell enacted that they were to work for anyone who wanted their services, and if they refused then they were to be subject to a fine of 20/-, and *"imprissonment"*.

No Trade Unions in those days. They also had to find security for their good behaviour in the future.

On May 26th, 1660, the Counsell enacted that a weekly market was to be held each Friday at the Croie of Weik, no doubt in the Market Square. Publication of this market was to be made at every Parish Church within the Shire, and no doubt the Weik merchants and burgesses had their own interests at heart in drawing trade to Weik.

Of the Tollbooth itself there are many references, giving a very rough idea of the layout. One featured our old friend, John Donaldson, wricht, who had appeared on the 15 September, 1665, accused for the blooding of Jon Sutherland, officer, by throwing of him over the Tolboothe stair in *"Seiking and demandinge"* payment for an unpaid unlaw, or fyne. Most probably the *"Tollboothe stair"* was a stone built affair on the outside of the building and, in the absence of the Health and Safety Executive, unlikely to have had a guard rail. Even much more recent history has record of the occasional broken neck from a fall over stone stairs of that nature, still to be seen in many a farm steading.

The Burghe Courts were obviously held there, and references to being *"thryis callit from dore and windo and nocht compearand,"* were common, resulting in a fine for contumacy and an order to be further charged.

The stair of the Tollboothe features again and a comment on the state of the wardhous is contained in the reference to Alex Abernethie, and others, who were previously in Court on 18 July, 1665, for taking the salt ox tails out of a barrel in Walter Bruce's boat, for which he was fined £5 Scots. Only a month later, on the 11th August, Alex Abernethie was again in the Tolbooth Court for *"Cming to the hous of Wm Sinclair, mchant yr, and withe Scandellous Speiches nocht worthe the puting in wreitt of the said Wm Sinclair & Mgratt Oswald his Spous, and thairfor the same being notoriouslie knowen, the Bailyies, for his demerites, ordainit Johne Sinclaire, officer, to put the said Alexr Abernethe in ward in the Lower hous thairof, qlk order being obeyed be the said officer, going doun the stair of the heiche Tolboothe to the Lower, the said Alexr Abernethe did throw doun the said officer and almost had braken his neik or bones. And thairefter being put in the said heiche Tolboothe for his mad misbehaver, Thair was ane barell full of Small Salt qlk was thairin for the Tounes use, qlk barell the said Allxr Abernethe did Brak violentlie in peices, Scatered the said Salt throche the flewr of the said wardhous qr thair most filthie excrementes of uther prisonners befoir, So that the said barrel of Salt was uterlie lost, all this Confest be the said Alexr Abernethie and Thairfor the Judges, Taking to Consideration the abooss & confusion abovespeit, the aboosing of the officer, the Braking of the Barell of Salt & Spoylling yrof, and for the aboossing of Wm Sinclair and his spous, It is ordainit that the said Alexr Abernethie pay for the said Barell of Salt £5 Scots money, and for the wronge done to Wm Sinclair & his Spous, that he stand twa houres in the Stokes at the Croie and the said £5 to be payit befoir he remove out of ward, qrupon act."*

So the floor of the wardhouse was as unclean as it could possibly be, not really at all a place in which one would want to spend any time. And that was the *"heicht"* Tolbooth which one would assume would be in better shape than the lower. William Sinclair and his spous Margrat Oswald featured later in January, 1669, in the case of Kathren Creak, thief. [See Chapter 9.]

In that same wardhous on the 18th December, 1662, Donald Ferguson, warder for the time being, was keeping Andrew Calder prisoner. Ferguson was charged with " *the stricking of Andrew Calder withe ane weitt old scheipe Skin upon the face, qlk was qualifiett in Judgement, & yrfra Dod Fergr cnvict in 50/-."* Can't have prisoners being treated like that! I would have thought a *"weitt old sheipe skin"* would have been a most murderous weapon wielded by some hefty Weiker.

There was also what in all likelihood was an even more noisome place of incarceration than the wardhous, which I assume was in the Lower Tollbuthe, i.e. *"the hoill under the Croie".*

On the 29 January 1669, William Hendersonn alias Gedok, was in Court for the blooding of James Sinclair, sonne to Wm Sinclair, merchant. William was arrested within the Tollboothe until he paid an unlaw of 30/-.

Nevertheless he went out of the Tollboothe without any order, so much for locks and keys. It would appear that in the Weik of 1660 prisoners at times just stayed there if told to do so. The record went on that Henderson *"being bot ane poor Critur and nocht worthe to pay anie fyne, Thairfor the saids Judges ordained him Sit in the stokes at the Croie Twa houres, qlk was done, and yrfr absolved."* I like the old usage of *" Poor Critur"*.

But Henderson returned to trouble with *"comeing under cloud and Silence of night to ane Murray boatt lying in the water of Weik qrof Thomas Younge was skiper, abusing the men of that boatt, Blooding and aboosing of Johne Suyrland, tounes officer, who was trying to get him to leave the boat and come to the Bailyies."* In Court Young deponed that Henderson came to the Boat drunk, threatening to kill the men and burn the boat. John Suyrland had stones thrown at him, cutting him in several places, the said stones being produced in Court. Sentence was to sit twa houres in the Stokes with twa pynt stoupes about his neck, a paper hood on his head bearing his guilt, and after the expiring of twa houres to return to "the hoill under the Croie, to remain there until Tysday nixt, to find Caution for his good behavour in Tyme comeing, utherwayes to be banished out of the precincts and Liberties of the toun, and nocht to return thairefter under the paine of *"loising of his right ear"*! What the *"hoill under the Croie"* was like is best left to the imagination.

Henderson promised to behave himself honestlie and civil-lie in all tyme coming, was again warned on the potential loss of his right ear if otherwise, and was reinstated in his *"office"* as the *toun pedler*.

Another breakout featured George Gun from Thrumster, appearing in Court on 3rd August, 1708. His offence was blood-ing, blaeing and beating our two aforementioned tydsmen friends, Walter Dalrymple and Thomas Hall, two of her Majesties servants, along with James Young, merchant in Weik, and *"breaking the roof of the Tolbooth of Wick & making yor escape yrof, and yrfor ought & should be punished."*

"As to the breaking of the roof of the sd Tolbooth the sd George

Gun confesses the same:" Whether the roof was of thatch or slate we are not told, but to a Gun neither would be much of a barrier. Gun was fyned £20 for blooding Mr Dalrymple, £10 Scots for abusing him and £20 Scots for breach of prison, and further had to remain in prison until his fyne was paid and a bond of Caution found for him.

It is of passing note that Scots money was always referred to as opposed to Sterling, though the two were used in common even in 1660, and there are occasional references to Sterling in the Counsell Book well before the Union of Parliaments in 1707, converting at £12 Scots to £1 Sterling.

Perhaps a final look at conditions in the Tollboothe for prisoners is contained in a case relating to two Rorie girls, Helene in Myrland and Margratt in Waster. They were "bleacheres" who had 12 elns of linen webs in their possession belonging to David Murray in Winles. They alledged it had been *"Stollin and awaytakin be Theives and Robers"* but were obviously not believed, and were *"in ward in the Tollbuthe"*. Wm Bruce, younger, in Myrland, became cautioner for Helene, and Johne Rorie in Waster for Margratt, to get them out of ward against *"triall at 24 houres notice"*. The entry ends with the ominous words *"the said prisoners being alyve."* and one can ask just what health risks a prisoner ran when in *"ward"* in the Tollbuthe of Weik.

40 shilling Scots of James II, 1688

One Merk Scots of Charles II, 1669

— Chapter 19 —

George Bruce, Skipper in Trouble

Trying to make full use of my computer to analysis the Counsell Book of Weik, I took one name which appeared more than the usual number of times and asked the computer to find all references to him. Our "hero", if we can call him that, was George Bruce, and the George I am interested in was a "skiper in Weik". There were other George Bruces such as George Bruce of Seater and George Bruce of Holland and George Bruce the merchant and Counseller in the newly reconstituted Counsell of 1660. There were also Walter Bruce, skiper, and his wife Kathrein Miller, parents of George Bruce the skiper. George the merchant had a son Walter so it looks by the name usage as if George the merchant and Walter the skiper were brothers, though I have not found that confirmed in the Records.

There was also Isobel Bruce, widow, who could have been a sister, the maiden name of married women being used along with "*spous of ?*" The other Bruces appeared quite frequently but George Bruce, "*skiper*", held pride of place and my interest, the only problem being to identify which is "*our George*".

First reference was on the very first page when the Counsell was being reconstituted after a gap of two years and George Bruce appears as a "*counseller*". This Bruce must have been the elder and the merchant. He appears in the list of merchants on the second page, dated 28 February, 1660, along with Walter

Bruce, younger, also a merchant. In the voting list of the election of October, 1660, appears Walter Bruce, elder, voting for Francis Mansonn.

George Bruce, "skiper", appeared sometimes as a witness and sometimes as the main man in some affair or other. Usually identified as *"skiper"*, he appears on the 14th March, 1660 , with George Mullikin, for *"pulling out the haire of utheres heads, blooding, and bleaing"*. *"Utheres"* in the Records means *"each other"* .

"Baithe the said pairties Compeirand in Judgement, the said mater and declarationn thairof was submited to the witnessing of Wm Cormok and Johne Innes, Schomakeres, quho were present withe the said pairties, whois Declaration efter aithe given to them followes. Wm Cormok, ane of the Witnesses forsaid, Deponed upon aithe that the said George Bruce did tak upe ane skoll [oar] and did threatin and menas the said George Mullikin thairwithe, So that thairby bothe the said persones did Enter in violence withe [each] utheres, and did grip utheres by the haires of thair heades most unhumanlie. Sicklyck the said Johne Innes deponed upon aithe ut supra, and morover that they had eneuch ado to gett the said persones Sundred from utheres, they being Tumbling & wretheing on the fleur most unnaturallie and unhumanlie." Fyned 50/- Scots each, a small fine, so the stramash not really taken too seriously by the Baillies.

Slightly less aggression, and probably George the merchant, appears as a witness on June 4th, 1660, in the deforceing of Francis Mansonne, toun officer, by Patrick Dunbar, glover in Weik. Mansonne was trying to collect Dunbar's *"penaltie"* as freeman of Weik, *"penaltie"* being merely his dues in this case and not a fine.

November, 1660, and George Bruce, *"our George"*, gets a *"decreet"* against James Watersone, younger, for £5 Scots. Trying to enforce the Court order, George Mansonne, officer, has a struggle with Watersone, called deforcement, a somewhat common occurrence. I suppose trying to part a Weiker from his money was no easy task in those days!

I do not know of any relationship between Walter Bruce, skiper, and George Bruce of Holland but on 10th April, 1661, Walter appears as a witness in the case of George Bruce of Holland who had a pewter plate thrown at him by Johne Mansonne after he had thrown a *"cupe of aill"* over Mansonne's head. Both Mansonne and Bruce were fined, equally to blame in the eyes of the law, it seems. They were both charged with blooding and blaeing [bruising] each other, and fined £10 Scots *"per peice"*.

George's mother Kathrein Miller appears on the 8th October, 1662, victim of Ephraime Readburne and Issobel Davidson his spous, who were accused and fined £6 Scots for *"the Beating, Blooding and Crewell aboosing of Kathrein Miller, Spous to Walter Bruce, Skiper, and pulling out the haires of hir head."* Conviction was done on the sworne oath of Kathrein Miller herself.

George Bruce, probably the merchant, gets James Blair, merchant, incarcerated in jail in the Tollbooth on 24th Febr, 1664, for a debt of £15 Scots. No doubt the money was paid and James Blair got out.

Local affairs must have been a failing of the Bruces as George Bruce, skiper, appears on the 17th October, 1664, on the list of retiring counsellers. His name is on the *"leitt"* or list, of nominations for the new Baillies for 1665, aiming a bit higher than a mere counseller. Unsuccessful, though, with Frances Mansonne and Andrew Baine being elected.

This election was held in the presence of Erle George, Erle of Caithnes, Lord Sinclair and Berridaill, heritable provost of Weik.

George's name then appears on the list of counsellers for 1665, the year to run from 17th October, 1664, to October, 1665.

"Qruponn they have given thair oathes of fidelitie To do all thinges Incumbentt Acording to the said office, and to Keipe Secrecie in all the effaires to be done to the weill and utilitie of the Burghe, qron act"

Next year, on the 2nd of May, 1665, George Bruce, skiper, was accused for *"wounding & blooding of Johne Pruntoche, mchant, in his head withe the Ratchet of ane pistell"*. Must have been a goodly thump because, though George Bruce appearing, but *"the said Jon Pruntoche being Seiklie in his Bed"*. Pruntoche put in a bill stating his inability to appear. The *"Ratchet"* of a pistol must have been the hammer on top of it, suggesting that George Bruce was holding it by the barrel, just slightly safer than loaded in the normal manner.

Johne Pruntoche put in a bill desiring that George Bruce, skiper, find a caution of Lawborrowes to Pruntoche for his safety in time coming. Bruce accordingly found his father, Walter Bruce, skiper, as cautioner that *"the said John Pruntoche should be frie and harmles of all Skaithe and Bodilie harme that he might do*

to him efter the dait heirof uther wayes nor be ordor of law & Justice,
under the penaltie of the Sowme of ane hundrethe punds Scots money
qruponn act. Sic Subscribitur".

G BRUCE

WALTER " ⌖ " BRUCE, *his mark.*

So George Bruce could at least sign his own name, well
written and probably educated enough at the local school of
the time. Walter, his father, made his mark with a well drawn
anchor, appropriate enough for a seaman. There was no reason
why some education in Weik in 1660 was not available, we have
referred previously to the building of a new school in 1683 at the
Shoar of Weik and to Andrew Sutherland the schoolmaster.
Kirkwall had a well established Grammar School at that time
with John Dischingtoune as *"maister"*, and mathematics and
navigation were taught as requirements for sea going. Trade
was well enough developed with the Norway, Baltic and
Holland connections, vessels going to Bergen and Danzig and
Amsterdam with grain and other agricultural products and
bringing back timber, iron, tar, skins, and of course, brandy and
wine and tobacco. Shopping lists of those times were surprisingly sophisticated as shown by some that have survived, see
Donaldson's *"Mey Letters"*. As for the blood given by George
Bruce, skiper, to John Pruntoche, confessed, convicted, and
fined £10 Scots money.

George was apparently spending too much time ashore for
only a month later on the tenth of June, 1665, he appears again
accused of the beating and blooding of James Doull, shoemaker.
They were both in the house of Thomas Hossack, merchant in
Weik, and so too, possibly unfortunately, were the two Bailies,
Frances Mansonne and Andrew Baine, who saw the wrong committed,*"bothe be evill and scandelous speiches & by the forsaid blood."*

So *"thairfor fynes & cnvictes the said George Bruce in ane unlaw*
of fortie punds Scots, and for cmiting the Same in the presence of the
Bailyies, XXlb."

Offending the dignity of the Baillies was a serious crime in
itself and not to be overlooked, even if George was a Counseller.
He was further inacted to keep his Majesties peace to the said
James Doull under the penalty of £100 if he failed. His very
legible signature *"G. BRUCE"* was appended, so again he obviously belonged to the educated Bruce's!

James Doull also did not get off though it was his blood that was spilt. For fighting with George Bruce, though possibly rather ineffectually as he drew neither blood nor blae, he was fined £5 Scots. For the much more serious offending of the Bailyies in their presence he was fined £12, the fines to be paid within time of law, under the paine of poynding.

The 18th July, 1665, we come across George Bruce's father Walter Bruce in the incident of the salt beef or ox tails taken out of a barrel in his boat by Alex Abernethie and others, and belonging to Wm Sinclair, merchant in Weik. Apparently at that time both Walter and his son George were both going to sea though quite possibly with the one boat, or vessel, and the barrel of salt ox tails would have been for export from Weik.

"Skiper" George appears in July, 1666, becoming cautioner for Alexr Mansonne that Wm Caldell shall be "*harmles and skaithles in his body, goods and geir in time comeing.*" This was following the episode when Alex Mansonne was accused and convicted for the "*crewell hurting, wonding and blooding with a chargit pistol, of Wm Caldell, merchant thair, being under cloud and silence of night, and as appearit to be of forthocht fellonie.*"

Caldell was not altogether blameless as he was accused and convicted of "*giveing ane blow to the said Allexr efter many evill speiches given to the said Wm and to the said Bailyies*", given in by Alexr Mansonne. It looks as if Caldell was the better man when it came to blows but Mansonne sought revenge in his own way. They were both ordered to find cautioners, hence George Bruce cautioner for Mansonne.

George Bruce, skiper, appeared again on 28/11/1666 for Allexr Johnsonn, schomaker, who was accused of receiving certain money stollin from Allexr Mansonne by Donald Ross, his servitor. The sum was 4/10d Sterling, again the use of sterling well before 1707. The matter was found to be frivolous and of small account, yet still the baillies " *have ordainit & be thir pntes, ordaines the said Alexr J'sonne & his spous That if ever they be found to cmit the Lyik falt in Tyme Cming that they ar cntent & consentes to be Banished the wholl Toune, and to pay the fyne to be Imposed upon them be the Judges, being sex punds Scots money.*"

George Bruce seems to have kept out of trouble for a while

until 27 November, 1666, possibly a *"long sea voyage"*. He then appears but under our old favorite of *"cloud and silence of night"*.

"George Bruce, Skiper in Weik, Indyted & Acused for the most unhuman dealling against Alexr Mansonne, mchant thair, In Cming to the hous of Elspett Sinclair, widow, under Cloud and Silence of night, being their bed tyme of night, and thair Cming with ane Sword and pistoll in ane hostile maner, Calling furthe and provoking the said Alexr Mansonne To cum out of the said hous, of Intenteionn to have Takin his Lyff, and provocation of him thairefter to ane Combatt or dewell, Contrair to the actes of pliament & lawes of this Kingdom."

Looks like a good night ashore for our seafaring hero, and what Allexr Mansonne was doing in the widow's house at their *"bed tyme of night"* I do not know.

Bruce compeired, and of course denied the whole claim.

Allexr Mansonne, persewar, takes the same to probationn.

"Comperit also Molus Thomsone in Howe, ane of the witnesses, admited & Sworne, who deponed in Judgement that George Bruce did cum to the hous of Elspett Sinclair, widow, withe ane Sword in his hand, and did Sitt at the part without the same qr the said Allxr Mansonne was, attending his furthcming, and thairefter the said Molus Thompsone did withdraw him To the hous of Wm Cormok, schomaker, to get ane poynt of aill, qr the said George Bruce did utter manie frivolous and bold Speiches, and efter Cming to the streitt qr Frances Mansonne, leat Balye, wis, the said George Bruce did offer to draw his Sword to him, he alwayes giveing him friendie admonitionn. In the mean tyme the said Molus Thompsone did kepe him from doing any harme yrwithe. Referes the remanet to the nixt Court."

"And Sicklyik the said Allxr Mansonne, acused for giveing of evill Language to the said George Bruce, qrthrow the mater did grow & Incres. And thairefter the said George Bruce & Allexr Mansonne In respect of thair Lybelles and Accusitionnes forsaid, the Same being Takin to Considerationn be the saids Bailyies anent the persewing of thair Bills & accusationnes, Ilk personne under the failye of fyftie punds Scots money. And in the mean tyme they to find Sufficient Cautioneres Ilk ane to utheres for the keiping of his maiesties peace befoir they remove out of prisonne, under the failyie of the Sowme of ane hundrethe punds Scots money, Ilk personne Contravener of this act qranent the saids pties hes Subt this pntt act and day, year & place forsaid - Sic Subscribitur.

*The mater being takin to Consideraon be Consent of persewer &
defender, George Bruce cnvict in Xlb. & Allexr Mansonne Vlb.
qruponn act.*

[signed by] GEO BRUCE   A.MANSONNE."

We say farewell to George Bruce, skiper, with a final reference on 3.03.1667 when he came to the aid of Frances Mansonn
who had come to the Croie of the Burghe with a staff or batten
in his hand seeking to damage Allexr Mansonne, who had previously been *"threatening and menassing"* Frances. No relationship mentioned. George Bruce and John Pruntoche were witnesses and had stopped further harm being done. Frances
convicted in 100/- Scots. The matter was not yet finished. Alex
Schand, couper in Weik, having parted the said Alex. Mansonn,
which looks like taking his part or side, drew a *"quhinger"*
[cutlass] to the said Frances and had almost killed him with it,
except George Bruce and Jon Pruntoche hindered the same.
Schand fined £15 Scots.

So George helped to keep the peace in Weik, at least once!

— Chapter 20 —

Breaking doon of the Brig of Weik

One of the incidents of Wick of 1660 was the breaking down of the Bridge of Wick by the shoemakers and glovers. This has been referred to before by others. It at first looked as if it was a serious and deliberate matter but it really centred around the curing of skins to make leather for use by both the shoemakers, the glovers and the cordeiners, as well as probable export. Complaint had been made by the Inhabitants of Wick to the Bailyies on the 22nd of October, 1665, that the shanks of the Bridge were being destroyed by the practice of the shoemakers and glovers of dressing their skins upon the Bridge. No doubt this practice included scraping and beating the skins, washing in the river and laying the skins on the "*Shank*" of the Bridge to dry or to be further beaten or scraped. It would have been very likely that the skins were fastened to the Bridge to avoid being swept away by a sudden spate of water, an occurence which resulted in my own loss of a sheep skin many years ago in the Isauld Burn! This practice was causing the dismantling of the stones of the shank and was a cause for concern. The "*shanks*" of an old bridge, simply built as would be the early Wick one referred to in 1665, were stone built pillars on which rested timbers forming the deck of the bridge, "*shanks*" being merely the old word for legs. The bridge itself was located at the site of the former dam which held back the Water of Weik to form the boating marina, now regrettably demolished. Progress?

There were some seven "*shanks*" in the bridge, according to the map drawn by Wm Campbell in March, 1802, and entitled "*Plan of Old Wick*". I found a copy of that map in Edinburgh in the Scottish Records Office in Charlotte Square and had it photographed. The Bridge in Campbell's map was almost certainly the one rebuilt on the old foundations about 1777 by James Sinclair of Harpsdale, who lived in Thrumster House. There were most probably more shanks than seven to cross the river with length of log being the controlling factor.

It was superceded by a three arched bridge built in the early 1800s in it's present Bridge Street location by Thomas Telford, or on his instructions and plans, and rebuilt at the end of the century. Accordingly it was ordained by the Bailyies and the Toun Counsell that in future, if any shoemaker or glover did the like again, they were to pay £5 Scots as penalty. No names were listed but a previous entry in 1660 itemises the shoemakers and glovers who were "*unfriemen*", and no doubt paid up. They were ordained to leave the Bridge alone, under penalty.

Offences against the laws of the Burghe were many and the importance of peats to the inhabitants of the Royal Burgh cannot be over emphasised. It appears that a closed shop of some kind was in being regarding the carrying of peats from the many mosses around Weik at that time because the Counsell, in June 1661, enacted that:

"Act anent bearing of peates.

The qlk day the saids Bailyies withe the advys & consent of the Toune Counsell and Remainanet Inhabitants within the Burghe, Ordaines that no Burdine bearers within the same [the Burghe] Carie or Transport anie peates from the Quoys of Brandsey, Heyland or utheres pteining the Inhabitants of the said Burghe, except Suche as Crples, unces, and cansst lead thair awin peates efter the daitt heirof. Ilk personne Contravener of this act to pay 40/- Scots money, Toties quoties, qrupon act."

And also another offence on peats, or at least offence against the Counsell views, was committed by Donald Malcome, weaver in Wick, accused for *"boolding his peates upon the Commonty of the Burgh,"* contrary to several previous acts against the practice. He had to remove the peats within eight days and never to build them on the Commonty again, and to pay a fine of £5 Scots. The Commonty is now Wick Airfield.

Peats were a very important commodity in 1660 and regulation by the Counsell was apparent. The first paragraph mentioning *"burdine bearers"* seems to indicate that an *"Inhabitant"* was limited in the amount of peats he could cut in a season by having to carry home his own, except perhaps cripples, widows and some other odd sods, who could have their peats carried by *"burdine bearers."* Carrying peats was done in straw cubbies or baskets on the back, or, in the scarcity of carts at that time, in straw panniers slung each side of some poor horse or nag, and I am afraid that the fair sex probably carried more than it's fair share, acting as beasts of burden. Photographs of such a practice exist from more modern times and are common enough. The second paragraph reference Donald Malcome building his *"peates"* upon the Commonty where no doubt peat cutting was carried out would again restrict the amount he could cut to the peats which he could carry away himself, and no doubt aided by his family, in one season. If allowed to build his peats upon the Commonty he could have cut more than others, an unfair advantage. Again, if he could employ *"burdine bearers"*, precluded by the act above, he again could cut more than his share. Therefore the above restrictions were one self regulating method whereby peat cutting could be controlled to some degree. Eventually Wick had cut all available peats within reasonable distance from the toun, leading later to well documented arguments on peat rights.

Middens on the Highway were another problem with a fair number of entries relating to Inhabitants having to remove the same within a given few days, along with fines. On the 6th November, 1660, it was *"ordainit that Wm Caldell & George Annand Try and veseitt the Calsayes of the Burghe that no midinges be Laid thairuponn qrof Iff anie be the awner of the midinges, to pay £5 Scots money thairfor, Toties quoties."*

The same day James Murray, alias Watersone, promised to take away his midden off the Calsay before Thursday next, the 8th of November, under the penalty of £5 Scots if he failed to do so. There were many other references to the problem, and it went on for centuries.

Controlling trading was a very important part of the Counsell work, reflecting that the *"Counsellers"* were all tradesmen with strong self interest at heart. This was shown in many a reference to *"forstallers and regraters"* and to *"unfriemen"*.

Though a "frieman and burgess of Weik", on 20 July, 1665, Allexr Manson, merchant, was in trouble with the Counsell *"Acused for forstalling in bying and giveing extraordinarie pryces for kiering and uther whyit fishes and frustrating the leidges, thairfor he was cnvict in Ten punds Scots money."* He was obviously outbidding the Inhabitants of Weik for any fish landed and cornering the market to the discomfort of the Weikers, an early example of free enterprise. No doubt he resold at a profit, just as reprehensible then as now! Can't have that! The Counsell, in March, 1707, referred, after complaints had come in, to a previously made enactment about the fair selling of fish to any who had need of them on landing the same at the Shoar of Weik. So the problem had been around for some time.

More interesting to me was this only reference in the Counsell Book to *"keiring and uther whyit fishes"* though there were references to fishing in general, such as the fight at sea between the crews of the two fishing boats and the borrowing without permission and damaging of the boat belonging to Sir James Dunbar at Staxigo by George Mullikin. The word *"keiring"* is well written and not mis-spelt or misread by me. It can only be *"herring"* though that fish was herring long ago, Dutch *"haring"*. I would not quarrel with the old spelling which could be just one man's writing of the name. The Germanic cum Dutch pronunciation with a more gutteral *"h"* could easily become a *"k"* rather than an *"h"*, there is not much difference.

No matter, many enquiries later by me to assorted fishermen has brought only an assertion that herring and mackeral are NOT white fish but "pelagic." Modern terminology, unfortunately, and unheard of 300 years ago. We are looking at 1660 and my personal view, at the risk of a basket of fish guts over my head next visit to Weik, is that herring in 1660 were just another white fish, which indeed its flesh is, and differentiated that type of fish from that other fish much sought after for long years later, the whale, whose flesh was indeed red. Whales are now called mammals, which they are, but they are also fish, and a much prized product of the deep sea. After all, the Japanese are still eating their way through masses of whale-meat for no other reason than *"helping with scientific research!"*

Early and fairly constant in the Record Book are references to *"forstalling and regrateing"* by *"unfreimen"*, again against the interests of the Burgesses and Counsellers, which of course stung the local shopkeepers where it hurt, their pocket. Nothing changes, I suppose, because I have seen but lately the shop-keepers in Thurso, or some of them, objecting to travelling sellers [pedlars!] hiring the Town Hall for a passing sale, and suggesting that such letting should not be allowed.

The Burgh of Weik had that all stitched up three hundred years ago.

On 26th May of 1660 the Earl of Caithness, taking his duties as Provest seriously, presided over a Burrow Court along with James Doull amd Allexr Cormok, Baillies, where were summond to Compeir within the Tollbooth a certain number of persones for these offences. They were accused of breaking the *" Lawes for forstalling, Scaffing & bying of crtn Comodities, Selling the Samyne to unfriemen Contrair to the Liberties of the said Burghe, [to the] greit Lois and Dampuage To the mchantes Burgesses &*

*Inhabitantes thairof, and absolutlie in manifest Contempt and braking
of the acts of pliament maid anent forstalleres & Regrateres, The names
of the said personnes followes, To witt:-"*

The following names were interesting in where they came
from in Caithness, i.e. *"Johne Nicoll in Easter Clythe, Dod Rioche
in Reisgill, Wm J'sonn thair, Andrew Sutherland in Forss, Allexr
Mcwillkeane thair, Frances Dunbar alias Dunbir in Latherone, Dod
Bayne, weaver in Forss, Mcailloches Sonne at the Water off Dunbeithe,
Allexr McMurchie in Breamoir, Mcwat Langwall in Beridail."* They
were *"Thryis Callit at the Bare and none Compeirand be themselffs,
nor no prors in thair names, The forsaid Noble Erle, withe cnsent of
the said Bailyies and Counsell of the said Burgne, Ordainit that ane
Certane Number of the yong men of the said Burghe qrter uponn the
forsaid personnes Disobedientes untill payment be maid of the
Contumas to be Inflicted uponn them, Ilk ane for thair awin partes,
and this by and attor thair fynes to be modifeit be the said Judges.*

*"And as for Thomas Kincaid & Walter Ros, Chapmen, forstalleres,
Johne Muirsonne, mchant in Weik, is becum Caur. for the said Thomas
Kincaid that he schal be Lyable to the Counsell of the said Burghe,
under the peniltie of fyve hundrethe mkes Scots money. Lykwayes the
said Thomas Kincaid is becum Caur. for the said Walter Ros, his
obedience, ut supra."*

So Johne Muirsonne became cautioner for their appearance
and any penalty that Thomas Kincaid and Walter Ross might
become liable for at the fairly high sum of 500 merks.

The other penalty of quartering was possibly quite severe.
It meant that some of the young men of Weik would be lodged
upon the named persons, to be fed and watered by them in
their own houses, until such time as they paid their fines and
penalties. This quartering is mentioned on other occasions and
it would not be a light affair to have a number of possibly rowdy
young men thrust upon you, or your wife, or your daughter.
Canisbey in 1652 had a similar situation when Cromwell's men
were quartered upon the locals, to such a degree that the elders
and members of the Church Session would not let their wives
and daughters go home alone from Sabbath Service because of
the *"Englishes quartered in their houses, the Session therfore being
unable to meet."*

There is no reference to any further action against the above
forstallers, so I expect they paid up.

On the 5th of May, 1668 William Innes, a merchant from Elgin, was accused for vending and selling tobacco and other merchant commodities up and down the Parish and adjacent parts of the County as freely as if he had been a freeman of Wick. It appears that he could have made an offer to the magistrates and Burgesses of Wick which would have solved his problems and allowed him to continue trading, which offer had to mean money. Innes maintained that he had made a Lawful offer but no one admitted any knowledge of it. Therefore he was fined £6 Scots.

The same day Peter Bowman from Peterhead was accused of selling, vending and keeping an open shop, or *"chope"*, within the Burghe, *"contrary to the actes and Laws of Borrowes and without any Libertie of the Magistrates"*. He confessed the indytment and referred himself in the will of the Judges. Fined £100 Scots, pretty hefty compared to the £6 of William Innes the same day. But all was not lost. A week later on the 12th May Peter again appears, and puts himself in the Will of the said Judges. They took the matter to consideration with the willingness of Peter Bowman to be made a freeman and Burgess of the toun, money no doubt talking, discharged him from the former fine of £100 Scots, and ordained him to pay 40 merks Scots and to provide a gun for the use of the Toun. What kind of gun was not stated, whether musket or cannon, musket would be the most likely.

We come finally to Hew and Donald Baine, from Tayne in Ross-shire. They fell out with the "Customer", Jon Nachtie, striking, beating and abusing him, no doubt over some Customs Dues he would have been trying to collect. They were fined in 10 merks Scots- £6.13.4, and that to be paid before they got out of the Tolboothe. What they were selling was not stated.

So a fairly constant battle was raged over unfreemen, quite a few from over the Ord, trading in Weik without forking out their dues to become Burgesses or freemen of the Burghe.

— Chapter 21 —

Trouble and Strife – the green eyed Monster

The green eyed monster appeared in Weik on the last day of January, 1665, when Arthur Dingwall was before the Court following a complaint made by Alexr Lambe, shoemaker in Weik. The Court carefully used, even as far back as 1665, that word made much of by Law Courts and Police and the Press of *"alledged"*, referring to some *"Jelosie"* between Lambe and Arthur Dingwall concerning Margrat Lambe, spous to the said Alexr Lambe. The matter must have come before the Church Session previously because it was ordained by an Act of the Session Book of Weik *"that the said Arthur Dingwall should nocht repair nor cum unto the hous of the said Allexr Lambe in tyme Cming, nor to have anie privatt or public meiting wt the said Margrat Lambe."* Church Session or no, Arthur Dingwall, upon the penultimate day of January, 1665, came into Alexr Lambe's house by way of *"quartering"*. This looks like the everlasting lodger moving in to get his feet under the table!

"And efter manie speeches passed betwixt Arthur Dingwall and Alexr Lambe, Dingwall threw a shoe at the face of Alexr Lambe, causing blood."

Reference was made in Court to the act of the Kirk Session previously made banning Dingwall from frequenting Alexr Lambe's house. Dingwall was fyned in 20 merks Scots and ordained never to habit Lambe's house in the future for the avoiding of any further possible trouble, unless with the consent and invitation of Allexr Lambe. I would have thought that a most unlikely invitation. They do not appear again on this matter.

The green eyed monster appeared again on the l9th January, 1674, in the guise of Donald Malcome, a weaver and burgess of Weik. The Baillies concerned in Judgement were Andrew Baine and Alexr Mansonne .

In this case it looks like covetous eyes on the effects of Margrat Adamsone, a widow in Weik, who *"committed the Cryme off Ipseare or selff murder."* Suicide in other words, and a name for such derived from the Latin *"Ipse"* meaning self. No time was lost because Donald Malcome was brought to Court the very next day after Margrat Adamsone had done away with herself *"yisternight"*. How was not stated but hanging was a fairly common punishment of those times, and a very possible and reasonably available first suicidal choice. Better than the cold sea, though there is record in Wick of that choice over the cliffs of the South Head.

The very haste with which this case came before the Court asks the question was it Donald Malcome who was suspect, or were the Baillies getting in early in case they might miss some of the spoils of Margaret Adamsone's Estate?

Malcome came to Court and was *"actit, bound, and obleist."* He oblidged himself, his heirs, his executors, his successors, to appear personally in Court in the Tolbuth on any Court day or days to be fixed upon Lawful citation and advertisement, to answer and be answerable to the Counsell of the said burgh *"for any goods, gear, Insight, plenishing, uticilles and domicelles, Gold, Silver: Cunyit and uncunyit abulyiements [clothes] & oyrs alledgit Intromitit with be him, or his wyff, or anie oyr to thir behoff, qlk appertenit & belongit to umqll Margrat Adamsone, widow in Week, who Comitted yisternight, being the 18 Day of this Instant, the Cryme off Ipseare or selff murder, and qt sallbe made out as said is. It sall be maid furthcomand to all havand entres [an interest] as accords off the Law And that under the paine off ffyve hundreth Merks Scots money to be payed be me & my forsaids In caise of failyie to appeir In maner and to the effet abovementioned, to the Theasurer of the said burgh, he alwayes being Laullie Somondit to any Court to be affixt & holdine for that effet, and also he sall noway absent himselff noway wilfullie from the saids Courts under the paine aforsaid.*

In witnes qroff he hes subt. yir pnttes wth his hand as follows, Day,
moneth, yeir and place abovewrn befor thair witnesses, Johne
Abernethie in Week & Johne Mansonne yr."

Donald Malcome obviously could not write himself as
Gilbert Omand, the toune clerk, signed in his name :- *"with the*
pen led be Gilbert Omand, toune clerk of the said burghe abovenamed,
at my comand becaus I cannot wryt."

"Ita est Gilbertus Omand, norius publicus, in premiss spe'all
Cognisitus Testan his meis signo et subrive manualibus. nor. pub:"

G . OMAND

There followed a series of entries relating to Donald Malcome
with William Caldell as his cautioner, reference to *"Criminal*
Indytments" and a quite substantial penalty of 500 merks in case
of failyie. *"Criminal Indytments"* suggests that Malcome and his
wife had already cleared out the widow's house, not by any
means the only time in history that that has occured, and faster
than a flitting.

However, all the sections which followed were crossed out
or over, though still quite clearly readable, which usually
signified that the matter had been cleared up satisfactorily at
a later date or hearing, of which there is no further record. This
is a not uncommon feature of the Old Records of Weik and
leaves one wondering what eventually happened in a
particular case. There are also instances of a penalty having
been paid satisfactory to the Baillies, and no further entry is
made, even if the party was guilty.

Family groupings for a bit of strife continued on the 26th of
June, 1707, when *"John Nauchtie, yongr., in Wick, Elizabeth Murray*
yor spous & Issobell Naughtie yor Daur, you ar Indytit & accused
for the violent beating, blooding, blaeing and ryveing the gravate of
Jon Suyrland, ygr, weaver yr, to the effusion of his blood And in calling
him ane comon theiff and rasckil, qlk you cannot Deny, contrair to
Acts made against scolding in the street."

"Jon Naughtie & his wife compeir & yr daur, and denyes. The
fiscal offers to prove be witnesses. William Lamb in Wick, sworne,
deponed yt Jon Nauchtie yr called Jon Suyrland purnie theiff, and yt
he did see Jon Nauchtie strick at Jon Suyrland wt his hand in the face
qrby he reced blood & blae on his nose. This he declaires to be of truth
as he sall ansr to God.

Dod McMurchie, yr, Sworne, Deponed that he did see Jon Naughtie give blood & blae ut supra [as above] & that Elspet Murray did take Jon Suyrland be hair & fast yrin qll he loosed hir hands. Cirstain Monro yr Sworne, Deponed that shee did see Jon Naughtie strick him twice & yrby reced blood.

Wick 12 Sepr: 1707. The Balyies, eftr revising the Indytment & depo'nes abovewrin, fynes him in ten pounds Scots ".

And of course the inevitable countercharge:

"The sd Jon Suyrland, you ar indytit and accused for blooding blaeing & abuseing the sd Jon Naughtie himself, wife and daur., qlk you cannot deny, & comeing to his duelling hous & provocked him in calling him theif & 40d. man. And his wife meeting him in the door he gave the said Elizabeth Murray two or three strockes in the bellie wt his foot."

"6 Juni, 1707. Cmpeirs Jon Suyrland & denyes, the fiscal offers to prove be the oath of the Defer [Defender]. In respect Jon Suyrland refuses to depone, the Bailyies holds as confest, & takes the samen to avisandy, and to be arreistit.

Wick 22nd Sepr. The bailyies, In respect the sd Jon Suyrland refused to depone, & holdin as confest, fynes the said Jon Suyrland in £10 Scots.

Slanging matches were a feature of Weik in the 1660s when *"Issobel Murray, spous to James Innes, schoemaker in Wick & the said James Innes, you ar both Indytit & accused for the violent scolding and abusing of Marie Groat in calling her Whoor & theeff & se'all tymes recept stollen ockjtes of theift from se'all persones. And yrfor ought to be punished conform to the act made agt scolding. And in Scolding and saying that one of her [Marie Groat] daughters did break oppen James McKean his packs."*

Reference to *"packs"* can only be to a chapman or travelling pedlar and they were with us into very recent times indeed. In several guises they are still with us though perhaps a bit more sophisticated in their "foot in the door" approach.

26 Juni, 1707. Issobel Murray and her husband James Innes were severall times called at the Bar and did not *"compear"*. The officer cited them again at their own dwelling house, and they were fined 50/- each in contumacy, and witnesses ordained to be led for proof.

"James Doull, weaver, sworne, deponed that Issobell Murray scolded on the Sabbath Day, the 22 instant & Imprecat in calling the sd Marie Groat Devill be in her Drunken womb & yt her daur broke se'all packes.

"Wm Anderson, merd, sworne, deponed that he did heir Issobell Murray say yt her daur did break ane pack, & yt Marie Groat said yt the sd Issobell Murray broke ane pack in Kirkwall. The Bailyie taks ye Indytment to avisandy: & yt oyr witnesses be led."

There was an obvious connection with Kirkwall with each side accusing the other of breaking packs there, a bit of cross Pentland Firth trading.

John Nauchtie, referred above, was really getting his day in Court on the 26th June, 1707, because *"Elizabeth Murray, spous to Jon Naughtie, yonr in Wick, you ar Indytit & accused for scolding & defaming of Anna Cuming, spous to Alexr Doull, late Bailyie in Wick, In calling her comon whoor & theiff In oppen streets. And yrfor ought & should be punished in yor person and goods & Banished out of the place to the example & teiror of uyrs To comitt the like in tyme comeing."*

"26 Junii, 1707. Compeirs Murray & Denyes. The fiscall offers to prove be witnesses viz: Issobell Murray, in Wick, [referred above], sworne, deponed that Elizabeth Murray called Anna Cuming whoor & Theiff & that shee cam to Caithnes with ane stollen Robb, & gave comand to Subve becaus shee canot wryt.

P. SINCLAIR. N.P.,

[Cumming is an old Orkney name.]

"Anna Calder, spous to Hugh Harrow, sworne, deponed that shee [Anna Cumming] never hade stollen Robbe as shee hade & yt shee wes A comon whoor as shee wes & yt shee never kent anie man except her own. This shee declares to be of truth as shee sall ansr to God."

[Slightly ambiguously written but essentially in the English usage of the time and defending Anna Cumming against the charges of Elizabeth Murray.

"Andrew Findley, chapman, sworne, deponed ut supra. This he declared to be of truth as he sall ansr to God."

The matter was considered by the Baillies and *"in Wick the Nynth of Septer, 1707. The qlk day In obedience to the act of avisandy on the oyr side, William Mullikin, Bailyie, Ordaines the said Elizabeth Murray to pay of fyne for her transgression ten pounds Scots for scolding of Anna Cumming, conforme to Acts made anent scolding in the toune books of Wick. And the sd Elizabeth Murray To find sufficient caution actit in the sd Books for her Civill deportment in tyme comeing And yt wtin ten dayes nixt of the date heirof with witnes, qron act.*

W. MULLIKIN."

"*The said day the provest of the said Burgh approves &
homolographs the abovewrin Ordinance, qron act.*
W. MULLIKIN,   CHA: SINCLAIR, Provest.

"*The sd day William Murray, bailyie of Wick, Inactis himself Caur
for the sd Elizabeth Murray, for her good deportment in tyme comeing.*
WILL MURRAY

"*Wick the tenth day of Septr 1T. V11 H. & sevin yeirs. For sameikle
as Wm Mullikin, Bailyie, and Charles Sinclar of Bilbster, provest, hes
recevd compleit peyt of the abovewrin fyne from Elizabeth Murray
herself & husband for scandalysing, scolding, beating as is contained
in the wtinwrin Indytment psued agt her be Anna Cumming, datit
the 26 Junii, 1707. And Wee yrfor Discharges the said Elizabeth &
her husband for now & ever, Subt. day & place forsd.*
W. MULLIKIN,   CHA: SINCLAR, Pvst

"*Wick 16 may, 1710. Court holdin yr be Alexr Doull, Bailyie &
remanent members of Court.*

"*Marie Grant, Brinebearer in Wick, you ar Indytit & accused for
comeing to Gate, Doors & windowes of Hugh Harrow, merd yr, & in
seall oyr places. And yr did oppenlie & unchristianlie & awowedlie
Scandaliz, traduce & Calluminating Anna Calder, spous to the sd
Hugh Harrow, in calling her ane Deboshed whoore & saying shee
hade bought Stircockes hous with guinies of gold that the sd Anna
Calder had gotten from Bailyie Calder for comitting adulterie with
him, and did express many more expressiones which the witnesses
can testifie qn called. And upon the 25 day of Apryll last you the sd
Marie Grant went to the hous of Patrick Sinclair, Clerk, And yr did
say upon the Sabbath day before, being the twentie third apryll, that
the sd Anna Calder, about 12 oclock at night, wes Scolding in the
Streets and wold make the samen appeir qn challenged to yt effect,
qlk you canot Deny.*

"*10 may, 1710. Cmpeirs Grant & Denyes & refer to probatne.
Compeir Ann Calder, psr, and adduces witness for proveing the
Indytment viz: John Brebner in Ackergill, being deeplie Sworne,
Deponed that he heard Elspet Calder Challeng Marie Grant for saying
that Ann Calder hade reced gold from Rob Calder for lying with her,
qch the sd Marie Grant owned, & knowes no more. This he declaires
to be of truth as he sall ansr to God. And Declaires he cannot wryt.*
P.SINCLAIR N.P., L.D.

*William Lamb in Wick, being deeplie Sworne, Deponed that he
did hear Elspet Sinclair, spous to James Doull, say that she did hear*

Marie Grant say That the guinyies Anna Calder gott from Rob Calder for lying with her bought the hous. And he replyed, "Marie lay yt under yor foot, for Anna Calder is known to be ane honest woman".

"And the sd Marie said shee own [knew] qt wes Spoke & desired him to goe to the Deivill. This he declaires to be of truth as he sall ansr to God & declaires he cannot wryt.   P.SINCLAIR N:P: L.D.

Andrew Keith yr, being deeplie sworne, deponed that he did heir Marie Grant say that Ann Calder got genzies from Robert Calder that bought the houss & on yt accot he did not know or heir, & declairs he cannot wryt.   P.SINCLAIR N.P.

"John Harper yr, being deeplie sworne, deponed that he did heir Marie Grant say efter shee cam out of Hugh Harrowes doors, that the sd Ann Calder had sitt up letter wt Rob Calder on ane Sabbath night & not so drunk. This he declairs to be of truth as he sall ansr to God & declaires he cannot wryt.   P. SINCLAIR N.P.

"The Bailyie, Considering the wtinwrin Indytment & depositiones, decernes the sd Marie Grant in ten pound of fyne for scolding & to stay in the haich tolboothe in prisone qll shee find cation for her Civill deportment in tyme comen. And remitts the Scandell to the Comissr: qron act   A.D. [Alex Doull]

"At Wick, 17 may, 1710. The sd day James Young, merd yr, Inacts himselff as Caur: for the wtin named Marie Grant for her Civill deportment in tyme comeing under the paine of fourtie libs Scots, toties quoties.

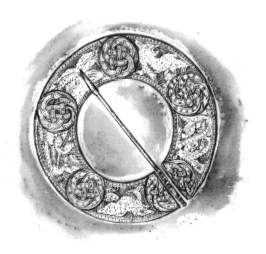

— Chapter 22 —

The Camps – Weik's Gateway to the World

Now I am not going to cross swords with all those eminent historians who have taken Wick to their hearts and have probably written learnedly more than I could ever read about that fair City. I am only slowly transcribing the Old Counsell Books of Wick, indeed I thought that if I did even the first one dating from 1660 to 1711 I would have excelled myself. It is done, beyond my wildest dreams from when I first saw it. Copies are now available in the Northern Archives in Wick, the Libraries of Wick, Thurso and Kirkwall, the Archives in Inverness, The Scottish Record Office in Edinburgh, and a copy or two for myself. It runs to about 120 pages.

Unfortunately, I unintentionally found myself starting on the second available book, which begins about 1739, or thereby, and runs to about 1770. It is in very poor shape with pages mixed up, obviously it has come apart at some time and been very badly rebound. There is a mystery about the intervening copy of the Records from 1711 to 1739. It existed, has been quoted from in the past, hopefully still exists, and if it does then someone may have it, or stumble across it, and take it to the Archives in Wick where it belongs.

Though I had not yet finished "Parish Life on the Pentland Firth" dealing with Vol 1, in this next volume there was one entry which took my eye. It concerned John Sutherland, Wick businessman, entrepreneur extraordinaire, developer and merchant, who saw a chance to develop a vacant piece of ground known as the Shore of Wick. This area is now generally called *"The Camps"*. He applied to the Counsell for their permission to build thereupon, which was granted, and I cannot do better than quote the whole Counsell Record word for word:

"Att Wick the twenty second day of April, IT.viiH. and fifty six years [1756]. The magistrats & Town Counsell, In Conjunction with Severall of the most respectable merchants and other Inhabitants of the Town, having viewed & Considered the ground which James Taylor, Meason, is now Clearing In order To build ane Store House for John Sutherland, Merchant of Wick, his Imployer, of thirty seven [feet] In Length & twenty seven in breadth all over, Walls, Dore, fynd That the whole Ground upon that part of the Shore is litle Enough for loading & unloading Bulkie Goods and for Containing Such ane Number of Horses and people as doe frequent the Ships and boats loading & unloading.

"Nevertheless seeing it may be usefull to the said John Sutherland To have a store house on that part of the Shore, Doe aggree To his building it of the forsaid Extent, provided it be founded as Near to the Waittir Side as Can be. That is to say, the North Wall of the said house at the East Gavell shall be fourty two foote Distant from the front of the Schooll house, and the North side of the West Gavell to be fourty Seventh foot Distant from the front of the said Schoolhouse, and that the West Gavell be twenty four foot Distant from the East Gavell of the fore house presently possest by John Sutherland, Shoemaker.

"The Ground upon which this Intended store house is to be builded was the highest Ground on this Shore where boats & timber used to be Cairied up for Security In time of stress or Stormy Weather. And this makes it necessary That the Camps between the Schooll House and the North Wall of the said Store House should be Larger in regard that it is the only place where the Scollers Can play and devert themselves within the view of thire master, and the place where the beef that is made in this town is usually pickled and tighted, And is Much and dayly frequented by many of the Inhabitants for ane Healthfull airing. And that part of the Camps between the New Schooll and the Old will be more necessary now than before the building of the Store house, as it will be allways necessary in the winter season for drawing up the boats and Securing the woods and timber that the merchants

are obliged to leave upon the Shore, as they have no Store houses nor Closes to serve the Same.

"And it is Understood that the intended Store house is to have noe priviledge whatsoever on the North Side wall Excepting only ane Entry to the Second Storie, and if a stair be found necessary on that side wall He shall Claime noe property to the Ground lying Either on the East or West side of the said stair.

> GEORGE SUTHERLAND, B:
> PATRICK HILL, B:
> JAMES ANDERSON, D of G:
> WILL CALDER, Clr:
> JAMES SUTHERLAND, Jr.

* a few word meanings for above.

The *"Gavell"* of a house is now Gable.

A *"fore house"* was a house with it's front facing the street, or in this case more likely the river i.e. a *"front house."*

Many houses in days gone by were built with the gable end either on to the street or on to the shore, Stromness in Orkney is still full of them, and it was a Nordic tradition, again well illustrated in Bergen. Therefore the fore house of John Sutherland, shoemaker, who from other entries I think was the son of John Sutherland, entrepreneur of the proposed new development, either faced the High Street on the North side of it, which I think impossible by the description of locations, or it fronted the Water of Wick, reasonably close to the water's edge and to the river side, and lay to the South of the lower end of the High Street. This would explain the 24 foot distance required by the Counsell between the East gable of his fore house and the West gable of the new store house, and would have given an entry down to the river between the buildings.

"Pickled and tighted" - Pickled needs no explanation to a Wicker, especially to a Wicker!, and *"tighted"* was merely the final tightening down or closing of the lid of a barrel in which the salt beef was finally stored. Pickling was certainly done in barrels or tubs and the beef would have been turned and salted a few times in the curing process from one barrel or tub to another before being completely cured and sealed. It would have been a considerably lengthier process than salting mere herring.

"Second Storie", and the stairs thereto. We have mentioned before now that the stairs of the Tolbooth were most probably built outside the building, a common enough access to lofts in farm steadings even today. This new store was to have a loft above the ground floor, or more likely a complete upper floor, timber joisted and decked. These outside stairs were very common, some being with us still, and left the whole upper floor free and unencumbered with a stair well coming through. Safety aspects did not exist, if you were daft enough to fall over the stair and break your neck, tough. One of my great uncles did just that!

"Camps" – the word around the which many stories are told. One is that soldiers came North at the time of Cromwell and set up a camp at that location. Some that soldiers of another period in history did so. A crazy way to live facing the wild and open North Sea to the East, and I do not believe it. Anyone seeing a South Easterly gale driving sea spray onto that area will appreciate the unlikely nature of a camp there. Soldiers were in practice quartered on existing inhabitants and in existing houses, living in these houses, being fed by the owners and at the owners expense. In the Session Records of Canisbay in 1652 at the time of Cromwell we find ample reference to *"Englishes"* being quartered in the local houses, and to the elders of Canisbay refusing to stay on after sermon to hold Session meetings and having to let their wives and daughters go home unattended!

A new school was built in Wick at the *"Shoar"* in 1683, according to our old records, which must be the *"old"* school of the above. A decision to build a new school was taken in 1751, also to be at the Shoar, after the Counsell had considered the need and cost of repairs to the old school of 1683 whose foundations were collapsing. The ground underneath at the Camps and Shoar is unstable, being mostly driven sand or gravel. Money was to be raised and the school was built before 1756, but when it was actually finished and occupied between these two dates I cannot tell. There was a reference in the Toun Accounts of 1754 to a payment of money laid out on the new school of £9.04.01 Sterling.

This has to be the *"new"* school referred to above, it could be no other. Neither school was referred to as being at the

"*Camps*" by way of location, rather using the description of "*Shoar*".

"*Camp*" had many meanings but the basic one is from the Latin "*Campus*" meaning a field. The widely known educational "*Campus*" referred not to the buildings, though that is possibly the more modern meaning, but rather to the area of ground enclosed or surrounded by these scholastic buildings. The tents of a mobile army, or the barracks and buildings of a static one, could be laid out around a "*campus*", a more or less level piece of ground or field. In army terms it would have been the Parade Ground, used for drill but also for recreation. Another meaning for camp is a lively activity or a romp, male or female. Yet two more in the dictionary are an oblong clamp of potatoes for winter storage, or an enclosure used for animals. Take your choice.

But the Old Wick Counsell Record states quite clearly that the Camps between the South wall or front of the New School, built but five years previous at most, and the North wall of the projected new store house to be built for John Sutherland by James Taylor, mason, was to be used by the "*Scollers*" for play. In fact, it was the School playground. Being close to the potentially dangerous waters of the river was but an added reason for the "Scollers" to play and divert themselves within the sight of their teacher. The part of the Camps between the old and the new schools was specifically referred to as being more necessary now, after the building of John Sutherland's storehouse, for the winter storage of boats. Obviously boats had previously been stored on Sutherland's site. The area of flat ground at the Camps was, indeed still is, quite limited in extent, and by 1872 in the first Ordnance Survey Map it was called The Burgh Quay, vying for usage with the cross river harbour of Pulteney, a separate town. The inhabitants of Wick also much used it for a "Healthful airing", so medicinal benefit from fresh air was not unknown in 1756. Then and now the "*Camps*" had a recreational value for Weikers. The other and more important aspect of the "*Shoar*" was that it was the entry point to Wick itself from the sea in days without any harbour whatever. The river, or "*Water of Weik*", was very much too shallow to take in vessels, even the smaller ones of those days, though no doubt they could come in on the high tide and lie aground against the shore when the tide went out. Other than a small bridge well up river there was no bridge capable of carrying loads across it from the South side to Wick Toun, fords having to be used. Cargo was landed or loaded over the beach and the Camps was at the junction of the river with the deeper waters of the North Sea. No doubt the state of the tide was an important feature in making a landing. On the Wick [North] side of the River there is little enough level ground even now at the side of the "Water of Weik", referred to in our records, to take a vessel close to.

So this small piece of ground was vital to Weik, to landing or loading cargo, sometimes taken out to the Bay in small boats to an anchored vessel. It was vital to be able to haul boats onshore when the weather became foul or threatening. It was high enough to be out of danger. It provided a winter haven to small boats many of whom were engaged in fishing in summer or in better weather. It provided limited storage to merchants to keep their bulky cargoes, either imports, wood and timber was mentioned, or exports, salt beef was mentioned.

No doubt as stated it provided the killing ground for cattle which were butchered, pickled and packed in barrels for export. It lay at the seaward end of the High Street, Weik's gateway to the world outside, the first step ashore for many an incomer.

So there it is. The Camps was the bairns playground!

— Chapter 23 —

Bigging the new school of Weik in 1683

"*20 mch, 1683. The Bailyie, wt consent of the Toune Counsell, Ordaines yt four qrtermasters may be choysen for attending for bigging ane school at the Shoar of Weik, & ilk inhabitant to furnish ane srvant for the said use, cnforme to the se'all qrtermastr yr desyre, under the failyie of 6/8d pr Diem, toties quoties, to be payed be srvant or mastr.*"

The above entry was the first I came across mentioning education and schooling in the Weik of the 1660s. Nothing more about schools was contained in the first Record Book of 1660 to 1711, the brief entry above giving little insight into what was a very important Burgh issue. I might have considered and thought a bit harder or longer on that statement, and although only conjecture, on what size of building needed FOUR quartermasters for the building thereof, as well as quite substantial penalties on the Inhabitants if they did not buckle to and help with the provision of labour, either their own or by providing a servant to represent their contribution. Presently I have no idea what were the dimensions of that school, but the location was at the Shoar of Weik.

Building in those far off days was relatively simple, stone being quarried locally and carted onto site, masons building with sweat of brow and skin of knuckle, lime being prepared from local sources for mortar. Obviously in Weik in 1660 timber had to be imported, a well enough known fact. That apart, materials and manpower were available locally at little cost other than organising and driving people to do the hard work. And the site was specifically at the "Shoar of Weik".

Next reference I found to education, of a kind, in Weik was the contretemps in the Records of the case heard on the 6th June, 1710, between the schoolmaster, Andrew Sutherland, and Alex Dunbar, one of the Weik merchants, who had to provide him with his living, or at least Dunbar's portion of the liability. This took the form of meal, be it bere or oat, and possibly the provision of whole grain bere to be malted for making some home brewed ale was the more important. In this fracas on the Loan of Weik in June, 1710, it was bere that was due from Dunbar to Sutherland as part of his schoolmaster's sallary.

They came predictably to blows with the persuer, Andrew Sutherland, our schoolmaster, deponing under *"sworne oath"* that Dunbar struck him on the mouth with his fist, that he loused one of his teeth, that there was great effusion of his blood and that he fell down upon his back, and declairing that he told the truth as he would answer to God. The bailyie found Dunbar guilty, fined ten pounds Scots before he removed out of prison.

Not to be outdone, Dunbar charged the schoolmaster with violent abuse, bad language and offering to strick him with his staff. The Bailyie considered the provocation to be light, and accordingly dismissed the charge.

In the second Record Book reference is made to the state of repair, or of disrepair, of the school built in 1683. On the first of April, 1751, *"the provost, magistrates and Town Counsell of the said burgh, having this day meett and having taken under their consideratione the necessity of repairing of the Schoole of Wick."*

The record stops at that point without stating any decision regarding repairs to the school and goes immediately on, and in a totally different and very small but clear and easily read hand of write, after the large words of *"IN ORDER TO HAVE ANE - deserving man to teach their children, therefore resolved to build a Schoolhouse of Twenty foot in Length and Sixteen foot in Breadth, Together with a fireroom fourteen foot in Length adjoining therto, the Side walls of which Schoolhouse and fireroom to be ten foot high, the whole house to be sufficiently Lofted with a Chimney in each of the Gavels above, with ane partition of staik and ryce in the Middle therof, or where ever it shall be found most convenient for the Schoolmaster's accomodation, and a Sufficient thick Roof over the whole.*

"And in order to make out the above Plan the Provost, Magistates and Town Counsell agree to dedicate the Current year's Town Publick towards the same, together with a Voluntary Contribution from the Inhabitants of the Town, which is believed to arise to about nine or ten Pound Sterling.

"And if it falls short of that Sum the Magistrates are to Stent the Deficiency on the Inhabitants as they shall see Cause, In which they are to have a special regard in Sparing those who may Contribute liberally of thire own Accord.

"And what sum shall yet be deficient is to be made up among the Heritors of the Parish by Voluntary Subscription, in which it is hoped every Heritor will Contribute in proportion to his Estate in the Parish, and will rather give more than what is required as the whole shall be faithfullie laid out in rendering the Schoolhouse and Masters accomodation more Commodious.

"And the Magistates appoint James Budge of Toftingall to go among the Heritors to get their respective Subscriptions, and To levy the Same, and to pay it in to the Person who shall be after Nominate to receive the Money, and to lay it out upon the Work. And also appoint John Sutherland, Treasurer, and Merchant in Wick, with Mr Patrick Kinnaird, Doctor of Medicine there, to go among the Inhabitants of the Town to endeavour to Levy a Voluntary Contribution, and to make report of thar Diligence to the Magistrates, and to take Counsell with them about what may be further necessary to be done in so Commendable a work. And it is recommended to the Collectors in the Town, and to Toftingall, to report their diligence in raising the Money to the Magistates betwixt and the first day of May."

and in Wick on the 14th June, 1751.

"We, William Calder, one of the present Baillies of Wick and John Sutherland, Treasurer of the said Burgh and . . . . . . Remanent Counsellors, having received a Petition agreeable to the Act of Council of date the first day of April last, do agree That as there has a subscription been taken up since the forementioned Act according to the order therin Contained, We order and appoint. . . . . to receive from each Contributor what they have subscribed for building of a Schoolhouse for the Town of Wick, as the old School is quite Ruinous and has no foundation to stand upon."

The *"Old School"* dated from 1683 above and was thus 70 years old.

Time moved on a year or two, and:

"Att Wick the first day of June, one thousand seven hundred & fifty four years, Patrick Hill & George Sutherland, Baillies, James Anderson Treasurer, William Calder, Dean of Gild, & Sir Patrick Dunbar of Northfield, Counsellers, being meet this day in Counsell wt John Anderson, James Frazer, William Anderson, merchants, & James Calder, mercht there, William Groat, Taylor, and John Calder, Barbar.

"Robert Smith, Schoolmaster, proposed To repair the School and make it sufficient and To ly out what money was necessary for that purpose, providing the Magistrates would give him Sufficient Surety for his repayment out of the Town's publick funds, when they would answer, of what sums he would be obliged To lay out upon that work.

"Both the Baillies reported that they had Imployed tradesmen To survie the present Condition of the schooll, who gave in ane Accot to them that the sufficient repairs of the schooll would stand about £10 or £12 Sterling.

Here I was puzzled because it was referred above that the old school *"is quite Ruinous and has no foundation to stand upon."* At first glance it appears to be the old school whose repairs are being discussed, after the Counsell agreeing to build a new school and to raise funds to that purpose. The extent of *"repairs"* at £10 to £12 Sterling is quite a tidy sum of money to spend on repairing a building shortly to be abandoned.

It was the equivalent of a third of the total money spent per annum on school and school masters sallary just a few years later in 1760. In today's money, relative to a schoolmaster's salary, we are talking about quite a few thousand pounds. In 1790 the Statistical Account referred to new house properties to be built in Wick in the new Town of Louisburgh requiring to be large enough to be valued at £10 Sterling, our £12 was thus quite substantial in 1754. So was Robert Smith then prepared to finish the work on the new school at his own expense if reimbursed by the Counsell at a later date?

I am prepared to go for the latter because by 1756 John Sutherland's new store house was sited at the Shoar of Weik in relation to and measured from the South or front wall of the new school, or school house, which was therefore by then built and finished. The word *"repair"* could have been applied to

FINISHING the new work rather than REPAIRING the old building. It also makes no sense to spend £12 Sterling on temporary repairs to an old school shortly to be disused, and that in a town perpetually crying out for money for *"publick service"*. All the above depends on our interpretation of the word *"repair"* but that word still has quite a number of differing meanings.

I rather think we should accept that Robert Smith took charge of finishing the New School. He was also possibly the new and deserving man referred to in 1751 when a decision was taken to build afresh. If so, then he would have been understandably interested in completing any outstanding work still required as it would be his own personal accommodation he would be completing. Education would appear to be quite seriously taken in those days because in the neighbouring Parish of Canisbay on the Pentland Firth, at a slightly earlier period, there was an entry in the Session Records reading:

MARCH 7, 1658.

"Some elders meitting: after calling upon ye name of God, notted that ye session, taking to yr consideration severall complaints put in by the schoolmaster of ye parishe shewing yt ye most pairt of the parents puts not yr childrene at all, and thes yt puts any take them away in ye midst of the quarter frome ye schoole, or before the Session sies that they have received instruction; therfore it is enacted yt whoso-ever puts not yr childrene to ye schoole, according to ye order, or taks them away yt ar presented till they be tryed by ye Minister & elders of yr profiting, sall pay 40s for contraveining ye act, and the quarter pay to ye schoolmaster."

So there was concern at least by the Church Session of Canisbay that children were not being sufficiently educated.

And on 28th October, 1660, again in Canisbay, the Session and the minister agreed to appoint Donald Reid *"to be school-master at CANNASBEY for teiching ye young children yt suld be sent to him, and for his paines 5 bolls victuall wes promissed him in the yeir, qlk he, thinking too litle, yit accepted to undertak ye charge and to enter wt all conveinent diligence, provydeing ye said 5 bolls victuall be duelie payed, and yt he may have forwt 3 of peats to supplie his present neid."*

Donald Reid was still teaching in Canisbay when that particular Session Records ended on 14th February of 1666, and was also reader in the Church.

The new school of Weik with dimensions of 20 feet by 16 feet with a fireroom of 14 feet length, which would have been outside measurements, would have given a main room of inside measurements of 11 feet width and, allowing only a thin partition between the fire room and the main room of neglible thickness, some 17 feet in length. This is based on side walls being 2′6″ thick and gable ends being 3′ thick, a width needed to incorporate a gable end chimney, measurements mirrored in Isauld House, the house in which I live, which was built of stone construction by George Innes not too long after 1751 at the turn of the century.

Such a main room would have crammed in a very limited number of "*scollers*", how many we cannot tell. I am assuming that the old school was abandoned and no longer used for pupil accommodation. Possibly only the children of the merchants and lairds would have been taught, though the earlier Canisbay record indicates a much wider local view of education.

The firerooom could have been kitchen and living room for the new schoolmaster, a stairs would have been somewhere built though a ladder was a possibility, still used in some houses not too long back. The upper story was to have two rooms, each with a fireplace and a chimney, and the partition upstairs, which was to be placed at the schoolmasters convenience, was of "*staik and ryce.*" This partition would have vertical wooden members, the "*staiks*", of about 4″x2″ timber, with "*ryce*", which was interwoven horizontal twigs or reeds such as we would still occasionally find as a wattle hurdle or fence in a small field or garden, more decorative now but at times also functional. Such a partition would have been very easy to move if you did not like it's position. In later days it would have been plastered to make a more substantial and modern affair, but still the same basic construction within, the lath and plaster of our own times.

A "*thik*" roof could be thatch but could also be of slate, and for some repairs done to the Tollbooth roof at that time a man was employed to "winn" slates, so it was not all thatch on the Burgh roofs.

Not a bad thing in Windy Weik.

The "*heretors*" whose subscriptions were required would have been much as found in the Valuation of Caithness of 1760 regarding school and schoolmaster's maintainence. Many a contributor to some good cause likes to see their name listed, so I can do no better than copy posthumously the names of those heretors of the Wick Parish Valuation of 1760, fairly sure that the heretors listed therin would also have been the willing contributors to the New School of Weik! The contributions to Schoolmaster's sallary, school and schoolhouse from each heretor were measured according to their assessed rentals in so many bolls of meal and so much money in pounds Sterling, a boll being 73 kgs present measure. Total sallary was expressed as £36.08.06d for school and schoolhouse and to the school-master 24 bolls meal. This was way beyond the 6 bolls needed annually for a household so no doubt the surplus could readily be converted to cash.

Heretors were James Sinclair of Mey for a part of Myrlandnorn, George Sinclair of Ulbster for Thrumster, Tannoch and half of Campster, William Sinclair of Freswick for Nybster, Sir Wm Dunbar for his Estate in the Parish, Sinclair of North Dun for the other half of Myrlandnorn and Sinclair of Barrock's part therof, Sir William Sinclair [Dunbeath] for Kees and Oukorn, Bridgend [Manson Sinclair of Watten Estate] for the Cleftside of Oldwick, Barrock for the Laird's Croft, also for Myreland, Quintfall, Crooks of How and the Milne thereof; Olrick [Sinclair] for Stirkock and Thurster, Wedderclett and Hauster, Over and Nether Bilbsters, Sibster, Heshwell and Quoylee, the Bankhead of Weik, Blingery.

Trace of the old school was not entirely forgotten in Weik because in a disposition of property at the Shoar of Weik, dated 30th June, 1890, from the Trustees of the late George McAdie to William Geddes, fishcurer, later of W. and A. Geddes, the property now John Sutherland's Waterfront was described as being "bounded on the West by subjects forming part of what were formerly known as the School House tenement, and have been disposed by us to Alexander Sinclair, Auctioneer, Wick." A long way from 1683.

Alexander Sinclair was the founder of Sinclair's Auction Marts, for three generations and over 100 years the farming focal point of every Thursday in the market town of Weik, and now but a whispering, distant and fading echo.

———≫·◆·≪———

Chapter 24

Harbour Facilities in Weik and Staxigoe in 1754

Today we can admire in comfort the extensive harbour facilities of Wick, the Boy Andrew lying in safe haven, a far cry from the old fourareen of the Shetlander no doubt mirrored in Staxigoe by the four oared boat belonging to Sir James Dunbar, taken without permission by Alex Mullikin to go afishing one evening in May 1708. Alex very oddly had no recall of those who helped him *"doun"* the boat into the water, there to be damaged by a probable bashing on the rocks of Staxigoe!

Shelter was nonexistent and safety for boats relied on the ability of strong men to haul their small open fishing boats onshore above the danger mark, referred to in the building by John Sutherland of his Store House at the Shoar of Weik in 1756 when particular mention was made of hauling up boats in times of stress or stormy weather, both previously onto Sutherland's site for his new storehouse, and then onto the Camps between the old and the new schools. Reports on harbour facilities, or the lack of them, were made at the turn of the century around 1800 by Rennie and Telford, eventually bearing fruit in the present Wick Harbour, particularly on the South or Pulteney side of the Water of Weik. Other notable men were also involved such as the Stevensons and James Bremner from Keiss.

But what of 1660, where the shelter, where the stone, where

the concrete and reinforceing of today, the interlocking steel piling better seen by the interested at Scrabster than in Wick. There was none in the harbours of Staxigoe, Boathaven and Wick, and of these Boathaven was little mentioned in the Counsell Records.

The Counsell met on the 2nd April, 1751, when the issue of school repairs was brought up, leading to the decision to build the New School at the Shoar of Weik to supercede the old one of 1683. At a later meeting on the first day of June, 1754, the Counsell discussed an offer from Robert Smith to *"Repair"* the school at his own expense provided he was reimbursed when the Town purse would answer, which I took to mean completing the new work. This was presumably accepted by the Counsellers though no record of such that day, but referred to in subsequent meetings.

Counsells being what they were, and no doubt still are, this meeting opened up discussion on another apparently much needed repair:

"Both the Baillies and the merchants present represented that the paulls & reigns of the harbours of Staxigoe and Wick were In such a bad condition that if they were not Immediatedly repaired Noe ships Could ly in those Harbours with safety. And for that purpose it will be immediately necessary to provide two sufficient new paulls for Staxigoe of about seven or eight foot Long, which will be worth teen or fifteen shillings a peice, And two new reigns worth about three pound Sterl. both, and that they would need about three paulls for Wick, all worth about twenty shillings."

And on the next page, continuing:- *"As the provost pays the Town's Cess and Missive dues and allows that Extent of the Customes to goe for the publick service of the Town, And that they Expect the provost [George Sinclair of Ulbster] will lodge with the town's treasurer the last recepts for the Cess and Missive dues, and that he will aggree To the yearly payment of Custome to come."*

"It is likewise proposed that the Provost & Baillies shall joine in reasuring or granting surety upon the publick funds of the Town For what money will be necessary for repairing the Schooll, And for furnishing Sufficient paulls and reignes for both the harbours, And To apply In the first place the yearly amercement of the Customes. And in the next place they propose to raise a yearly stent of about five pounds Sterling from all the burgesses and Inhabitants to be

proportioned by stent masters to be chosen out of the men of the Town of best knowledge and Judgement, which they think will be best raised, And which Customes & Stent if yearly well managed will in a short time pay up the money now necessary to be raised, and they Expect will make a fund for severall oyr publick Services. And they recommend to the Baillies To send a Copy of this to the Provost and to the non resident Counsellers for there approbatione and Concurrence."

Time was not standing still in this matter because on the 27th August a further meeting considered the resolution of the meeting of the 1st June, 1754, approved of the Resolutions, and George Sinclair of Ulbster, Provost of Wick, agreed to pay the Cess [Taxes] and missive dues of the Town of Wick. There was a slight catch, however, to this helpful gesture from the Superior of the Burgh :*"So long as the Burgesses of the Burgh shall maintain & support his Interest in the Election of the Magistrates & Town Council."* Nothing for nothing, but not too surprising after the long series of Court actions in the Court of Session in Edinburgh, particularly the five Interloquiters of 1749 involving George Sinclair concerning the rights of the Superiority of Wick and his power and influence in local Elections. This Superiority had been purchased in 1723 from John Campbell, the Earle of Breadalbine, by John Sinclair of Ulbster, George's grandfather.

George Sinclair certainly had a great interest in the Provostship of Wick and the control he exercised as Successor to the Earle of Breadalbine in the Superiority of the Burgh. It gave him entry to other aspects of National life further South, Conventions of Royal Burrows, General Assemblies of the Church of Scotland, possible membership of Parliament in Westminster to represent the group of five Royal Burghs of Tain, Dingwall, Dornoch, Kirkwall and Wick, who collectively had the right to one member to represent them in Parliament. There was an undoubted social and *"high society"* aspect to such positions.

He also did take his Provostship seriously by attending as Provost a great number of the Counsell meetings in Wick, even though he lived at Thurso East when not in Edinburgh. However, the political machinations of George Sinclair and of the Counsellers are not for this chapter.

Sufficient that George Sinclair took upon himself certain payments to Government on behalf of Wick, no doubt temporarily, and by so doing released the Customes dues to be spent by the Counsell on the school and on the repairs to the Harbours of Wick and Staxigoe.

"*The Provost and Baillies therefore, with the consent of the town Councill, assigned & disponed to and in favour of Robert Smith, School Master, and in favour of the undertakers who were to be employed for the furnishing of the new Palls & Rings to the Harbours of Wick and Staxigo, who were to be named by the Town Council for that purpose, the whole yearly product of the Customs of the said Burgh, after deducting fifty shillings sterling allowed to the Clerk & officer.*"

The further sum of five pounds Sterling was to be yearly stinted upon the inhabitants of said Burgh, beginning the first years payment of the said Customes & Stint at the term of Candlemass "*next to come*", and yearly & termly thereafter until the money that was to be expended upon the said school & the rings & harbours be fully satisfied & paid.

"*The Magistrates & town councill appoint William Manson and James Sutherland, merchants, and Andrew Bremner, weaver, to be stent masters for stenting the said five pound sterling yearly upon the Inhabitants & ordain the said stent to be paid into James Anderson, treasurer, and his successors in office, and ordained the present Tacksmen of the Customes and his successors Tacksmen therof, and the Town treasurer for the time being, to pay into the said Robert Smithe & the undertakers for the Polls and Rings for bothe harbours, such soums as they shall expend upon repairing the School & the said Palls & Rings according to an account to be given in by them, for which They shall obtain the magistrates Order, & the said Magistreates & Council Bind & oblige them & thire successors in office to pay to the said Robert Smith and the said undertakers for Polls and Rings what They shall expend for these purposes out of the first money which shall arise out of the Customs of the Burgh, The Clerk & officers fees Excepted, & out of the said yearly stint, & promise That the magistrates will decern the Tacksmen of the Customes & the Town Treasurer & Collectors of the stint to pay them on the first Complaint & appoints & Ordains the Town Clerk to give Extracts of ther presents to Robert Smith & to the Undertakers for their Security. And The magistates & Town Council appoint George Sutherland, Baillie, James Anderson, Treasurer & John Anderson, merchant, or any one of them, to undertake the management of the Polls & Ringes.*"

Followed the usual list of signatures of the Provost and Counsellers.

I suppose Council meetings and their minutes are dry reading at times but on this matter of repairs to school and harbours the Records are quite extensive. They went on the next month with:

"Att Wick, the twenty fourth day of September, 1754.

"Patrick Hill and George Sutherland, Baillies, James Andersone, treasurer, William Calder, Dean of Gild, Counsellers, being this day meet in Counsell and having heard read before them the resolutiones of the Town Counsell meet the first day of June last and there [their] Enactment upon the said Resolutions made and signed By the provost Baillies and Counsellers in appointing Stent masters for stenting the Inhabitants of the said burgh in ane yearly stent of five pounds Sterling a year to be put out in repairing the school and in furnishing palls & rings for the harbours of Wick and Staxigoe, and in appointing managers for the same, Doe in consequence of the said Resolution and Act of Counsell theron, And accordingly the said William Andersone and James Sutherland, merchants, and Andrew Bremner, weaver, stent masters nommated, being met in Counsell and required To accept, they accordingly accepted and Deponed that They would Exerce that office in terms of the said act of Counsell and accordingly signed.

  PATRICK HILL, GEORGE SUTHERLAND, B:,
  and the stentmasters signatures:
  WILLIAM ANDERSON, JAMES SUTIIERLAND,
  ANDREW BREMNER.

That was more or less the extent of the "minuits" of the Records relating to the raising of additional taxes or moneys from the Inhabitants of Wick for the finishing of the new School and for repairing the Harbours of Wick and Staxigoe to make them safer havens for vessels trading into and out of these two ports. "Paulls" were what today we would call bollards and were doubtless tree trunks of eight feet in length and a probable two feet in thickness, though I judge that from seeing similar in my own time set up behind the beaches in the fishing village of Whitehall in Stronsay and to which small fishing boats could fasten a line.

They were sunk into clay or other hard ground to a depth of about six feet, leaving two to three feet above ground level. They were usually set leaning slightly backwards from the sea which gave a better and safer grip for ropes. They were used where the ground was deep enough to dig in for placement.

"*Reings*" were iron rings which were used where the shore was rock and palls could not be sunk. Holes were drilled into the rock and the ring was fastened to an iron shaft driven into the drilled hole and probably fastened tight with molten lead. To this ring the ships would fasten their ropes or cables and suspend themselves between an anchor holding in the sea and to a rope or hawser to the ring on the rocky foreshore. Scrabster had such well known rings below the present lighthouse, shown on a map of 1841 which I had but which has now gone missing after I gave it to the Harbour Trust! Pity.

The rings at Staxigoe in particular were needed due to the rocky foreshore. A vessel could suspend or moor itself with a rope to either side of the harbour but Wick would have had to use palls at the Shoar of Weik which was more sand and gravel thown up by the sea.

This method of mooring ships or vessels stayed much the same until the new developments of harbour facilities circa 1800. Not one to appeal to a shipmaster in a South East gale coming onshore but that was all that Weik and Staxigo had to offer.

Little wonder then that we had the case of the vessel cast away on 13th March, 1661, within the "*Road of the saide Burgh and the Water Mouthe thairof.*" I wonder if it was a Friday!

— Chapter 25 —

Customs Dues and Trade of Weik in 1766

Having centred upon the Shoar of Weik in 1756 for John Sutherland's new store house, for the new school to be built in 1751 to replace the one of 1683, for the repairs to the harbour of Weik in the year 1754, we should perhaps consider what went on there, if any information survives.

The healthful exercise which the inhabitants indulged in on the Camps and on the Shoar were not the only reasons for concentration on that tiny and low lying portion of the Burgh of Weik. Cargoes came and went, ships ran aground or were wrecked, small fishing boats were hauled to safety above high water mark. Cattle were killed and salted. Doubtless pigs and sheep likewise. Timber was brought in by ship, landed and stored on the Camps. Onlookers loved to see others working. Still do. It appears that the very life of Weik centred at that spot, comings and goings by sea, keeping watch a bit further out for Dutch enemies in 1665, a favourite spot for a duel or a fight between friendly Weikers in September, 1663. So do the records tell us anything about the trade of Weik so long ago?

Perhaps we can take the table of Customs dues in 1766, written by William Calder, the then Toun Clerk of Weik, and guess here and there what went on in trade over the Shoar of Weik.

Table for the Customes of the Burgh of Wick.   £. S. D.
                                                                  (Ster

1st	Victuall the Chalder of bear to unfreemen	- .10.08d
2nd	Double Trees Each dozen	- . 2. 00d
3rd	Single Trees Each dozen	5. 00d
4th	Birks Each Dozen	5. 00d
5th	Dealls Each dozen	5. 00d
6th	Learge Couple leags, Each dozen	2. 00d
7th	Small Do	5. 00d
8th	Bark, per boll	5. 00d
9th	Each beef that Comes to the Css	5. 00d
10th	Each mutton	6d
11th	Each pork	6d
12th	Each Double Stone butter & Cheese	5. 00d
13th	Each point of oyll of Export	4d
14th	Ships in Staxigo or Wick, Each tun is	8d
15th	Each boat for Ankerage	3. 04d
16th	Each yeard of Cloath wooling or linning	4d
17th	Each pound of wooll	4d
18th	Each boll of meall that comes to the meall house	-
_	for seall or Shypt on the shore by ane unfreeman	5. 00d
19th	Each hyde to ane freeman	4d
20th	To each Stone of tallow to ane unfreeman	1. 00d
21st	Each last of beef to ane unfreeman	10.00d
22nd	Each Brewer that brews for Each Browst	1.00d
23rd	Each Ancker of Aquivity sold in the Burgh	3.04d
24th	Each pair of Cairt wheels landed in Wick & Staxigoe	1.00d
25th	Each Mill Stone landed at Wick or Staxigoe	2.00d
26th	Each Grave Stone landed at Eyr. places	1.00d
27th	To Each boat load with fire stone left to the	
	Shoarmasters Discretion In proportione to	
	the Lastage or fraught to be paid.	

The above *"Customes"* levies were not collected by the Council, but were annually rouped to the highest bidder, who then had the right to collect the dues and, if possible, to make a profit on his bargain. This was a different Customes from the ones where we had the officers of Excise appointed under the Crown, and whose activities are not referred to in the Records other than their occasional fights or witnessing same, particularly Walter Dalrymple and John Hall in 1666, sometimes called *"tydewaiters"*. Their most likely work would have been against smugglers of whisky, both imported and exported from the illicit stills in the heather hills, some of them reputed to be still there!, brandy, wines, silks and satins and other prohibited or taxable goods, and against weapons of war being illegally taken into the Country. No doubt there were many other contraband articles in their remit. The Customes we are looking at were the ones used by Town or Burgh for local usage, and were levied on much of the tradeable produce comeing to the Toun, either inward or outward.

The above list we may comment upon in order given:-

"*Victuall*":- This was food but particularly grain or meal with which the farmers of those days paid their rent in the first instance, and traded with any surplus for cash. Yields were very low indeed compared to 1997, measured in relation to seed sown as "*to the thrid pickle*" in the case of oats, and to the "*fourt*" pickle in the case of bear. "*Victuall*" was also the measure of "*sallary*" for both Minister and Schoolmaster, and continued until comparitively recently in farm workers wages, 6 Bolls of meal a year, 3 each of bere and oat being the yearly amount for a married man. A woman servant got half that. A "*Chalder*" of bere was just over two tons.

"*Double Trees*" and "*Single Trees*":- Obviously timber of differing sizes but as "*Couple legs*" are mentioned below it would appear that the trees above were just that, trunks of wood which could be put to whatever use and cut the owner wished. I do not understand why Double were at 2/- a dozen and single at 5/- a dozen. Did the writer transpose in error?

"*Birks*":- Good old Scots word for birch, a traditional Scottish timber now much loved by conservationists but of little real timber value, giving nevertheless a rather nice, smooth, clean wood. Large birch timber is hard to find now. Possibly used in 1750 for smaller houses or cottages of a cheaper style or cross members between stouter couple legs.

"*Dealls*":- Sawn boards or planks of timber usually imported from Norway and appearing often in old Orkney records of 1600 in shipping manifests. Grain, tallow, hides, were exported to Bergen, a busy Hanseatic League port in Norway with a 1650 population of around 15,000. The ships then went north to Alesund or Kristiansund or South to Haugesund or Stavanger to the woods to pick up and load their return cargo of timber for Wick, Thurso or Kirkwall.

"Couple leags." :- Large or small, used for roofs and a term still with us. They would appear to be already dressed to size before coming across the Shoar of Weik. Again, as large were at 2/-d a dozen and small at 5/-d a dozen, which seems nonsensical, perhaps our Clerk transposed the Customes. It would be always better to import already cut and dressed timber for reasons of space onboard ship.

"Bark" :- Measured per boll, a quantity measure. Used probably in large quantity to cure hides and skins into leather, and the boiled liquor of which was used to preserve herring nets and no doubt ropes made of flax or hemp. "Barking" the herring nets from the fishing drifters of my Stronsay days was one of the activities I remember.

Each *"Beef"*, *"mutton"*, *"pork"*:- Cattle, sheep and pigs taken to town for killing and salting down and barrelling at the Shoar of Weik. Still the product of Caithness farms but preserved in different manner.

"Butter and cheese.":- Again, farm products, but little produced now in Caithness. Very marketable in former days, though the quality was probably less than our Environmental Health friends would find acceptable.

"Oyll" :- Paid Customes Dues if exported but if sold locally in Weik it carried no duty. Sources were various, melted down from whales if any came ashore, or harpooned at sea if they could, from seals if they could be caught, from sea birds young and old off the cliffs of Caithness and from fish livers, particularly cod.

"Shipping":- Using the ports and paying according to the tun. There must have been a rough and ready measurement used for that purpose.

"Ankrage":- A lesser charge for anchoring a ship in the Roads of Weik.

"Cloath, woolling or linning.":- The product of weaving but could be imported or exported. Freswick in particular grew flax or "lint".

"Pound of Wooll.":- Self evident.

"Boll of Meall." :- Either for export or home use. Unfreemen obviously paid the Custome dues so suggests that freemen traded in meall free of charge.

"Hydes" :- Presumably cattle hides rather than sheep skin which was too thin to make durable leather. Sheep skins would have been fairly scarce in those pre clearance days in Caithness and were probably mostly cured as sheep skins rather than as leather, used on the linoleum floors of many a bedroom until short years ago! The glovers of Weik would have used sheep skin leather.

"Tallow" :- In the Caithness Valuation of 1701 Wick pays feu duty tallow of ten stone valued at 4 merks [£2.13.4d.] per stone. Looks like a valuable byproduct of killing cattle and, when sold to an unfreeman, paid Customes.

"Each last of beef.":- Quite a weight and quite a price. One of the main exports of Weik. A *"last"* was about 1.5 tons, approx. twenty barrels of salt beef.

"A Brewer for each Broust.":- Just a small charge on drinking. Unfortunately it set a precedent which every Government since then has extended.

"Aquivity.":- Whisky, surprisingly. Sold in the burgh in a small barrel called an anker. When they asked you in Weik in 1766 would you like a dram they meant it, hence the phrase *"no half measures."*

"Cairt wheels.":- Could have been for cart or carriage. Contrary to popular myth that Caithness had no carts until 1800 I have a map of Castlehill of 1778 showing carts as small vignettes. John and James Donaldson, wrights in Weik in 1660, without doubt could have made you one.

"Mill stones":- Landed at Weik but heavy things to carry. There was but lately a mill stone quarry, or *"quarrell"*, at Dunnet Head, or rather Dwarwick, still with unfinished stones lying there. Transporting the mill stone by sea to Weik would have been sensible enough.

"Grave stones.":- Usually sandstone and, if of 1766, then some surviving specimens still to be seen as flat and readable stones in the Kirkyard at the Parish Kirk of Weik. Canisbay also has a goodly share. Quite possibly some of those still existing paid Customes at the Shoar. I do not know their source but there is an old sandstone quarry at Sandside Bay below Isauld. Any offers? Or more likely Dwarwick Head at Dunnet.

"Firestone.":- Some would have it freestone as a safer reading of the old word but it is *"firestone"*, which was a very soft and

easily worked sandstone. Whether *"firestone"* eventually became called *"freestone"* I am not too concerned. Some of the harder specimens are anything but free as a dirling hand from hammer and chisel has told many a mason. Firestone was used for just that, building the jambs of a fireplace where Caithness flagstone would split with the heat after but a short time. The lintel above the fire place was usually a large slab of flagstone but set vertically giving a good space behind for the chimney to *"draw"*.

Of quantities we have no knowledge but the trade was constant. Of shipping we know but little but Thurso had two vessels of 30 tons burden in 1656. Wick is credited with none. The Thurso vessels were above average and a more common size for the time was about twenty tons. Some of these were half decked but little detail available. They did, however, cross the North Sea to Norway and as far as Danzig in the Baltic.

Hamburg, Amsterdam, London, Ipswich, Leith, Glasgow, were among their ports of call. Never let it be said that the North was isolated from the main stream of National life.

May we quote again from Aeneas Bayne's Survey of 1735:-

*"***TRADE.*** Having thus briefly spoken of the severall parishes, we shall now say something as to the Trade of the Shire.*

"The Trade of export of the Shire of Caithness consists mostly in Corns, wherof they export in any good year 16,000 Bolls, at the Ports of Thurso, viz:Scrabster Road, a small way West of the Town , and at the River mouth [Thurso], and at Staxigoe Harbour near the Town of Wick, half meal, half bear. They likewise transport a great deal of victuall to Strathnaver in Sutherland, Inverness and Ross. It is remarkable that no grain agrees so well with the soil & Climate of Caithness as common bear & small oats, which last readily yields half meal, so that a Boll of this oats, when milled and fanned, will produce half Boll of meal & sometimes more at 9 stone weight pr Boll. The victuall is commomly bought by merchants at Edinr. and sent to Norway, or to the West of Scotland, and sometimes purchased by their own merchants who carry it to Norway & oyr places beyond sea, and have bounty money allowed by Act of Parliament for Encourageing the Exportation of Corns which is 20 pence pr Boll for bear or meall, and in return they carry home wines, Iron, Dales, fir trees & other small Timber for the use of the Countrey as they can best dispose of it. They likewise drive considerable trade with Leith by Exportation of

Tallow, barrelled Beef, pork, Hams, Geese, Skins & Hides, feathers, calf skins & oil, etc. There was once a considerable fishing on the Coast of Caithness which is now in great measure decayed for want of suitable Encouragement.

"I have spoke already of their Several pretty salmond fishings, Herring are rarely had on the Coast, they send great quantities of Excellent Butter and Cheese to other Countries yearly and severall parcells of Black Cattle to the South of Scotland and England. As to their Imports, they have some quantities of Wines from Burdaux, Lisbon, etc. Some commodities from Norway & Holland. Some from London but more from Leith and Glasgow. The merchants furnish the Countrey very well with Iron, Salt and other gross wares. Besides, there are Severall Itinerant petty Traffickers & Hawkers frequenting the severall fairs, which makes the Countrey well furnished with other small necessaries. There is a fishery still encouraged by the Tralls of Dunbar at Clyth & Wick."

So even in 1735 we had subsidies for the *"fairmers!"*

— Chapter 26 —

Town Accounts of Weik in 1660

Accounts of the Burgh of Weik in 1660, or slightly later, were more than simple, they were almost nonexistent. No banks in those days, so any money available was set out in the hands of various credit worthy people who were responsible for the principal and for the accrued interest when called upon to produce the same by the Counsell.

The Tolbooth was in perpetual deficit and the cost of keeping a prisoner was met either by the prisoner him or herself, or by the person who had incarcerated him, or her, for whatever reason. This was called *"aliment"* and there were cases when the *"persuer"* would not pay any further aliment so the prisoner was accordingly released. No charge on the taxpayer.

On the 30th September, 1741, the Counsell considered that there had been no regulation of jailer fees or Tolbooth maills [rents] from any person confined within the prison of the Burgh, nor any regular application of the same. They were probably fed and watered by their friends. It was therefore enacted that in future any prisoner of Good Condition, i.e. a small bit of wealth, should pay six shillings eight pence Scots [half a mark] each twenty four hours inside. If of *"Lower Circumstances"* then they had to pay *"three shillings and four penys"* per diem. This had to be paid before such prisoner was set at liberty, and to the treasurer of the Burgh, – *"To be furthcoming for the behoof of the burgh In defraying the Expense of repairs upon the prisone, and paying the jaylor and keeper of the prisone and paying his fees, Which is herby Declared to be one third part of the money soe to be paid in."*

The same day *"The provost & baillies, Considereing that the Town Clerks yearly Salary being twelve pounds Scots is not adequate to his trouble, Therfor they have Enacted & herby Enact that the towne Clerk's*

Salary in time Comeing be twenty four pounds Scots money yearly,
and ordaine the treasurer of the burgh to make payment of the Same
yearly to the town Clerk for the time being out of the resources of the
town, and ordaines him to have twenty four pounds for the past year."

So the Toun Clerk got a rise in pay.

Still on the problems of the jailers of the Tolbooth of Weik, on 17th September, 1755, there was another record relating to the escape, or *"elopement"*, of David Campbell, prisoner there. Three persons were to blame, and for each of them a cautioner had to stand security in £100 Scots if they did not appear when called to answer to the charges.

In the first William Anderson, merchant, stood cautioner for Robert Craige, late post in Wick, accused of neglect or being an accessory to David Campbell's elopement. *"Late post"* appears to be just that, the Weik postman of those days. Next was James Miller, merchant also, standing cautioner for Alex Bremner, pensioner in Wick. Pensioner only referred to anyone who had been formerly in the armed forces, army most likely, so Bremner had served his time or been invalided out, and received a small pension from a grateful government for his service. We came across a few others.

William Anderson again stands cautioner for a third culprit, Donald Lyall, Couper in Wick & town Jayllor.

I did not come across what David Campbell had done nor his eventual fate, but this does occur at times where an entry leaves one in limbo regarding the final solution. Possibly they never caught up with him.

David Campbell did leave a splash on the calm surface of the Burgh's affairs because on the 2nd February, 1756, following his escape, the Counsell considered the neglect and omissions of the Touns office and took steps to correct it, or to have a monetory fall back on to Cautioners.

Referring to David Campbell's elopement, they required that cautioners be found for Donald Durren, elder, Toun officer, and Donald Durren, procurator fiscall, for their good behavour, fidelity and watchfulness in time to come. The Durrens had to find cautioners before they left the Barr of the Tolbooth under the penalty of twenty pounds Scots "per peice".

They found James Miller, merchant in Wick, who enacted himself as Caur: for Donald Durren, Junr, and Alexr Durren, shoemaker in Wick, enacted himself for Donald Durren, Senr. in terms of the Enactment signed by the magistrates. Witnesses then signed the principal copy and the Caurs. signed their hands at Wick the second day of February, 1756.

One Donald signed with his mark, "D.D.", and the other Donald his own signature, presumably the younger though not stated.

In Wick, 14th April 1756, the magistrates and Town Counsell of the burgh of Wick considered the need for repairing of the street of Wick, which had to be the High Street, running from the Parish Kirk to the Shoar. They nominated and appointed John and William Andersone, merchants in Wick, to be stent masters on those inhabitants who had been warned several times by the towns officers. The inhabitants apparently ignored the requirement of the Counsell to repair the street themselves, presumably being liable for the portion each had adjacent to their shop or house, usually the same building and still well known as *"living above the shop"*. Indeed did not a very recent Prime Minister do likewise! Probably a Weik connection!

The Andersons accepted the duty of stentmasters for the repairs.

In 1755 we come across a Counsell Meeting where *"John Sutherland, merchant in Wick and late treasurer of the said Burgh, presented a Copie of ane accot Current for ther approval, ane Copie of which is as follows, To Witt:*

[Two pages of accounts, left side Dr. right side Cr.]

"The magistrates of Wick there Accot Current wt John Sutherland, there treasurer."

This looks like John Sutherland squareing the books on demitting the office of treasurer and getting the Counsell's final discharge for his transactions, sometimes called intromissions.

The accounts below tell us at least something about the Burgh's finances, though we have already mentioned the new school at the Shoar of Weik and the repairs to the rings and polls in the harbours of Weik and Staxigoe. Although not so stated in the Accounts, I am quite certain that they are expressed in Sterling rather than in Scots money. In 1741 the Clerk was to have a pay rise to 24 pounds Scots but below in the Accounts it is £2.10/for Clerk and Officers Fees, which equates with

conversion to Sterling at approx 12 Scots to £1 Sterling. Perhaps
after 1745 official accounts became more Anglised, though the
mix of Scots and Sterling continued for quite some time.

"1748: [page 1 on left hand side.]   *Dr.*

To Cash Pd. for mending the lock of old	
door of the Tolbooth	*£-.03.00*
To do/ to a man to Winn Slate	*-.04.06*
To flooring flags for the Tolbooth	*-.05.00*
To Laying with sand & Carriage	*-.03.06*
To Bigging holes above the window	*-.02.06*
To Dozin Crown glass	*-.01.00*
To Mending the Bridge	*-.03.00*
To Clerk & offrs fees for 1748	*2.10.00*
To do/ for 1750	*2.10.00*
To do/ for 1751	*2.10.00*
To do/ for 1752	*2.10.00*
To Wm Anderson Bill Given up	*3.00.00*
To James Calder do/ given up	*3.02.06*
To Ball: of Geo: Suth'ds do/ given up	*-.10.00*
To Cash Laid out on the Schoolhouse	
as per Particular accot	*9.04.01*
To George Horn for naills given	*-.07.06*
To Don'd Durran for Slating the back Part	
of the Tolbooth	*1.11.01*
To John Anderson's Bills given up	*7.15.00*
	£36.12.08

*Both parties having Perused there Accompt of the Same &
Mutually Discharged each other of all Preceeding this fourteenth Day
of February One thousand seven hundred & fifty five years.*
Wick February 14th 1754. Errors Excepted.

PATRICK HILL

*NB. I owe Twenty Bolls Lime to be used
for the schoolhouse. Jno SUTHERLAND*
*GEORGE SUTHERLAND
Jno SUTHERLAND.*

[page 2 on the right hand page.]

1748 Feb: 2nd   Cr.

By Two accepted Bills of Wm Anderson for the
    Customes paybll at Lammas 1748 & Candlemass
    1749   £5.00.00
[Note that Lammas 1749 is missing, see below.]
1750 feb: 2nd By James Calders Bill for do. Paybll
    of termes 1750 & 1751   6.05.00
1751 feb: 3rd By William Andersons Bill forsd of
    Paybll of termes 1751 & 1752   6.00.00
1752 feb: 3 By George Sutherlands do/ of for do
    Paybll said termes 1752 & 1753   4.10.00
1753 feb: 2 By John Anderson do/ for do/
    Paybll Sd terme 1753 & 1754   7.15.00
By Ball: due John Sutherland for which the
Baillies have given an Order on James Sutherland
    their Present Theasurer Paybll by equall
    moyeties at Lammasmas & Candlemass 1756.   <u>£7.02.08</u>
                                                        <u>£36.12.08</u>

On the income side above we have entirely the monies
coming in for the Customs and no other Income, not much to
run the Toun accounts. The year of 1749 was set to Wm
Andersone at £4.5/- but is not entered and we do not know
where that money went. Possibly quite properly spent on something else but should have been in the accounts. Each year the
bid was a "crown" more than the amount shown in the accounts
except 1750 when the amount was £6.5/-. Possibly a mistake.
In all other years and according to the articles of the Roup, a
Crown was to be taken off the first of the Customes *"for a treate"*,
and indeed was as per accounts. The *"treate"* was quite
blatantly for a booze up for the Counsellers at the taxpayers
expense, covered up as *"administration expenses"*.

A great tradition nonetheless. Does it still go on?

On the expenses of the Counsell out of that meagre income
we have at least part payment for the new School on the Shoar
of Weik of £9.4.1d, which again has to be in Sterling but it does
not say to whom, so we do not know the name of the Contractor,

and a further reference by John Sutherland to owing 20 bolls of Lime to be used for the Schoolhouse, presumably for mixing mortar rather than whitewashing the exterior. Perhaps Sutherland was the contractor but equally he could have been a merchant supplying materials. It would appear that the schoolhouse was not yet built, or at least not yet finished. This is consistant with Robert Smith, schoolmaster, on the 1st June, 1754, offering to *"repair"* the schoolhouse, i.e. to finish the building of the new school in my interpretation. That is certainly the largest amount in the expenditure above. The accounts of the various persons are not detailed so we do not know what work or services they represent. John Anderson's Bill at £7.15.00d is a major sum, it must have represented some major construction work. As John Anderson was involved with the repairs of the Harbours of Weik and Staxigoe, and as the amount of money is reasonably near what was quoted for that work, I would stick my neck out and say that was the work he did.

There was also a reference in 1751 to *"Old Tolbooth"* but I do not think a new one was built. The Counsell Record of 1739 to 1771 in the Archives in Weik was certainly taken apart at some time, or fell apart, and was rebound with pages out of sequence and with a possibility of missing pages, or else the possiblity that the still missing Record between 1711 and 1739 has reference to a new Tolbooth to be built. There is no evidence of that to my present knowledge. What is in the Records is a sale, on 30th September, 1751, of several parts of the Old Tolbooth to some obvious friends of George Sinclair of Ulbster There is the missing Record Book which might have given a clue, or possibly there was an even more ancient Tolbooth than the one which features so much in the Records and to which we do have access. The answer is not yet available. So I do not think Anderson's account can be for anything other than the harbour repairs.

A small amount of 3/- was spent on repairs to the Bridge. The clerk and officer fees were paid at £2/10/- per annum, but again a mystery around 1749 when no payment itemised. Could have been a set off with some other small expenditures, a balance of the Customes of that year of £1.15/- after paying the fees.

The other expenses were solely on the Tolbooth, repairs by their size. The lock and old door were repaired for 3/-. flooring flags purchased for 5/-, laying the flags with sand and carriage cost 3/6d. For the uninitiated laying flagstones on a floor by bedding them on dry and loose sand was an art form in itself. It still is, and the Flagstones Restaurant at the Tech College in Thurso is a modern example of an old Caithness Craft. A man to "winn" slate" at 4/6d, Donald Durren for slating the back part of the Tolbooth at £1.11.1d, naills from George Horn at 7/6d, are consistent with a reroofing job. Building up the holes above the windows at 2/6d and the purchase of a Dozen Crown glass at 1/- looks like window panes. A glazier appears somewhere in the Records.

And that in 1750 was the extent of the Toun Accounts of Weik!

— Chapter 27 —

Brotherly Love in Weik in 1660

Brotherly love and friendship did not always hold sway in the Weik of 1660, nor sisterly, nor paternal either. On the 25th August, 1662, Marion Smithe, spous to James Donaldson, wricht, brother of John Donaldson whom we have already met, along with her daughter Cristane, were accused for the most unnatural abusing of James Donaldson, he being clothed *"onlie naiked in his sark."*

Fairly difficult to protect oneself in those circumstances and, save for the timely intervention of George Bruce, skiper, and Kathrein Sinclair, spous to Thomas Young, merchant, coming to the house presently, mother and daughter *"had almost strangled the said James."*

However, Marione, *"in Respect of hir povertie"*, was fined only £3 Scots. What her loving husband had done to deserve such treatment at the hands of wife and daughter was, unfortunately, not revealed to us.

Povertie appears to have been a hallmark of the Donaldson family as John on another previous occasion had been put in the stocks at the Croie due to his *"povertie and inability to pay a fyne."*

In another incident of family affection John Pruntoche got into trouble for coming to the house of his sister, Agnes Pruntoche and, without any legal order, throwing out of the house *"Sundrie Chystes"* without any warning or other justification. Their brother James must have been there at the time and John threw a stool at him, cutting his face and blooding him. When the matter came to Court on the 2nd May, 1665, Johne was lying sickly in his bed, to which fact Wm Sinclair, merchant, and Johne Cormok, weaver, gave testimonie. He was ordained to *"compeir the morne"*, the 3rd of May, to answer the charge.

Did not appear, though, therefore convicted of Contumacy and fined 50/- for that offence. He was also ordered *"nocht to Trowble or molest the forsaid hous of Agnes Pruntoche in Tyme Cming under the paine cnteinit in the Act of Pliament, and ordainit to be Sumondit to the morne for the Caiss abovewretin, and being Lallie warned, Called & nocht Compeirand, the sd Johne Pruntoche cnvict in cntumacy L./-. Inde bothe £5."*

John Pruntoche continued obdurate and there were many other incidents concerning him. However, in the matter of *"brotherly love"* he again appeared on the 10th October, 1661, in a Borrow Court held by Frances Mansonne and Allexr Cormok, Baillies. This time it was for *"the most unnatural aboosing of Euphane Doull, his mother, by casting hir uponn her awin fyre within hir Dwelling hous, and aboosing, Beiting and Striking of Agnes Pruntoche his sister, qlk being Complained uponn be the said Euphane Doull, and showing the Same to Frances Mansonne, Bailyie and George Bruce, skiper.*

"Compeirit Johne Pruntoche & Denyed the Lybell. James Watersonne, yonger, takes him to prove the same, qlk wes Refered to the witnessing of the said Frances Mansonne, Bailyie, George Bruce, Skiper, [our old friend!] and David Mowatt, Schomaker. The said personnes, uponn oathe being admited, deponed as followes, To witt: Frances Mansonne affirmed, as Lykwayes George Bruce, that the said Euphame Doull did honestlie Complaine to them anent the said cmitit, and that she did show them hir Cloithes quhilk wes Scorced & brunt uponn hir be the casting of hir in the fyre."

A fire in those houses of 1660 would almost certainly have been of peat, would most probably have been in the centre of the room, either against a flagstone back or a small stone built wall, with the smoke finding it's way out through a hole in the possibly thatched roof rather than a more modern fireplace with a chimney in a gable end or interior built wall. It would have been all too easy to fall into a fire so placed if helped by a loving son! This was not by any means the only reference in the Counsell Book to such a misadventure.

But Euphane Doull had a neighbour, i.e. David Mowat. He deponed that *"Imediatelie efter the casting of hir in the said fyre, and he, being nearest neighbor Richt doore to door, that she Callitt upon and did show him the forsaid Clothes as they wer Scorced & Brunt, And thairfor the forsaids Bailyies, for the said unnaturall sin, cnvicts the said Johne Pruntoche in ane unlaw of £50 Scots money for the quhilk, and finding Cautionn to pay the Same, he was areistit within the Tolboothe of the said Burghe."*

"Quairuponn followed that the said Johne Pruntoche did most baislie and cntrair to the Lawes of this Kingdom, abooss the abovewretin Bailyies withe his viperous tonge, nocht wurthie to be exprest, and thairfor he was cnvict in ane unlaw of £40." Quite a heavy fine.

So he could not keep his mouth shut to the Baillies, and he therefore paid for it.

On 25th August, 1665, William Petrie, schomaker, was accused for the blooding of Dod Petrie his brother, *"which being refered to the said Dod his aithe of veritie, Deponed that the said Wm, giveing ane blow to him and, he making to Eshew the same, he did fall uponn ane Deall [beam of timber] lyand by qrthrow he receavitt sum Blood uponne his lege, and thairfor the Judges, withe advyis of the Counsell cnveined for the Tyme, fynes & cnvicts the said Wm Petrie in £5 Scots money."*

Does not sound too severe a case but appealed to the Court all the same.

On the 18th day of Apryll, 1707, a Court was held by Wm Mullikin & Wm Murray, Bailyies yrof, & *"remanent members of Court"*, to consider the case of Muriall Mckurchie in Wick & Margaret Smith her mother. Both were *"Indytit and accused for comeing to the dwelling house of Alexr Horne and charged with the violent beating, blooding, Rugging & ryveing of Ann Suyrland, spous to the sd Alexr Horne And scolding & abusing her in her good name & reputatione qlk you cannot deny. Compeired both the Defers & denyes. The fiscall offers to prove."*

"Marie Grant in Wick, being admitted witness, sworne, deponed yt Muriall Mckurchie cam in to Alex Horne's hous & did scold & abuss the said Ann Suyrland in calling her yt shee could say also much to her at schee wold say to her. [Takes a bit of working out,

doesnt it.] *And being seall tymes put to the door & the door shut, the said Muriall did cast in at the windowes seall peices of trees & oyr things which if not preventit might have done skeath [damage or harm] to the children & oyrs wtin the hous, And yt shee did see Margaret Smith offere to take off Ann Suyrlands clothes."*

Looks like a good going stushie developing!

"Barbara Manson, sworne, deponed ut supra. The Bailyes, considering the above deposone, fynes ilk ane of the defers in fyve lb Scots per piece And to be secured [imprisoned, normally in the Tolbooth] *qll peyt & to find Caution for yr civill deportment in tyme comeing, qron act."*

So in quite some detail we have a neighbourly chat between friends in Weik in 1707.

True to form, as in most cases in the old Record Book of Weik, we have counter charge to answer the first charge, and Ann Sutherland, the victim in her own house of the attack, was also:

"The sd Ann Suyrland, you ar Indytit & accused for the violent beatting, blooding & blaeing of the said Muriall Mckurchie with ane top tree on the back, & casting the said Margaret Smith in the gutter befor the door, qch you canot deny:"

I do not know what a *"top tree"* was but it sounds suitable for the task in hand. Possibly a branch or the thinner top end of a tree. I cannot think what use such might have been unless for firewood. This charge must have been laid by Muriall Mckurchie and her mother Margaret Smith in retaliation for being themselves charged. They could find no witnesses to corroborate their version of events so, for want of any probation [proof], Ann Sutherland was assoylied [cleared] of any blame.

Wick, 18th August, 1749. Compears Donald Oliphant, indweller there, and Enacts himself that John Sutherland, Shoemaker in Wick, shall not for the future disturb the peace of his wife by useing her bad, but doe her that justice that becomes ane Loveing wife, providing she allways demain herselff as becomes ane affectionate wife to a husband, and Craves that she may be heard upon his first Complaint and Enacts himself for the sum of fourty pounds Scots, the principall for the caur. relief.

Signed by both parties. JOHN SUTHERLAND,
DONALD OLIPHANT.

So wifebeating is nothing new, apparently.

On the 26th September the same year James Doull, elder, weaver, was accused *"for the violentt awaytaking without anie order of Law or Decreitt, of Thrie Longe Tries aff of the Scheip hous pertaining to Allexr Doull, weaver, his Brother, and thairefter the said Allexr in most humble manner did Intreat the said James Doull, his Brother, To restor back againe the said Tries without anie farder Trouble or questionn, Sieing it was notorlie known be all the nichtbores that the said Thrie Tries onlie did belonge to the said Allexr. Nevertheless the said James Doull did absolutely refoos bak the same bot most unnaturallie did aboos his said Elder Brother withe most odious and vyle Speiches nocht worthie to be exprest or put in wreitt. And thairfor the Bailyies fynes & Cnvictes the said James Doull in ane unlaw of £5 Scots , and iff ever he beis fund to Speak the Lyik words to his said Brother in Tyme Cmg, to pay Xlb. Toties quoties, qruponn act."*

Not that Caithness at that time was noted as a sheep county but it is apparent that sheep were kept indoors in a sheep house in the winter time, and quite possibly that they were milked in summer time for human consumption as well. Norway still has quite a sheep milk cheese industry and their goat milk cheese, or *"gamalost"*, though too strong a flavour for myself, is considered a delicacy. Therefore a sheep house would be a useful if not a necessary building.

Sheep were again the problem on 21st May, 1708, when Elspet Calder, spous to Donald Brebner, weaver in Wick, was *"indytit & accused for coming to the Barnyeards of Papigo belonging to Sir James Dunbar of Hempriggs, yonr, and at yor own hand wtout advyce, consent or witnes of any of the Srvants belonging to the said Sir James Dunbar, did violentlie & masterfullie break open his doors, (or) At least did oppen ym with ane uyr key not belonging to the lock of the sd door. And did carie away out of the sd houss se(ver)all sheep & oyr goods pundled for Eating of the corne belonging to the sd Sir James wtout any order or witness to yt effect. Therfor you ought & sould be punished according to the lawes & acts of pliat made anent breaking of pund hous & making use of falss Keyes."*

Elspet confessed to opening the Pund House without a *"pundler"* present. The *"Pund hous"* was for the old but not out of date right of a landowner or farmer or Town Council to impound, or *"pund"*, straying livestock against payment of damages, and the *"pundler"* was a man so employed. In this case Elspet's sheep had strayed onto Dunbar's corn. She must have been a resourceful girl. She appeared again in July, 1708, in another incident, along with Kathren Doull and with Marsall Bain for bashing up David Duncan, Chopman, on the King's High Street, and calling him a liar and cheating knave. Punishment was meted out but not recorded, referred to earlier. Marshall Bain was involved somewhat later still in June, 1710, with Agnes Roull and her depredations

A final episode regarding sheep, or rather sheep stealing. And as so many families either side of the Pentland Firth explain their presence with an *"uncan"* name on the *"wrong"* side of the Firth to the long gone folk lore sheep stealing of an ancestor, we may as well mention William Calum, fisher in Weik. On 2nd October, 1741, Calum was in Court charged with the theft of a sheep from out of the Cree of Robert Begg at the Head of Weik. A *"Cree"* was an old Caithness word for shelter or animal yard, sometimes spelt *"Crue"* or *"Cruive"*, even the Icelandic *"kro"*. Appears in Lincolnshire as *"Crewe yard"* for cattle, a loose yard or fold. Nordic word.

William had stolen the sheep during the night of the 4th September and killed it at the Mid Dick of the Park of Weik. A search made next day by Robert Winchester, one of the Baillies, and Donald Lyall, the fiscall, found the remains in Calum's house, the *"Head, feet, skin and four leages."* As any farmer knows, the skin is most important for identification as normally there is a farm mark of paint, or tar in days gone by, upon it.

Calum, confronted with this indisputable evidence, confessed in Court on the 2nd October, 1741. He was given a choice, either face a Criminal prosecution for the *"cryme of theft"*, with the hazard and possibility of hanging, or be liberated from his imprisonment in the Hole under the Cross of Weik, no doubt rather more noisome than the Tolbooth, on condition that he became the hangman for Weik and for the Shyre of Caithness, under the authority of the Magistates or of the Sheriff of Caithness or his Deputy.

As George Sinclair of Ulbster was both Provest of Weik and Sheriff of the County, it does not seem to be much of a difference. Really an offer Calum could not refuse, in the circumstances, so he bound and obliged himself to that duty. Oddly I found no reference to any hangings whatever in the records so far studied, whether the mere threat was sufficient or not I cannot tell. One man was banished from the County on pain that if he ever returned and was apprehended, he would underly the possiblity of death.

Earlier in the Weik Records than William Calum, on 13th August, 1675, we had another hangman appointed, Donald Harald. In obedience to the Sheriff of Caithness he became enacted to exercise the office of an executioner within the Burgh of Weik and the Shyre of Caithness during his lyfetyme. If he did not exercise his office *"Lallie and Legallie"*, his own life was to be in the Sheriffs will. Looked like a permanent appointment with certain risks! Judged from Calum's case with the sheep, I think Harald probably was also in trouble, and that this was a standard method of finding a hangman.

Makes a change from probation!

— Chapter 28 —

Cromwell in Cannesbey.
1652 - 1655

Of course everyone in Orkney and Caithness knows about Cromwell and the presence of his soldiers in Cannesbey and in Kirkwall in the 1650s, of the legend that their horses were stabled in the Cannesbey Kirk, his men quartered on the locals. Everyone knows what they were doing in Cannesbey, or do they? Who were Thomas Carre, John Clegge, John Gudelad, James McConile, Glengarrie, Lt.Roy. What trace still exists of their presence after some 340 years, if indeed any at all? They have been referred to previously in Chapter 3, "Visitors to the Parish", but I thought a wider view would be worth doing.

Well, there is Cromwell's Brig lying in the lee of Houston's John O' Groat's Mill, easily seen and many times painted by budding artists. And not very much else.

Having studied somewhat the presence and names of Cromwell's men in Orkney from 1652 to 1663, some 110 recorded in the Christenings and Marriages by Thomas Dischingtoune, the Praecentor and keeper of the Session Records in Kirkwall, I took a thought as to whether they were recorded in Caithness to any extent. There just HAD to be a reason for their presence in Cannesbey for some 4 years, and the peaceable parishioners of Cannesbey did not require the presence of "Inglish" troops to keep order in that most distant of Parishes.

Therefore a look at the map of Caithness was indicated, and indeed that of Scotland, plus a quick look at the history of the times. The Scots were creating trouble, again!, and Montrose had invaded Scotland from Denmark via Orkney and Sannick Bay to meet disaster at Corbiesdale in April, 1650, his later death by execution after betrayal, capture and trial.

It would have been on Cromwell's mind that Scotland needed some form of *"protection"* and so his troops proceeded Northwards, leaving Aberdeen early in 1652 and being recorded in the Session Records of Cannesbey on the 24th March of that year. They were still getting a mention in late 1655 so they were there, off or on, for at least 4 years.

So what did they do to keep them in order and under discipline, other than the normal pursuits of the *"licentious soldiery"*. Road making was always the order of the day, and bridge building was but a part of that. Sannick Bay was only a few miles to the east of Cannesbey so a goodish or at least passable road along the coast would have been a strategic requirement, including Cromwell's Brig at the Mill, for the movement of guns. But what else? and why?

The main base of Cromwell's men was said to be Ackergill Tower and again a glance at the map of Caithness shows that Ackergill covered Sinclair's Bay. Cannesbey covered Sannick Bay to the East of John O'Groats in Dungasbey and, more particularly, Gills Bay at Cannesbey itself. A detachment of men quartered at Freswick Castle, or House, though the present one was not yet built, would cover Freswick Sands.

These were the days of sailing ships dependent on wind and tide and Gills Bay was a lee in which to shelter, waiting for the Eastbound flood to change to the Westbound ebb and permit a passage through the Pentland Firth to the West past Dunnet Head, or to shelter in Gills Bay from the all too prevailing West wind against which sailing ships could make but little headway, and, against an East going flood tide, none at all.

So where better than Cannesbey to place some troops to either prevent another invasion or landing such as Montrose's recent debacle, or to prevent the French and Dutch, with whom Cromwell was having trouble, from either landing at Gills Bay or using it by privateers [authorised pirates!] for shelter against the elements.

Having worked all that out, I thought there should therfore be some defensive or offensive works at Cannesbey, if they could be found, justifying the expense of Cromwell keeping troops so far North, though the expense must have been minimal judged by the small payments made by the Session now and again to *"a poor soldier."* A glance at the map indicated a look at the Ness of Quoys as the most strategic point covering the Eastern approaches to Gills Bay, menacing the channel between Stroma and the Mainland, and giving a reason for soldiers being in Cannesbey.

Sailing ships would have had to tack back and forth to make a passage against a West wind and each successive tack would have brought the ship close enough to the Ness of Quoys to be within range of any cannon available, even if their range did not cover all the distance to Stroma. The threat of even one lucky shot dismasting a ship would have greatly deterred in these fiercely tidal streams.

I had previously seen a gun emplacement in Orkney at the Ness of Tankerness covering the entrance to Deer Sound, locally credited to Cromwell, with a very ancient cannon of antique construction still there in situ, of length some 7 feet, of bore some 3.5 inches. There had been at least three known cannon at that site, one is now used as a bollard on a pier at Tankerness House, one is known to be just under the sand on the beach where it ended up while being transported to the same pier from the Ness. Protecting the battery site to seaward was a substantial embankment. The presence of that battery suggested defensive requirements by Cromwell's men against invaders, and Deer Sound was until very recent years an acknowledged shelter and anchorage, with a history of convoy collection during the Napoleonic Wars, and more recent usage in modern times.

So I thought a visit to Cannesbey might bring dividends, and there I went one sunny Sabbath. My calculation was that I should find some trace of a similar construction to that on the Ness of Tankerness, covering the water towards Stroma and the entrance to Gills Bay. Bear in mind that many of the soldiers mentioned as being in Kirkwall in the 1650s were classed as *"gunner"* and one as *"Master Gunner"*.

And there it was, on the shore at the point of the Ness of Quoys, the very visible trace of a rectangular construction, heavily walled on the seaward side, medium walls to either side and a lighter wall to landward. The surface was level and was underlain with stone but a few inches down, giving the lie to the local suggestion that it was a plantie cru for the growing of cabbages. Anyway whoever would grow cabbages with sea spray coming over on the point of the Ness would deserve to win the local Seed and Root show. The beach was composed of very good stone boulders easy to build and a gun emplacement of this nature would have had turf and earth banking on the danger side, i.e. the sea. Some 50 metres to the East was another construction which would have done excellently as a magazine for the storage of gunpowder, again heavily walled to seaward and out of line of shot directed towards the gun battery. Again, the broadside cannon of most men of war did not have any great range, being designed for smashing a ship close alongside with heavy cannonballs, some made even of stone. The guns for long range firing were normally placed on the bow or stern of these Men of War, a different type of gun altogether and designed for dismasting in pursuit or retreat rather than smashing power.

The surviving walls are admittedly very low but after all the passing years would one have expected more. They are still very well defined. From that site cannon could have covered any approach from the East and it would have been most unwise to try sheltering in Gills Bay. No excavation was attempted, nor would there be without permission, but I would have liked to try a metal detector over the site. Who knows if the odd cannon ball might not still be there!

I must say this find was very satisfactory as I had calculated on it's being there and was not trying to explain something which I had already seen or found. And there it was.

But a wider view of Caithness at that time was indicated so I looked again at the map of the County. Within Canisbay Parish the other possible landing beaches were Sannick Bay of Montrose fame and round Duncansbay the Bay of Freswick. Sannick may well have been of value to small boats from Orkney which could run up onto the beach to off load but the Bay itself is not sheltered from the tide and a foreign ship trying to land men and guns by small boats would find it very inconvenient. Further search round that shore found no trace of anything resembling a gun emplacement. I wrote Sannick off.

The only other beaches of landing capability on the East of Caithness are Freswick and Sinclair Bay, and I have no knowledge or suggestion relating to that save one. There was in the Cannesbay Session Records in 1655 a Capt. Wood in Freswick who had a chyld "libbed" by a local witch, a "*libbe*" being a spell spoken over someone unwell. The Record stated on the 23rd May, 1655 :

"Janet Groat delate to be a charmer & charged, called, compeired, who, being desyred, did say ye words used in ye LEBBE forespokin as follows:

"Bittin be they yt beatt; beatted be they at ye heart roole, yr tooth and yr toung, yr liver & yr lung, yr heart within yr breast. If it be a maiden, God give sche murne, if it be a wyff, God if sche spurne, if it be a kneave chylde, a scharpe sword to his breast bane till he turne his tounge again".

"Sche libbed ANDRO STEVIN in OKINGILL and Captaine WOOD's chyld in FRISWICK. This libbe is done with small salt.

After inquirie, ther being no more, etc. "

So we do not know if she was punished or no. As for the "*libbe*", it makes no more sense to me that I expect to any other reader. Still, that was the National Health Service of 1655. Perhaps it worked just as well! Small salt would have been fine ground table salt rather than coarse salt for fish or meat curing.

That one reference to Capt Wood was the only one I found mentioning him between 1652 and 1666, the name occuring but once. Was Capt Wood a Cromwellian soldier and was there another detachment, other than the one at Cannesbey, covering Freswick Bay from a possible landing from the Eastern Sea.

But if my ideas are correct, which of course they are!, then there should have been other signs of gun emplacements on the Caithness Coast other than at Cannesbey. Again, I expected to find such. At Freswick on the south side of the bay at Byke Yards there is another banking on the cliff edge which could have sheltered a gun or two. There is no other reason for that bank to seaward.

Back around the coast Harrow is another very good and remarkably sheltered possible landing. Perhaps it is not without significance that the more modern gun battery built there for training purposes in the later 1800s was constructed just where one would site a gun to protect the approaches, and its construction would have obliterated any previous emplacement. Further west is Dunnet Bay. On the Point of Ness at Dwarwick there is again a seaward embankment. Guns there would have precluded a landing on the beach within Dwarwick. But Dunnet Bay is quite a distance across, what of the Castletown shore?

The strategic promontary sticking out into the bay is quite obvious but guess what. There is another training gun battery built just where one would have sited cannon in 1650, the two embrasures pointing just west of Dunnet Head. That was as far West as I cared to go, Murkle Bay should have had a look, Thurso and Scrabster also. But to return to the East Coast I went to the North Head at Weik, still to me St Niniane's Head. Wonderful lookout point for Dutch shipping as we have already mentioned, both North and South. However, the ground has been absolutely messed up with various constructions over the years and there is no chance at all of finding any trace of a possible simple gun emplacement of 1650.

Now all this is long gone, perhaps my imagination was working overtime. The fact remains that Thomas Carre, John Clegge, John Gudlad, James McConile, and the others under the command of Lt Roy, probably Glengarrie, built the battery still to be found on the Ness of Quoys, Cannesbay, and the old bridge at the Mill of John O'Groats, leaving to themselves a lasting memorial still to be seen on the face of Caithness.

— Chapter 29 —

William Shakespeare visits Weik?

Among the half a million varied items of the Dunbar papers out of Ackergill Tower and now in the safe keeping of the Wick Society I was given one and challenged to read it, if I could. Two pages of old writing which I would hazard a guess by the style of writing at dating around early 1600, if not marginally before. Clearly enough written and well preserved except for the right hand edge which was slightly frayed. It was entitled:

"The Originall of the familie of Kilcowie, whyle Stuart."

I assume that the family of Kilcowie was a part of the genealogy of the Dunbars and I am NOT writing a history of that family, containing myself to the two old pages from the Ackergill papers. But for all that, the immediate impact was in the very first line and the very first paragraph, i.e.

"After the defeat & slaughter of the usurper Mackbeath, the death of Banquo & of his sone Fleanche, Walter, sone to the sd Fleanche begotten be him upon Wode, not only daughter but airess to the K: [king] of Wales as being his only child, and so the only airess of the Brittish blood, & who had never more children but this Walter. Which Walter, coming from Wales to Scotland, becam singularlie favoured to Walter Canmore, & was by him creat at the par: [parliament] of Forfar, Earle of Bute & Lord High Stewart of Scotland, whence it is sure the Sirnames are for all of his posteritie being called Stewart."

So began the House of Stewart.

I suppose that among the very best known of William Shakespeare's tragedies is Macbeth, and here in the very far North of Scotland in this Parish on the Pentland Firth was a reference on old paper and in old writing to the very facts on which he based his play. It is accepted that Shakespeare did not stick too closely to historical fact, unfortunately not unknown among so called historians even today, but still near enough.

So here in one paragraph was reference to Shakespeare's characters, to Macbeth, slain in 1057 at the Battle of Lumphanan in Aberdeenshire, to Banquo and his son Fleanche, to one of the Welsh Kings. It was some time later, 1284, that Edward 1st, Hammer of the Scots, extended English power over Wales, though running battles and revolts broke out there from time to time against English domination and arrogance, as in Scotland.

The reference to Walter Canmore is obscure as the records state that **Malcolm** Canmore succeeded Macbeth. A possible error in transcription of Walter above unless he answered to both names, or that he adopted the name of Malcolm as King, a not too unknown practice.

The old document went on with:

"In the 2nd generatene after this Walter, viz: a grandchild of his, receaves for patrimonie from the paternall familie of Bute a considerable portione of the Lands of Lorne, And so he & his familie downwards are called Stewarts of Lorne, Which familie of Stewart of Lorne, being in good accott In the days of K:J: the First [King James] of blissed memorie. The sd K: then maried the Duke of Summerseat's daughter, which Duke was the K: of England's sd broyr, and qn the sd K:J: of Scotland married her She was then representative airess of England, though it happened oyrways because her uncle the K: had afterwards children."

"This princess had manie children femeall, almost all matched to Kings, and on(e) sone, afterwards K:J: the 2nd, K:J: the first being murthered at Pearth by the contryvance of the Earle of Athole, his fayr broyr, & the Tutor of Strathern, who both was forfeited upon yt accot. Tho afterwards the Earle[dome] of Stratherne was regifted to the aires, the honours containing forfeit, The aire being created Earle of Monteith, and the Earledome of Athole was annexed to the Crowne."

King James the First was for many years a prisoner in London of Henry 1V of England, captured at the age of 12 by the English in 1406 on his way to France, lodged in the Tower of London which was then a Royal residence rather than a prison, learning there of his succession to the Scottish Crown in that year. He returned to Scotland from his captivity only in 1424. As stated previously he married the daughter of Henry's brother, the Duke of Sommerseat, and heiress of the English throne until Henry IV had family of his own. I am assuming that the marriage took place while James was still a prisoner in London, or at least an involuntary guest. A good Marriage of State between the English Crown and the King of Scotland and by no means the only one in History. Probably an early attempt to unite the Kingdoms by peaceful means and not by any chance the only such attempt.

The old document continues :

"In the meane whyle on(e) Sir James Stewart, creat Knight barronet be the French King for the notable vassalages done by him In that Kingdome, famous in our historie by the name of the Black Knight of Lorne as being the 2nd sone of the familie of Stewart of Lorne, this Sir James, coming from France, is fancied be the Queen Dowager & moyr to K:J: the 2nd, & is privatlie maried to her."

The Queen Dowager was that same daughter of the Duke of Somerseat who married King James the First. Interesting to find the word *"fancied"* used so long ago with unaltered meaning!

Service in foreign countries was not uncommon in those days, including in the year 1612 Col. George Sinclair, a natural son of David Sinclair of Stirkoke and his 900 mostly Caithness men, who were ambushed and annihilated by the Norwegians in the Pass of Kringalen in the Dovre Veld mountains in Norway on their way to service with the King of Sweden. The Douglases did similar service in Europe.

"The Queen Dowager proving wt child, The Counsell challenged the matter. But the Queen owning the mariage, the challenge ceased. Sir James had by her John the eldest & David, afterwards Bishop of Morray. This John, being broyr uterine to K.J. the 2nd & favoured by him, was by his Majestie creat Earle of Athol & gott the estate yrof from the K:, & is knowen to this day by the name of Old Jock of Athole."

"The K: married this his broyr uterine to the Lady Katharine Dowglase, only child to Dowglase the forfeit Earle of Morray, and gave him in tocher wt her the Lo: of Balvenie as being a pt of the sd Earl's her fayrs forfeitur upon this Lady Katharine Dowglase."

The Douglas family, descended from the famous Douglas of Bannockburn fame, had become very powerful landowners, mostly in the Borders and also in Morayshire, but were brought to heel, temporarily, by James II in 1455. The extent of the Lordship of Balvenie I do not know but Balvenie Castle is in Dufftown and there is a notable whisky distilled there. Dufftown is slightly inland from the other lands mentioned lying towards the coast but I think the totality of the lands of Balvenie would have run from Dufftown to the sea.

"The Old Jock of Athol begetts John who succeedit him in the Earldome of Athol, William, Lord Invermeith, & Robert, upon whom is bestowed the barronie of Leuchars, wt some oyr Lands ther which wer then a pt of the Earldome of Athole. This Robert Dyes Leaving behind him a sone named Henry, and I judge so called becaus the K: of England to qm they had ye honour to be so wer in blood. The Duke of Summerseat's daughter wes so often named."

The Leuchars above is land lying between Elgin and Lossiemouth, not the Leuchars in Fife.

"Whyle this Henry was a young man Mckulle of Lorne killed Stewart of Lorne & whyle in bodie persued the slaughter. This Henry persued it & outLawed McKulle & having desyred his two Cussens german, the Earle of Athole & the Lord Invermeith, to revenge the blood of the chief man of this familie of their Immediat descent, they ayr denyed or delayed. Wherupon he went wt some of his sudends [students?] which hazarded wt him to Lorne & killed McKulle & manie of his relatones, for qch vassalage K:J: the 4th then reigning made him Shreff of Banff & purpossed to have given him the Earldome & created him Earle of Rose."

King James IVth reigned from 1488 and was killed at Flodden in 1513, so we are dating the above slightly as we go on.

"But a vaine & selfish man, on(e) named Stuart, also then Bishop of Rose, opposed the matter, & so the K: gifted the sd Henrie the barronie of Kilcowie in armanoch, Also the Earle of Athole gave the sd Henrie the lands of Newtonne & divers oyr Lands in Balvenie In Duchus as it was then worded, And finallie after this Henrie begott

Henrie, he Robert, he Henrie againe, he Sr James, who would have been Earle of Rose be K:J: the 6th favour had he lived but sex weeks.

"*This Sr James had a broyr called ... Stuart of Newtoune whose Liniall heir Henrie Stewart of Towienovie is and yr being noe ishue of the sd Sr James Stuart, the sd Henrie Stewart of Towienovie is Lykewayes the sole Liniall heir of the honorable familie of Kilcowie.*"

The "*lands of Kilcowie*" is now Kilcoy in the Black Isle and "*armanoch*" is the old name for the South facing part of that same Black Isle, being Gaelic of "*ard*" meaning high ground and "*manoch*" meaning between or middle, i.e. the high ground between Inverness and Easter Ross. How it came to be called the Black Isle is not for me to sort out, there are many theories.

There is one "*Newtoune*" in the North facing part of the Black Isle, formerly called Cromartie Shire in the map drawn in the early 1600s by Timothy Pont, one time Minister of Dunnet. Other Newtons are two a penny, including around Lossiemouth.

"*Towienovie*" I will take a rain check on, it may be recognisable to a student of Scottish History, or perhaps someone more familiar with Dunbar history and genealogy than I. Suspect "*Towienovie*" lies in Morayshire but got a suggestion that it may lie as far as Aberdeenshire. "*Duchus*" became "*Duffus*".

The writing of this old record is close and similar to the Record Book of Wick Counsell of 1660, I would certainly not date it later and it is quite possibly a good bit earlier but not much before 1600. This of course is an amateur's guess. Shakespeare lived 1564 to 1616 so we are in the same period.

There is land called "*Lower Hempriggs*" to the East of the Findhorn Estuary towards Lossiemouth. Local Caithness folklore holds that the name of "*Hempriggs*" was so called because hemp or flax was grown there. There is still land called "*The Hempriggs*" at the North end of the sand beach in Freswick, facing South, and flax was very definitely grown and processed there, both on the land with Wm Cogill and his wife from Mey coming before the Kirk Session of Cannesbay for going to Freswick on a Sabbath in 1658 to see their "*lint*", and in mention of the "*Flax pools*" with lint belonging to Johne Warrs of Dungasbey being allegedly stolen out of the pools by Margaret Groat in October, 1653, also recorded in the Session Records of Canisbay.

The first reference I found to a Dunbar holding ground in Caithness was in Latheron Parish in the Valuations of Caithness of 1683 where he held land valued at £332 Scots and was designated *"Hempriggs"*. He also held lands at that date in Wick Parish of Stamster, a part of Noss, Gallowhill, Feallquoys, and four pennyland at Weik, valued at £533.06.08d Scots. The Dunbars had come to Caithness well before 1683.

It is a fact that a name often went with a man to some other location, witness George Sinclair taking the name of Barrock with him to Lyth when Sinclair of Rattar in approx 1678 redeemed the wadset George Sinclair held on the lands of Barrock, Dunnet. By that time George was known as George Sinclair of Barrock, which he never owned, and the name went with him to Lyth where he began buying land from the Bruces particularly, from Sinclair of Dun and from Sir William Dunbar. Barrock House and Barrock Mains continued his Barrock nomenclature though the Estate was entitled the Lyth Estate.

Similarly the Dunbar who first came to Caithness could well have been called Dunbar of Hempriggs from the lands in Morayshire, and the name coming with him to the lands he first purchased in Latheron in Caithness as a kind of pseudo title rather than being imposed on land growing hemp, or flax, near Wick, and a crop credited by folk lore to Dunbar.

What else there is in the Dunbar papers I cannot tell. The Dunbars were around Caithness for a long time. Do not take me too seriously when I suggest that perhaps William Shakespeare was a house guest of the Dunbars in Ackergill Tower!

Epilogue

Under the wide and starry sky,
Dig the grave and let me lie,
Glad did I live, and gladly die,
And I lay me down with a will.

This be the verse you carve for me,
"Here he lies where he longed to be,
Home is the sailor, home from the sea,
And the hunter home from the hill."

Robert Louis Stevenson wrote those timeless words as his own epitaph. They are graven on his tombstone on the hilltop where he lies on the Island of Samoa in the South Pacific and where he ended his all too brief life at the early age of 44.

I quote them as they seemed to be appropriate when applied to this Northern portion of Scotland, the wide and starry skies of both my native Orkney Islands and my domicile county of Caithness, to the hunter home from the hill, the sailor home from the sea. They are rather more than appropriate because R. L. Stevenson had the Lighthouse building traditions in these Northern waters of his great grandfather Thomas Smith, his Stevenson grand father and father, his uncles and cousins, all engaged in civil engineering projects with the Harbour at Wick, with lighthouses all around the Pentland Firth, lighthouses to guide the sailor through the tides and eddies and hazards of the Pentland. The stories I have tried to tell in this short book are also of the tides and eddies and hazards of life as lived on the shores of the Pentland Firth more than 300 years ago, by sailors home from the sea, by hunters home from the hill, all long gone.

Robert Louis Stevenson himself lived in Wick for a short time in his youth, describing it I believe as "The coldest place on Earth."

His "Treasure Island" was one of the very first books I remember reading as a small boy, certainly before I went to school. What boy has not fancied himself as "Jim Hawkins", some disliked uncle or schoolmaster in the role of "Long John Silver"? Did the land and the islands and the seas around the Pentland Firth colour Robert Stevenson's early life, a seed sown to grow into his love of adventure stories, a backdrop for his "Kidnapped"? In any case the lighthouse of Dunnet Head, featured on our cover and watching ceaselessly over that Pentland Firth, was built in 1831 by Robert Stevenson, grandfather of Robert Louis Stevenson. The family were inveterate lighthouse builders, starting with Thomas Smith building the two Pentland Skerries lighthouses in 1794, and, in the days before revolving lights, one to face East, one to face West. Thomas Smith married, in 1792 and third time round, Robert Stevenson's widowed mother and, in course of time, in 1799, Robert married Thomas Smith's daughter Jean by his first marriage. Robert had also earlier, in 1790, aged 19, entered Thomas Smith's business of lighthouse building as an apprentice, being associated with Smith in the construction of Start Point lighhouse in Sanday in Orkney in 1806. The Stevenson family, through three generations, went on to build the lights of Dunnet Head in 1831, Noss Head in 1849, Cantick Head in Hoy in 1858, Auskerry near Stronsay in 1867, Sule Skerry far out in the wild Atlantic to the West of Orkney in 1895, Stroma in 1896, Copinsay, farmed by my great great grandfather at one time, in 1915, Duncansby in 1924. The final lighthouse of the Firth was built as recently as 1958 at Strathy Point on the North Coast of Sutherland by P. H. Hislop.

Robert's simple verses are known world wide when perhaps their author is forgotten, at least as the writer of these lines. No matter, such is humanity.

But they do distil and can be applied to the haunting beauty of this Northern land and sea scape, the wide sweep of the skies, the far look round to distant horizons, the consciousness, one day one summer, when Nettie and I and my sister Anne and her husband Sandy Muir from New Zealand stood at the Lookout Point just above the Lighthouse on Dunnet Head, of the green fields and endless, heather-brown moors of Caithness stretching behind us to Morven and Scaraben to the South, to Ben Hope and Ben Loyal and Ben Arkle rising to the West, to

Cape Wrath jutting into the far sea beyond, the look across the Pentland Firth to the near distant cliffs and The Old Man and the Hills of Hoy, the sweep eastwards over the Orphir Hills of Orkney to Wideford Hill and the sharp spire of St Magnus in Kirkwall when, on a clear day, you can see forever.

Nearer, the entrance to Scapa Flow between Cantick Head in Hoy, with its lighthouse, and Hoxa Head in South Ronaldsay, further on to Swona, to Stroma, that Isle of my mother's mother, further on still to the distant Pentland Skerries, and in the East the lift of Duncansby Head with yet another lighthouse. In the whole of Scotland you will not find a panorama to compare.

And in between the cliffs of Hoy and of Dunnet Head the Pentland Firth 300 feet below us writhing in the grip of the tide.

And at Dunnet Lighthouse with Nettie one rare but memorable evening long ago, clear and frosty, autumnal, no moon and pitch dark, visibility sharp as a razor, the flickers of light from all these lighthouses, some directly seen and some a mere reflection in the sky such as Start Point in Sanday and Auskerry at Stronsay, out of direct line of sight.

I only refer to Robert Louis Stevenson as he was one who has gone before, who saw these lands and seas for himself. The stories I have tried to tell have been of people who also have gone before, to "sailors home from the sea", to "hunters home from the hill", mostly very ordinary people who were not really ordinary at all, but each a giant in his or her own way.

There is much more left to tell but I must finish this present book at this time. It is only a selection of stories out of the old records of which there are many more, though I probably chose the better ones. I must move on as there are other things I would like to do while I have still the time.

I have enjoyed the many hours of challenge and work entailed in reading and deciphering the old records. If I have succeeded in making some of them better known and more available to more people than before, then I am well content.

> "The Moving Finger writes; and having writ,
> Moves on; nor all thy Piety nor Wit,
> Shall lure it back to cancel half a line,
> Nor all thy Tears wash out a Word of it."
>
> Omar Khayyam

Timotheo Pont, circa 1600